# FILMMAKERS SERIES

### edited by
### ANTHONY SLIDE

## In Preparation:

# James Whale

by
## JAMES CURTIS

Filmmakers, No. 1

THE SCARECROW PRESS, INC.
Metuchen, N.J., & London 1982

Library of Congress Cataloging in Publication Data

Curtis, James, 1953–
    James Whale.

    (Filmmakers ; no. 1)
    Bibliography: p.
    Includes index.
    1. Whale, James.  2. Moving-picture producers and
directors--United States--Biography.  I. Title.
II. Series: Filmmakers (Scarecrow Press) ; no. 1.
PN1998.A3W4772  1982      791.43'0233'0924 [B]    82-5965
ISBN 0-8108-1561-3                                AACR2

For David Lewis

# CONTENTS

## ACKNOWLEDGMENTS

Numerous people helped this project along in the seven years between inception and publication. The late Carl Laemmle, Jr. graciously consented to see me, and it was he who introduced me to David Lewis and began my research. Peter Barnsley allowed me use of his material on Whale's early days, and David Stewart Hull championed the project with commendable faith.

For assorted involvements I am also indebted to the Academy of Motion Picture Arts and Sciences; Ned Comstock of the Department of Special Collections, Doheny Library, University of Southern California; William K. Everson; Paul Frizler; Bob Gitt; Mike Hawks; Charles Higham; Ronnie James; Miles Kreuger; Bob Porfirio; Anthony Slide; and Marc Wanamaker.

I owe a special debt of gratitude to the friends and co-workers of James Whale who generously contributed memories of an especially private and uncommon individual: Lew Ayres, Larry Blake, Mae Clarke, Irene Dunne, the late Robert Florey, Pierre Foegel, Curtis Harrington, Louis Hayward, Ted Kent, John King, David Manners, Alan Napier, Le Roy Prinz, Gloria Stuart, and Jane Wyatt.

James Curtis
Los Angeles
1982

The Scarecrow Filmmakers Series will focus on a varied group of film people, both present and past, active and inactive, and it is perhaps appropriate that the first volume in the series should be devoted to James Whale, a director whose output was immensely varied. Whale is, of course, best known as the director of such classic horror films as Frankenstein, The Invisible Man, and The Bride of Frankenstein, but, in fact, he directed many features of originality and style in a variety of genres. It says much for his talent and his unique abilities that Whale was able to direct productions as varied as Hell's Angels, The Old Dark House, and One More River. The quality of his directing is not surprising, but what is unexpected is that Whale has never before been the subject of a book-length study.

Perhaps writers have been unwilling to undertake the amount of research upon which James Curtis embarked. This book was developed, on and off, over a period of seven years, during which time Curtis interviewed an assortment of Whale's friends and co-workers. Piecing the puzzle together, Whale emerged as a director of great sensitivity who functioned well in the familial environment of Universal studios under the ownership of Carl Laemmle, and whose later efforts were hindered by his failure to cultivate an arrangement as conducive to work at the larger, impersonal studios where his later films were made.

James Curtis is a Los Angeles-based writer and editor, whose background includes instructional design and technical and promotional writing. He is also the author of a recently

vii

published, highly acclaimed biography of writer-director Preston Sturges.

Anthony Slide
Series Editor

# INTRODUCTION

We are usually reduced to a series of speculations whenever evaluating the work of a motion picture director-- watching for trends, researching biography, questioning the medium, exploring attitudes and colorings. No single med- ium melds as many disciplines--acting, writing, photography, design, music--or as many creative talents.

The director's name usually comes last in the credits, as large as anyone's and with a card to itself. What has he contributed that we can see? A particular line of dialogue? an actor's expression? a cut whose preciseness meant a bellylaugh instead of a titter? If we investigate, we may find he wrote the original story, got the studio to agree to it, cast the film, rewrote the script, altered the lead perform- ances, cut the result, and oversaw the projectionist on open- ing night. We might, on the other hand, find he replaced two other directors and allowed a good film to be made in spite of himself.

In the case of James Whale, he never appeared on camera, rarely gave interviews, and failed to live long enough to answer the questions of the current generation of film en- thusiasts. Where do the contributions of others leave off and his begin?

The fascination with the work of James Whale stems-- for many--from the masterful "horror" films he made at Universal in the early 1930's. Literate and atmospheric, three of these films have survived through constant showings on television, each time titillating a few new devotees along

with the countless others seeing one of the films for the fifth
or tenth time.   With a few notable exceptions, Whale's films
are the best of this genre because they work on more than
one level.   The broad themes established so straightforwardly
in Frankenstein are carried over into Bride of Frankenstein
intact.   Those looking for an exciting, well-paced monster
movie are not disappointed.   But adults and the more sophisticated can enjoy Bride as not so much a horror show as a
whimsical fantasy and an exciting piece of cinema.   Bride is
frequently hilariously funny.   What distinguishes it from a lot
of other such films is that the humor is entirely intentional.

Whale's approach to his horror films--and the fact
that they've proven themselves so resiliently commercial--
tends to obscure his work in other genres.   Frankenstein,
Bride, Invisible Man, and even The Old Dark House contain
distinguishing elements attributable (from this distance) only
to the director.   And since Whale acquitted himself so successfully in making these films, it's easy and acceptable to
dismiss his other works as the wanderings of a horror di-
rector--the job for which he was clearly created.

There's an element of truth in the contention that
Whale's best films were his horror films, but these accounted
for only a small portion of his total output.   To dismiss his
ventures into practically every genre (except the western) as
ill-advised and undistinguished is to deny Whale's position at
the time as a respected and highly cultured man whose pri-
mary background was that of an artist, and whose films, regardless of genre, were approached with great insight and
skill.

Whale's films seem to divide neatly into two categor-
ies that could easily be labeled "jobs" and "projects."   Jobs
were things he more or less felt--through contractual obliga-
tions or career considerations--compelled to do.   He approached these films as the skillful director of undistinguished
product, efficient but only as good as the material he was
given.   They were usually made in less than hospitable en-
vironments in which Whale felt disinclined to experiment or
embellish.   The early jobs, made for the Laemmles at Universal, do not compare well with Whale's best work, but they
do contain things that suggest to the interested observer that
James Whale was indeed the director.   Whale's later jobs
were less successful, owing to an unfortunate chain of events
that robbed him of the comfort and respect he enjoyed under
the Laemmles.   Aside from Warner Bros.' The Great Garrick,

which was delightful but not commercially successful, they
reveal little of Whale's influence.

Whale's projects--films he wanted to do and developed
with a special enthusiasm--account for his finest moments.
With but two exceptions, these were made at Universal between the years 1931 and 1937, when Whale was at the peak
of his creative powers.   It was here that Whale made his beloved "horror" films, interlaced with commendable excursions
into a number of other classifications.   He in fact had emerged
as a specialist in war movies by the time Frankenstein came
about in the summer of 1931.   His reputation as a stage director was based almost exclusively on the phenomenal success of Journey's End, R. C. Sherriff's grim drama of death
and despair in the British trenches before St. Quentin.   After
directing the original West End and Broadway productions, he
came west to California where he was soon recruited by Howard Hughes to direct the dialogue sequences of his own
Hell's Angels.   Placed in the somewhat unusual position of
remaking a silent film while preserving the integrity of some
truly spectacular aerial footage, Whale approached the task
as a learning experience, subjugating any creative impulses
of his own to those of Mr. Hughes.   When not airborne,
Hell's Angels became a film of remarkable dullness.   There
is little, if any, hint of the style Whale would later develop.
If he carried anything away from the experience, it was at
least partial responsibility for the stardom of Jean Harlow,
whom he disliked intensely.

Whale's emergence to the rank of full director occurred
with the film version of Journey's End in 1930.   Cautious and
stagy, the picture probably suffered from Whale's over-
familiarity with the material.   The famous dugout set, re-
produced faithfully, implied the proscenium arch of the stage.
Actors faced the same unseen wall with, in some cases, em-
barrassingly broad performances.   Interestingly, Journey's
End hints at Whale's potential command of the medium only
when it moves into the trenches.   Here we meet most of the
main characters, dramatically backlit amidst loud bursts of
light in a dark, tangled maze of barbed wire and mud.   Con-
trasting the bright, daylit battles of All Quiet on the Western
Front, Whale took a budget roughly $1 million less and turned
his limitations to a grim advantage.   Journey's End, for all
its lack of scope, presents a mysterious and more brutal war
than All Quiet.

At the core of whatever power Journey's End possesses

is the performance of Colin Clive.  Weary, driven, at the
very edge of madness, Clive presents a masterful portrait
of a tortured soul, a performance that won him a prominent
career as featured player with frequent modifications of the
same compelling qualities.

The bubbling madness of Clive's Captain Stanhope was
doubtless the inspiration for his Henry Frankenstein of the
next year.  By the time of Frankenstein, Whale had defined
much of his approach to filmmaking with an excellent adaptation of the Sherwood play Waterloo Bridge, made under a new
and promising agreement with Universal Pictures.  A story
of doomed love in wartime London, Waterloo was expanded
and improved upon in a screenplay commissioned under
Whale's auspices from playwright Benn W. Levy.  Levy's
structure of the script bears similarities to Whale's most
personal later productions.  Supporting a strong central performance from actress Mae Clarke, Whale directed the love
interest, in this case Kent Douglass, to a point of blankness
that detracts little from the plight of the protagonist.  Ethel
Griffies and Frederick Kerr then add an accent of humor in
supporting parts that relieve and, in some ways, intensify
brief passages of agony at the heart of the story.  Clarke,
a supporting player of considerable ability, was directed with
sympathy to one of the great unsung performances of the
early sound period.  Her acting is very naturalistic, but
never to the point of inadequacy.  The key to her character
is her unwillingness to accept the love that has found her.
She fights it with an almost self-destructive intensity that
tracks with Whale's most successful characters:  Frankenstein, Stanhope, and even the Monster himself.

From a purely visual sense, Waterloo Bridge is carefully detailed.  Whale, a former stage designer, worked well
with fellow Englishman Charles D. "Danny" Hall in suggesting
an authentic, if sometimes stylized, wartime London.  Moving from an awareness, almost exclusively, of stage effects
for sound, Waterloo Bridge far outdistances Journey's End,
where the backstage suggestions of bombs and snipers' bullets
were transposed intact to the screen, the rhythmic beats on
a kettle drum constituting more of an ominous musical score
than a series of jolting shellbursts.

Whale also began to discover camera mobility, a device of importance to him as his career progressed.  A special favorite was the lateral dolly, used at length to follow
movement, or slightly arced to observe action from a distance

or emphasize a mood.    Waterloo Bridge featured some un-
usually fluid camerawork for 1931.    Perhaps Whale enjoyed
an advantage in being from the stage, where dialogue was a
natural component of drama and not something to be accorded
extraordinary respect or indulgence, as directors from silent
days were inclined to do.    Whale never seemed particularly
concerned about illogical camera placement or movement.
The medium of film excited Whale for the things it permitted
him to do that were impossible on the stage.    He loved camera movement for its own sake, as he did the traditionally
spare close-up.

      It was fitting that Whale next chose Frankenstein, a
subject of considerable cinematic potential.    Here, however,
Whale seemed to understand the almost overpowering qualities
of the story in keeping his film wide-eyed and relatively un-
adorned with trickery.    Whale's emphasis was with the Monster as almost a protagonist and not simply a plot device.
He therefore structured his film so as not to detract from
the flamboyant performances of both Colin Clive and Boris
Karloff.    Karloff, buried under pounds of grease paint and
nose putty, created a genuine sense of pity for the beast, an
unfortunate byproduct of Clive's restless scientist.    Whale
kept the creature voiceless and the issues simple.    Again
trapped by his own inner energies, Clive played Frankenstein
to the same ragged edge as he did Stanhope.    They are, in
ways, remarkably similar men.    His controlled hysteria at
the Monster's creation is not unlike Stanhope's quiet agony at
the loss of his friend Osborne in Journey's End.

      In light of Whale's later work, Frankenstein contains
remarkably little humor.    Whale's penchant for comedy shows
only in brief moments with Dwight Frye as Frankenstein's
dwarf assistant, and in Frederick Kerr's grumpy, irascible
Baron.    In a sense, Frankenstein is a textbook exercise in
horror, drawn from study of the German silents, told plainly
and with a genuine purpose to shock.    Even a half-century of
imitation and parody has not seriously diluted its effect.

      Whale followed Frankenstein with a programmer called
The Impatient Maiden, a picture he did with an apparent sense
of duty and boredom.    Here, he concerned himself little with
performances, which didn't interest him, and with matters of
writing over which he had no control.    As Lew Ayres, the
star, later revealed, Whale spoke little to him, rarely even
acknowledging an acceptable take.    Impatient Maiden plays as
it was doubtless filmed--ground-out in a workmanlike manner,

pausing only for interesting, unrelated bits of business.
Whale regularly dollies through a succession of breakaway
walls, following action with no apparent concern for the reality of the scene.  In contrast, the action builds predictably
to a climactic appendectomy which Whale carefully details
with actual operating room procedures.  In both cases, these
were features added merely for their own sake; moments of
brightness and originality in an otherwise dismal and com-
monplace production.

Whale returned forcefully to his element with The
Old Dark House, proportedly a horror thriller with as many
wicked laughs as shivers.  Although extremely faithful to the
novel of J. B. Priestley, The Old Dark House bears the
stamp of an especially wry and cynical sense of humor.
That the same elements crop up again in later Whale productions prepared by other, unrelated writers can only attest to
some nebulous involvement on the part of the director.  The
Old Dark House features much of the original Priestley dialogue, carefully pared of its surrounding significance and delivered with piping elegance by a handpicked cast of pre-
dominantly British actors.  Whale's influence on casting is
obvious by the dominance of actors with whom he worked in
England in the twenties:  Ernest Thesiger, Charles Laughton,
Raymond Massey, and Eva Moore.  Thesiger, who had absolutely no standing in the American film industry of the time,
was accorded the prize role of Horace Femm, master of the
house and deliverer of a lot of the film's best lines.  He is
alternately commanding, frightened, and forboding.  He is
apologetic when the lights dim ("We make our own electricity,
but we're not very good at it"), and stern when the boister-
ous Laughton interrupts his dinner ("Have a potato!").  Whale
generally accents his lines with an appropriately angled close-
up, according a different cut--for emphasis--for practically
every sentence.  Whale's style enjoys a further advancement
when dealing with such subjects, his manner of cutting be-
coming far coarser and, where applicable, even jolting.
Boris Karloff's introduction in Old Dark House is similar to
the same moment in Frankenstein:  quick, only slightly altering views of the face, timing the response of the audience
and underscoring it with a decidedly ragged series of shots.
Here, Whale, as with Frankenstein, is less concerned with
matching his shots as he is with heightening the effect of the
drama and, if need be, throwing his audience a little off
balance.

This particular quality is especially evident in The

Kiss Before the Mirror, an ironic drama of jealous murder
that starts off almost as light opera.   Beautiful Gloria Stuart
glides toward her rendezvous with lover Walter Pidgeon as
the latter waltzes and sings his way through preparations for
their early evening tryst.   She smells the flowers, observes
her reflection in a pool of water, answers his melodies with
piano accompaniment.   The dialogue is saccharine almost to
the point of parody, but on the horizon looms husband Paul
Lukas, who advances to the bedroom window, draws a revolver, and shatters the glass with his blasts.   The film
then goes dark, very dark, as attorney Frank Morgan seeks
out Lukas in a dingy jail cell where Lukas broods remorse-
fully and describes his realization he was a cuckold as he
observed his wife's reflection during a kiss before her vanity
mirror.

Whale balances the dire circumstances of the crime
and its prosecution with the cynical asides of Morgan's spin-
sterish assistant and the dimwitted Charley Grapewin.   When
Morgan sees the same elements of doom in his own marriage,
and suppresses his murderous inclinations in the defense of
his client, Whale highlights his emotional and memorable
courtroom speech with a full 360° pan of the set, studying
each observer as might one of the spectators, or the defendant himself.

The Invisible Man was, in many ways, Whale's favorite film, licking the problems of story that stumped a number of hapless screenwriters before his friend R. C. Sherriff reasoned the best approach was simply the one most
faithful to the H. G. Wells original.   Once written, the problems of filming were technical, employing a host of innova-
tive tricks developed by John P. Fulton, and political as
Whale sought to replace lead actor Boris Karloff with his
own choice, his friend Claude Rains.   The dazzling success
of his adaptation, the careful blending of comedy (the first
appearance of shrill and nosey Una O'Connor as Rains' land-
lady balanced well the early moments of mystery and suspense) and tragedy (Rains' love for Gloria Stuart perverted
by the unforeseen effects of the chemicals on Rains' mind),
helped prevent what could easily have developed into a hopelessly mechanical morass of wires moving objects and limited
movements mandated by the special photography and limitations of the character's invisibility.

Rains' soft, resonant voice proved ideal for the quiet
madness he portrayed without benefit of facial expressions or
exceptional makeup.

After an elegant, Lubitschesque comedy called By
Candlelight, a job for which Whale replaced the inadequate
Robert Wyler and one which was marred by the inability of
Paul Lukas to play his role with anything other than thudding
exaggeration, Whale did the film version of Galsworthy's last
novel, One More River.  A social drama of modern England,
Whale managed a sense of understated class into which he
thrust Colin Clive as Diana Wynyard's brutal husband and
Mrs. Patrick Campbell as the heroine's aunt and principal
comedy relief.  Whale carefully manipulates the elements of
sound and picture, straining the screeching of the wireless
to hilarious effect, and giving Mrs. Pat the opportunity to in-
ject one of her delightful one-liners ("Lawrence does something to ours with a penknife").

Whale next filmed what is debatably his masterpiece,
The Bride of Frankenstein.  Bride, more than any other film,
shows Whale's mastery of the medium and all of its elements.
He structured it, as his friend David Lewis so aptly put it,
as a "hoot," setting a plausible premise for a decidedly im-
plausible story.  Opening on young Mary Godwin fancifully
spinning an amendment to her earlier tale, he travels back to
the burning mill where the Monster was supposedly destroyed
at the end of the first movie.

Glibly, Whale dollies in on the dispersing crowd, alternately balancing tragedy (the grieving parents of the
drowned Maria) with comedy (hawkish, dowdy Una O'Connor).
Hans ventures closer to the ruins, to see for himself the
bones of his daughter's killer.  With Mary Gordon pleading
him to stop, the floor crumbles beneath him as he plops into
the water where Franz Waxman's swelling score cues us that
the Monster still survives.  In a truly startling shot, the
monster menacingly emerges from behind a timber and angri-
ly strangles the helpless villager.  Gordon, still calling from
above, reaches eagerly for the emerging hand of the Monster,
thinking naturally that it is the hand of her husband.  Karloff
climbs completely to the surface, pulling the old woman down
in his stead.  Immediately following this brutal and shocking
opening, Una O'Connor wanders into the scene, notes the
creature towering above her, rolls her eyes, hikes her skirt,
and waddles off at high speed as Karloff does the slightest of
double takes.  It sets the mood for the whole film--very mo-
bile camera, complex construction, horror countered with
humor almost back-to-back.

As he did in Old Dark House, Whale spotlighted

Ernest Thesiger.   Here, as Dr. Pretorius, he is the villain
of the piece, a part obviously written specifically for him.
As David Lewis is quick to point out, Whale himself was not
a writer and professed no particular skill with words.   He
did, however, see to specially written parts for both Thesiger and Una O'Connor in this film, as well as others.   In
each instance the character is a collage of mannerisms,
catch-phrases, and broad expressions.   And, as with his
other works of the horror genre, Whale cuts intricately and
joltingly; in lieu of dollying in to a close-up, he is generally
inclined to use two or three successively closer shots,
bracketing individual bits of dialogue.   Thesiger especially
benefits from such exposure, the careful editing adding extra
emphasis to an already finely-wrought performance.

Colin Clive is again the tortured soul of the earlier
film, beset by both the Monster and Pretorius.   The story
however, shifts more toward the Monster, as he is given a
voice in a perversely memorable manner, with a blind hermit adopting him as a friend to whom he presumes to teach
English.   (The hermit's tearful prayer of thanks is joined by
Karloff's restless creature, tears also rolling down his
cheeks. )   The Monster develops into adulthood:   he not only
speaks, he drinks wine and smokes cigars.   Karloff reportedly found these circumstances less amusing than Whale:   he
revered the Monster's character; Whale, by contrast, wanted
to do away with him for good.

It is not difficult to imagine Whale envisioning whole
scenes, sometimes outrageous, sometimes without dialogue
or point.   Whale's acute perception of each character could
probably have been mimicked and dialogued in conference
with a writer like John Balderston, who could communicate
easily with him and understand the various effects he wished.

Bride was not without its problems.   As with most
Whale projects, it ran both over schedule and over budget.
Judging from the original screenplay, the film ran closer to
85 minutes in conception than the 75 it runs today.

After Bride of Frankenstein, Whale eschewed the horror genre as if he had stretched it as much as his imagina-
tion would allow and wished not to repeat himself.   He prepared to move on to bigger and more spectacular productions:
Show Boat, Good-Bye, Mr. Chips, The Road Back.   It was
only while awaiting a starting date for Show Boat that Whale
decided to make Remember Last Night? a comedy-mystery

cut from the same cinematic mold as Bride.    Again, camera
movement is maximized.    At one point, a scream heard in
the living room brings the respondents through two breakaway walls and up a flight of stairs in a single shot.    There
is no payoff; the shot is there simply because it's exciting.

Show Boat, when it was ready, proved to be Whale's
biggest and most mainstream production.    He handled the
chore thoughtfully, hinting at the darker traditions in his work
only during the "Ol' Man River" number when he circles
Paul Robeson, pushes into a very tight close-up, and then dis-
solves to a montage of expressionistic shots illustrating the
song.    Show Boat was an overblown, problematic experience
that allowed Whale less control than his cheaper, more personal excursions.    Show Boat is therefore less distinctively
Whale than The Road Back, another troubled venture for which
a special camera crane was built that facilitated long, lateral
traveling shots of the advancing soldiers on a stylized battlefield with movable farmhouses and cycloramic background.
The film's early moments of battle are filmed with a relentlessly advancing camera, catching the brutal violence with
almost panoramic grace.

Afforded the use of more sophisticated camera equipment than he had previously employed, Whale took a special
delight in shooting the film's uproarious mob scenes perched
high atop a crane that allowed him to follow and then ex-
plode the advancing crowd by simply pulling up and back.    It
is a trick he employs several times in a finished product
that alternates between the flamboyant and the hopelessly
banal.

Faced with problems of censorship and political pres-
sures at the "New" Universal, Whale departed for Warner
Bros., where he made the stylish and elegant Great Garrick,
and to M-G-M for the relentlessly boring Port of Seven Seas.
For the first time in his career, Whale was adrift as a free-
lancer, no longer able to employ his favorite actors and
technicians.    He merely toyed with his later films, unable
to influence the writing and production values as he once had
with the Laemmles.    Sinners in Paradise is an undistinguished
and silly movie, made back-to-back with Wives Under Suspicion, a better film in which Whale opens with an imaginative
montage of a convicted killer's final days, zooming in on
shots of the judge and prosecuting attorney, and carefully
traveling across electricity lines, past HIGH VOLTAGE signs,
and into the death house itself where the switch is thrown and

the lights dim.   By the time of <u>Man in the Iron Mask</u> and <u>Green Hell</u> (his last complete feature) he is merely going through the motions without troubling himself with the particular capabilities that had so enthralled him only ten years earlier.

He retired in 1941, seeing friends, painting, and directing plays in a little theatre in the Santa Monica Canyon. Since Whale lived quietly, and left the motion picture industry so completely, he aroused little attention in later years. Unfortunately, he died before a revival of interest in his work and therefore became somewhat of an enigma.   Questions concerning Whale's early retirement and mysterious death were raised and only compounded by an early version of the book <u>Hollywood Babylon,</u> which implied Whale was murdered in a homosexual rage.

His films are remnants of a unique period of experimentation and development.   What kind of man was James Whale?   What was it about his background and personality that aided his development?   In understanding Whale the man, we can only then fully appreciate his approach to the new and influential medium of the talking film.

# CHAPTER ONE

"Dudley," J. B. Priestley once wrote, "seemed to me a fantastic place. You climb a hill, past innumerable grim works and unpleasant brick dwellings, and then suddenly a ridiculous terra-cotta music hall comes into sight, perched on the steep roadside as if a giant had plucked it out of one of the neighbouring valleys and carelessly left it there; and above this music hall were the ruins of Dudley Castle. The view from there is colossal. On the Dudley side, you look down and across at roofs and steeply mounting streets and pointing factory chimneys. It looked as if a great slab of Birmingham had been torn away and then tilted up there at an angle of about forty-five degrees. The view from the other side, roughly, I suppose, to the north-east, was even more impressive. There was the Black Country unrolled before you like a smouldering carpet. You looked into an immense hollow of smoke and blurred buildings and factory chimneys. There seemed to be no end to it."

The Black Country of the English Midlands was a highly industrial region that made an unlikely birthplace for the distinguished aristocrat James Whale would later become. He was born in the family home at 41 Brewery Street, Kate's Hill, on July 22nd, 1889. His father, William Whale, was a local blast furnaceman of modest means whose wife, Sarah, bore a total of ten children. Only seven, however, survived past infancy.

The Whales, especially Mrs. Whale, were devoutly religious and regularly attended Dixon's Green Methodist Church, where James' puritanical background was reinforced

1

as a boy. He became a student at Bayliss' School on Tower Street, and later at the Dudley Bluecoat School. He worked for a while at a cobbler's shop in Eve Hill and eventually landed a boring job pounding embossed designs into sheet metal fenders at Harper and Bean's in Waddam's Pool, where he grew into adulthood.

Uncommonly reserved with a bean-pole physique, young Whale longed to study art at a four-year institution but, at age 21, his parents could hardly afford to support him. He managed to enroll as an evening student at the Dudley School of Arts and Crafts, where he exhibited a remarkable talent, and gradually began to separate himself from a tradition of manual labor.

John Hadley Rowe, who later became Vice-Principal of St. Martin's School of Art, was Whale's best friend during that period. In an interview some sixty years later, he remembered Whale's manner and bearing as "distinctive" even as a schoolboy. "Whale looked and behaved like a gentleman and kept himself a little apart," Rowe's questioner, historian Peter Barnsley, concluded, "though he was by no means aloof. He had an artist's introspection and chose his company to suit himself."

Rowe and Whale often went sketching together, perhaps to the Castle, or "Wren's Nest," or even the Fox Yards. James purchased a "Matchless" motorcycle, and the two would then go to Wombourn Common to draw and paint. On occasion, they would also attend the melodramas presented at the Dudley Opera House, where Whale got his first intro-duction to the world of theatre with such works as Alone in London, The Span of Life, and The Face at the Window. "His outlook on drawing was unusual," Rowe said, "because he had a pronounced sense of selection for essential charac-teristics. His portrait drawings, which were many, varied considerably by the skillful change in technical methods sug-gested by the personality of the subject. I well remember his wash drawing of a Bluecoat School boy complete with chequered cap band and ribbon being resolved magnificently in indigo blue; a result which would startle students even now at the Royal Academy schools or the Slade."

After the outbreak of World War I, Whale became a volunteer YMCA worker at the Army training camp at Litch-field. Reluctantly, he developed into a candidate for officer's training, joining the "Inns of Court" Cadet Corps, and was

commissioned a Second Lieutenant in August of 1914. He
was assigned to a Worcestershire regiment, sent to France,
and served on the Somme, at Arras, and Ypres.

On the night of August 25th, 1917, Whale led a company of the 2/7th Battalion in a frontal assault at the Steen-
beek, Belgium. "My platoon had been told off to do a stunt
on a pill box at midnight," he said years later, "and we had
gone into a well-laid trap. It all happened so suddenly I was
stupefied and found it impossible to believe myself cut off
from everything British and in the hands of the Huns."

After a few days in a camp at Karlsruhe, the twenty-
eight-year-old Whale was moved to Holsminden, near Hanover.
To keep from going crazy, he made hundreds of line-and-
wash drawings, many with theatrical themes drawn from memories of the theatre at Dudley. Soon he was organizing a theatrical company within the camp, spending the fifteen months
he was confined with 1400 other men designing modest sets
for their original productions and even directing some. He
also played a lot of bridge, wagering with absent and non-
existent fortunes represented by checks written on the backs
of old cigarette wrappers. Many of his friends came from
wealthy families; Whale did very well. After the armistice
and exchange of prisoners, he hurriedly returned to England
ahead of his comrades, where he promptly cashed the checks
he had won before payments could be stopped. He also sold
a number of his drawings and wound up with nearly £4,000.
Rather than return to the factory life he had grown to detest,
he signed on as a staff cartoonist for The Bystander and began an extended period of self-education on the subject of the
London theatre.

Within a year, he had quit the paper to enroll at the
Ryland Memorial School in Birmingham, where he developed
a special interest in Barry Jackson's Birmingham Repertory
Theatre. Backstage, he assisted in most every facet of production, and understudied small parts. John Drinkwater's
Abraham Lincoln was first performed there in 1919: Whale
played several parts--including Booth when the need existed--
although his regular role was that of an orderly whose big
line (in scene five) was, "A dispatch, Sir." Its size and
weight mattered little; with each show, he gave the line a
different reading, and prided himself on never delivering the
dispatch quite the same way twice.

It was later that year, on August 30th, that James Whale

made his formal stage debut as a supernumerary in Jackson's production of Beaumont and Fletcher's The Famous Historie of the Knight of the Burning Pestle.   He found himself on the payroll only a few weeks that year, but began thinking of the stage as a promising livelihood.   He curtailed his art studies and traveled to Manchester, where he played a small role in the Christmas production of The Merry Wives of Windsor. He first met actor Ernest Thesiger there, whom Whale impressed as a "frail ex-prisoner of war with a faun-like charm. "

Come 1920, Whale moved on to Stratford-on-Avon, where he acquired some Shakespearean experience and began to learn the art of stage direction in earnest.   It was there that he was seen by Nigel Playfair, a prominent writer-actor-director who invited Whale to join his Repertory Company at Liverpool.   For Playfair, Whale made his London debut in September of 1922 at the Regent Theatre in Body and Soul by Arnold Bennett.

During this period, Whale met--and subsequently became engaged to--Doris Clare Zinkeisen, a thin, Scottish-born designer in her early twenties, whom Playfair had discovered in Liverpool.   She was hired to design the sets and costumes for The Insect Play in March of 1923, and remained thereafter.

"Miss Zinkeisen, " John Gielgud recalled in Early Stages, "was very good looking and wore exotic clothes. "

Whale, he observed, was "a tall young man with side-whiskers and suede shoes who was stage-managing for Playfair at the Savoy. "

To Whale, Zinkeisen was a special woman who appealed to him as no other in his life.   They never married and Whale remained devoutly homosexual through the rest of his life.   Zinkeisen later became the wife of Captain E. Graham Johnston, and distinguished herself by designing for Evergreen and Words and Music, as well as by authoring the film The Blue Danube and a book called Designing for the Stage.   She, like Whale, shared a passion for painting and it is her murals that decorate the Queen Mary.   Until Whale's death in 1957, they remained good friends.

[Opposite:]   Second Lieutenant, August 1914.   Whale is farthest left, fourth row from the top.

Whale as John Wilkes Booth in <u>Abraham Lincoln</u> (1919).

Doris Zinkeisen

In the case of The Insect Play, besides Gielgud--
whom Whale considered the finest actor he had ever worked
with--was Elsa Lanchester.  It was her first stage part, that
of the Larva, that began her trek to local stardom.  Playfair
had seen her at the "Cave of Harmony, " a non-professional
avant-garde "night club" she and some friends had made out
of a children's theatre in which they had been involved.  He
frequently visited, and performed in some of their productions,
as did Whale.  "We gave old and modern plays and cabaret
turns at midnight, and never had a drink license--it was
more like a midnight play production club, " Lanchester later
wrote.  In 1924, Whale aligned himself with James Bernard
Fagan's Oxford Players for three seasons.  The company included Tyrone Guthrie, Virginia Turleigh, Flora Robson,
Reginald Denham, Alan Napier, Glen Byam Shaw, Peter Cres-
well, and Mary Grey as the leading lady.  Dorothy Green,
Doris Lytton, Minnie Rayner, and Raymond Massey appeared
in selected productions.

> Reginald Denham and James Whale helped Fagan
> with the producing [said John Gielgud], and Fagan
> and Whale took turns in designing the scenery,
> which we all used to help paint and construct be-
> tween Saturday night and Monday afternoon.  Some
> of the effects were quite ambitious.  Whale did a
> wood for Deirdre of the Sorrows consisting almost
> entirely of a few light tree trunks cut in three-ply,
> and we had a most regal tent scene in Monna Vanna,
> contrived from the rose-colored curtains used at
> the Court for the Moscovitch Merchant of Venice
> Trial Scene.

Recalled Alan Napier,

> A season at Oxford coincided with the academic
> semesters, and Jimmy was hired for the Spring
> semester of 1924 as scenery director and, he said,
> "assistant director, " but he never did any directing,
> as Fagan did it all.
> He also played parts in two of our productions
> that were taken to the West End in London.  The
> first was a play by Richard Hughes, who wrote A
> High Wind in Jamaica, and it was called A Comedy
> of Good and Evil with Mary Grey and me.  He
> played "Gas" Jones and was frightfully good with
> this eccentric business of a little Welsh village.
> Here is the old impoverished minister and his wife

with a wooden leg.    There is a storm outside--and
a cry--and there appears a beautiful golden-haired
girl, who was played by Jim Fagan's daughter,
Gamma.
   It turns out that she is a child of the Devil, because as she touches the Bible, it goes up in
flames.    The terrible metaphysical problem arises--
Should a good Christian parson take in a child of
the Devil or not?
   They determine to, and the next morning, the
wife wakes up with a beautiful new leg with a silk
stocking on it, and it seems to have a life of its
own.    There she is--lighting the fire--and the first
person who calls is Evans the Post.    Of course, in
no time, everyone in the village knows that the parson's wife has a new leg.

The play culminated with both Heaven and Hell grap-
pling over the then deceased Napier's soul.

It was an amusing play [Napier concluded], but it
was like caviar to the general audiences, and we
only ran three weeks because it went into some
heavily metaphysical stuff.
   I got frightfully good notices.    Jimmy, after
reading them, said, "Alan, you'll never look back, "
and I've been looking back ever since.

There was hard work at Oxford.    "It was once-a-week
repertory--with a new play every week--so we had a scant
six days to rehearse, " Napier said.    "Then we would break
for holidays and in-between semesters where, if we were
lucky, we'd go to the West End.    Otherwise, we'd all dis-
band until it was time to work again.    We all had families
to go to, but one wondered where Jimmy Whale would disappear to.    We'd go away and when it was time to work
again, there he was. "

Whale earned £0 a week at Oxford.    "It was possible
to live on £4, " Napier added, grimacing.

We were always very easy together, and I've
always felt that he was a bit sorry I wasn't homosexual myself.    He had a wicked, sardonic smile
and a very bizarre sense of humor.    I remember
one afternoon after a hot matinee of Good and Evil
in London, I had my shirt off and was removing my

make-up. I could see James come up behind me in
the mirror. He put his hands on my shoulders and
said, "I know somebody who would be crazy about
you. Yes ...," " and I said, "What? What are you
talking about?"

He said, "These shoulders ... Yes ... He would
absolutely love you. "

Shortly after, he prevailed upon me to go to a
party--all men--to meet the putative admirer of
my torso. A nice little fellow, in fact, but the
gathering convinced me that such goings-on were
not my cup of tea.

Jimmy was a monkey--a kind-of Bohemian upper-
class with very precise, clear speech patterns.
Being from the Black Country, he had a lot of accent to lose. He must have worked hard to acquire
this upper-class manner of speaking that was so
important to him. The clean-cut phrasing was
probably a result of having to learn it.

There existed a very definite "class" system within
the English theatre of the early twentieth century, and the
appearance of proper regional origin was all important. The
way one spoke was clearly the key to one's being accepted
as a gentleman. James Whale's drive was to rise above his
origins; storming the snobbish fortress of the West End and
its elite became an all-encompassing goal. Actors not making
the grade were naturally relegated to touring companies, although an occasional exception might be made for a character person who specialized in comic maids and the like.
Whale shuddered at such a thought, working diligently at his
speech and manner.

"He was a superb craftsman and a good actor, " Napier felt, "who was limited by an odd appearance and dry
manner. He was very sure of himself, but he also had some
great, basic insecurities. "

A Comedy of Good and Evil had come to J. B. Fagan's
attention through a performance by the "300 Club" the summer
before. The club was one of many theatrical groups that
proved most useful in promoting new plays to the theatrical
community.

"The Sunday Societies, " as they were known, grew out
of the Sunday Observance Act of 1781, which forbade the opening of public entertainments on the Sabbath. The Stage Society

became the first, in 1899, to regularly hire a theatre for
private performances on Sundays.   As a rule, there was
only one performance, with an occasional Monday matinee
for reviewers and word-of-mouth business.   Under this system, they pioneered the original presentations of You Never
Can Tell (1899), Candida (1900), Captain Brassbound's Con-
version (1900), and The Admirable Bashville (1903).   Soon,
other subscription clubs followed, including The 300 Club,
The Sunday Play Society, The Lyceum Club Stage Society,
and The Repertory Players.   Primarily, they were a showcase for new plays that had little popular appeal.   Being
private, they also enjoyed a freedom from censorship:
Shaw's Mrs. Warren's Profession found its first exposure
with The Stage Society in 1902.

     In May, Whale played Epihodov in Chekhov's The
Cherry Orchard, Fagan's second show to make it to the West
End that year.   Considered by many to be the author's finest
work, the play had been introduced to London before the war
by The Stage Society where the audience, in part, walked
out.   John Gielgud, Alan Napier, and Mary Grey were in the
new version and it became the first successful Chekhov on
the English-speaking stage, running 136 performances.

     "We could have run even longer," said Napier, "but
we had to get back to Oxford to prepare for the new season.
It was an amazing success."

     During the run, Whale also acted in The Prisoners
of War for The 300 Club with Raymond Massey and Colin
Keith-Johnston.   Then, at summer's end, he broke with Oxford and established lodgings at 402A King's Road in Chelsea.
There, he designed and built set models of cardboard,
sketched costumes, and read everything he could find on the
theatre.   In October, he did The Sea Gull at The Little Theatre, again with Gielgud, directed by A. E. Filmer.   He
played Semyon Semyonitch Medvedenko, as well as designed
the sets and costumes (as he had done for The Cherry
Orchard).   In all, he did over thirty productions in the 1925-
28 period in London.

     Immediately after Mr. Godly Beside Himself, a 300
Club play for Nigel Playfair, Whale went to work on Playfair's Riverside Nights, a grab-bag musical comedy-drama
revue that enjoyed immense popularity during most of 1926.
Whale designed the sets, costumes, and played a small role
in the second act.

The show was put together by A. P. Herbert and Playfair, who also directed and co-starred in a company of 18
that included Marie Dainton, Kathlyn Hilliard, W. Earle Grey,
and Elsa Lanchester. Containing two complete operas, a his-
torical drama in three acts, and a "translation of a new play
from the Russian" (Chekhov), besides songs and dances, it
opened at the Lyric, Hammersmith on Saturday, April 10, to
exceptional notices. Of the parody of "The Three Sisters,"
The Times said:

> It is not only amazingly funny, but it has the
> true quality of parody in that it is also a just criti-
> cism, especially of translations from the Russian.
> It is Miss Marie Dainton, who made a welcome re-
> turn to the stage as the commere of the show, and
> remains, in her own words, "as brisk as a bee,"
> gave us a delicious impression of Mrs. Patrick
> Campbell's intensity. Mr. Miles Malleson, who
> was all through one of the bright stars of the even-
> ing, excelled himself as a newspaper seller, an-
> nouncing in the true depressive manner, "All the
> losers!" Mr. James Whale stood oddly out of the
> picture, as if you had put a real vase into a still
> life; for his part was almost a reproduction of
> Epikhodov [sic].
> The performance was received with great en-
> thusiasm, for which Mr. Playfair returned thanks
> in a graceful speech.

Again for the 300 Club, Whale designed the scenery
and costumes for Don Juan by James Elroy Flecker; and
played Baptiste in The Would-Be Gentleman, a gay farce
adapted by F. Anstey from Molière's Le Bourgeois Gentil-
homme, with Nigel Playfair starring and directing. Next
came The Beaux' Stratagem, a Playfair comedy with Edith
Evans, which he designed and in which he had a featured
role.

In May of 1927, Whale did the sets for an ambitious
300 Club production of D. H. Lawrence's biblical play David,
directed by Ernest Milton. Actor/playwright Miles Malleson,
Whale's colleague in several outings, then had a part for him
in his Love at Second Sight: Collins the butler. Malleson
directed, reminding Whale of his own ambitions to one day
become a director. But he had done only minor direction
for Barry Jackson, and had merely assisted Mr. Playfair.
Still, he yearned for Malleson's chance to direct in the West

End. Love was not a success, but it served to renew
Whale's determination.   He began actively seeking a directing
assignment and went to work on the designs for The Kingdom
of God, which opened at the Strand in late October.   It was
a Spanish play about the long, simple life of one Sister Gar-
cia (Gillian Scaife), who, at eighteen, joins the Order
of St. Vincent de Paul and ends her life as the Mother Su-
perior of a tiny orphanage.   Whale had a small part in this
also, but it, too, was unsuccessful despite favorable press.
The year 1927 was a steady one, but it was 1928 that was
to mark the turning point in Whale's life.   Early on, he was
in Benn Levy's adaptation of A Man with Red Hair, in which
Charles Laughton starred as Crispin, his perverse, sadistic
father (although Whale was actually ten years Laughton's
senior).   It was a story of torture and pain that inspired in-
tense reactions from all who viewed it.   An outraged Times
critic wrote,

> Crispin is the centre of the play, with his mad
> son, sketched with a sickening skill by Mr. James
> Whale, and his Japanese servants.   The whole
> dramatic strength radiates from him; everything is
> seen in his light or in his shadow; and Mr. Charles
> Laughton has made so subtle, so revoltingly bril-
> liant a study of his sadistic obsession that the man,
> and through him the play, is well-nigh intolerable.
> Mr. Laughton by face, by voice, above all, by
> imaginative bodily movement, compels suspension
> of disbelief.   You see before you a fanatic who has
> raised a lust for the infliction and the endurance of
> pain to the level of a faith.   And for two hours you
> watch him at his vile, pseudo-philosophical game.
> That his victims escape at last, that the lovers
> are united, that the torturer is flung over a cliff--
> all of these things are of no account; they are weak-
> nesses, too weak to be compensations.   Cruelty
> and torture dominate the stage.   There is no es-
> cape from it.   Mr. Laughton's acting we are bound
> to admire, but we owe an evening of something
> very near misery to its skill.

After Whale appeared in a brief revival of London's
Grand Guignol and the Stage Society's highbrow Paul Among
the Jews, he finally landed a chance to direct in the West
End.   It was producer Anmer Hall who cast Whale in the
title role of Fortunato and then agreed to engage him to direct it.   Fortunato and The Lady from Alfaqueque were two

Spanish plays by Serafin and Joaquin Alvarez Quintero to be
presented in tandem, the former being a "tragic farce," and
the latter a mild comedy.   In the casts were John Gielgud,
Anthony Ireland, Margaret Webster, Miriam Lewes, Gracie
Leigh, and Elsie French, among others whom Whale had known
previously.   Producer-dramatist-actor Harley Granville-
Barker and his second wife Helen had translated both plays
after his retirement from the theatre to teach and collaborate
on such things.   The rehearsals went well and the usually im-
posing Granville-Barker was nowhere in evidence until one
day, when word at last came that the great man would sit in.

        "We were all extremely nervous," Gielgud recalled.
"Everyone whispered, people smoothed their hair and walked
about, and Miriam sat, dressed in her best hair and frock,
beating a tattoo with her fingers on the arm of her chair.
Granville-Barker was certainly a revelation.   He rehearsed
us for about two hours, changed nearly every move and arrangement of the stage, acted, criticized, advised, in an
easy flow of practical efficiency, never stopping for a moment.

        "We all sat spellbound, trying to drink in his words
of wisdom and at the same time remember all the hints he
was giving us, none of which we had time to memorize or
write down.   Everything he said was obviously and irrefutably
right.   Even when he announced that James could not possibly play Fortunato and that O. B. Clarence must be engaged, everyone gasped but nobody ventured to disagree."

        Whale could do nothing but press on as best he could.
"There were long, long waits," wrote Margaret Webster in
The Same, Only Different, "while (Granville-Barker) went into a private huddle with the director.   After this, he would
deliver to the company a pontifical--and fascinating--lecture
on the history of the drama, on psychology, on Spanish literature, habits and domestic architecture.   After this, he
would disappear completely for a week.   When he came again--
the company by this time was brimful of Spanish lore--nothing
Spanish would be mentioned at all.   But he would take one
tiny section of the play and go over it again and again and
again, leaving other major sequences completely untouched."

        The experience was humiliating for Whale, and the
plays, as he had feared, were not popular.   "For some reason or other," Gielgud reasoned, "English audiences always
seem suspicious of a double or triple bill, and I do not think

a programme of this kind has ever succeeded in the West
End. "

The Times said:

> ... They are melodious plays, and that accounts
> for their delicious strangeness--for melody is a vir-
> tue which in the theatre has become a trifle strange.
> Let it be confessed that the melody of "The Lady
> from Alfaqueque" drags before the end, the duping
> of our tender-hearted provincial being too long
> drawn out; but "Fortunato, " which does genuinely
> deserve the name of a tragic farce, is beautifully
> sustained alike in its sadness and its gaiety, and
> ends with a scene that is a little gem of prepared
> theatre-craft.  And though in all instances the
> casting has not been very happy, there is much
> that is delightful in the performance.  Miss Gillian
> Scaife, though she has not all the Latin vivacity of
> Alfaqueque, very ingeniously elaborates the ami-
> able follies of Fernandita; there is admirable work
> by Mr. Gielgud, Miss Miriam Lewes, Mr. Eric
> Stanley, and Mr. Geoffrey Wincott, and a remark-
> ably brilliant and moving performance by Mr. O. B.
> Clarence in the first piece.  The plays have been
> decorated and produced by Mr. James Whale, who
> never fails to make his own manner an accompani-
> ment to the dramatists' melody and an enrichment
> of it. "

The Lady from Alfaqueque and Fortunato hung on for
a month, then died a quiet death.  Whale liked the plays,
but knew the London stage too well by then to overextend
his hopes.  He had entered into rehearsals as an actor for
High Treason, a play by H. Pemberton-Billing about a
Bishop (H. A. Saintsbury) who shoots a Prime Minister to
prevent a declaration of war, when he received another directing assignment on the strength of Lady and Fortunato.

The play was The Dreamers, written by Anthony Merryn on the basis of the Pythagorean transmigration of souls:
two lovers from a former life meet again while involved with
others.  There were only four characters in the cast, played
by Clare Harris, Sidney Seaward, Gwen Ffrangeon-Davies,
and Ernest Milton.  Whale worked hard on the new offering,
and did not have Harley Granville-Barker to hamper him,
but was appearing concurrently in High Treason at the Strand

Theatre and couldn't muster much faith in it.    Notices and
receipts again were poor.

He continued with Treason at £5 a week.    One day
Geoffrey Dearmer of The Stage Society submitted the script
of their projected December production, Journey's End, to
him with an offer to direct it.    Whale read the play and immediately fell in love with it.    That evening, after work, he
repaired to his flat and went about designing its one set,
that of a British dugout before St. Quentin in March of 1918.

The lead character was that of Captain Dennis Stanhope who, with his command, has come up to take over some
of the front line:    after three years of war, he is the idol of
his men and an example of sheer courage.    He is also an
alcoholic of great note.    Stanhope's companions are his sec-
ond-in-command and only friend, Lieutenant Osborne; Second
Lieutenant Hibbert; Second Lieutenant Trotter; and Private
Mason, the cook.

The play concerned the arrival of a new officer, Second Lieutenant Raleigh--just out of school where only a few
years before the clean-living athlete Stanhope had been his
hero.    Stanhope worshiped Raleigh's sister, and Raleigh looks
forward to fighting on the same team with him at last.

Lieutenant Osborne tries to prepare the new arrival
for the real Stanhope; when the Captain returns, his first
thought is for whiskey--the thing that allows him to carry on.
Raleigh's presence only triggers a great resentment within
him, and the greeting he extends is anything but cordial.
That night, Stanhope tells Osborne of his love for Madge
Raleigh--he knows she thinks him an honored hero and fears
her brother will spy on him and write to her the truth.    He
is a nerve-raw wreck, and his censorship of Raleigh's letters is the only answer.    To his puzzlement, however, Raleigh only writes in praise of him.

Hibbert, a coward at heart, at one point asks the
Captain for permission to report sick and be sent to the
rear.    Stanhope, in turn, gives him thirty seconds to take
his place or be shot as a deserter.    Hibbert stands to his
gun, but Stanhope can't bring himself to fire.    He tells him
that but for the alcohol he consumes, he too would be driven
to the safety of a base hospital.    In reality, though, Stanhope drinks for his nerves, not his heart.

As a German offense nears, the Colonel orders a raid on the enemy trenches to capture a prisoner from whom details can be learned. Osborne and Raleigh lead the party, but only Raleigh returns. Stunned by the death of his friend, Raleigh refuses to join in the fragile spirit of hilarity that characterizes that evening's dinner. As the others drink themselves into forgetfulness, Stanhope flies into a vicious rage against the man who openly mourns the loss of Osborne.

Finally, the German attack comes and Raleigh himself is fatally wounded. Carried back into the dugout, Stanhope keeps him from knowing that he is dying and sits dazedly beside the body when death does come. He resents himself and his treatment of the boy. Stiffly, the Captain mounts the steps to face the Germans who have broken the British line. A shell bursts on the dugout roof and Stanhope goes under in the crumbling structure.

It was as grim a war tale as Whale had read, and he could see the truth within it; the author had obviously been there himself. Whale also recognized the fact that it was not a commercial piece and that he had the script only because three or four other directors had turned it down. The Stage Society prided itself on presenting things like Paul Among the Jews; when they took a liking to something, it was a good bet that no sane commercial producer would touch it.

Its author, an "outdoor man" for the Sun Insurance Company named Bob Sherriff, was told to come meet with his director backstage at the Strand.

"I went to the stage door, " he remembered in his autobiography No Leading Lady, "and was taken to Whale's dressing-room, where he was making-up for his part. He scarcely looked at me: he kept his eyes on the mirror as he rubbed on the grease paint, and talked to my reflection in the glass where I sat in a chair behind him. He didn't seem very enthusiastic about Journey's End. I gathered that it was to be a stop-gap production because the one originally planned by the Stage Society for December was a big expensive affair postponed for a month to get the right people to act in it.

"He said little about the play beyond the comment that certain scenes were too sentimental and would have to be brought down to earth or cut out. I gladly agreed to do anything he suggested. I would have cut the whole play and done it again if this got it any nearer to the West End. "

R. C. Sherriff

Sherriff had written several plays on an amateur basis
to raise funds for the Kingston Rowing Club, of which he was
a member.   They showed some limited success, but after
that period of his life had ended, he dabbled with Journey's
End without much thought toward commercial production.
When agent Curtis Brown took on the property, he was pleas-
antly surprised, although he entertained no delusions about
its lack of commercial potential.   Whale invited Sherriff to
his lodgings that next afternoon to see the model he had built,
and then left to perform.

"I went to his flat in Chelsea and he showed me a
beautifully constructed model.   I had envisaged little more
than a squalid cavern in the ground, but Whale had turned
the hand of art to it.   By strutting the roof with heavy tim-
bers he gave an impression of vast weight above:   an oppres-
sive, claustrophobic atmosphere with a terrifying sense of
imprisonment for those who lived in it.   Yet with this,
through innumerable small details, he had given it a touch of
crude romance that was fascinating and exhilarating.   Above
all, it was real.   There may never have been a dugout like
this one:   but any man who had lived in the trenches would
say, 'This is it:   this is what it was like.' "

James Whale was a lucky accident for the Stage Society.   It was all a second-level situation, and he lavished
care into it that a more established director wouldn't have
bothered with.   The same was true of the casting process.

Laurence Olivier was playing at the Royalty Theatre
in John Drinkwater's Bird in Hand.   It wasn't much of a
part he had--simply half the love interest--and he certainly
wasn't very well known.   Established performers such as
Leslie Banks and Robert Loraine had balked at Journey's
End, and Whale soon turned this to an advantage.   The entire cast should be relatively unknown, he determined, as a
star would throw it off; try the reality of it.   Whale offered
Olivier the part of Stanhope--the young actor could easily
recognize it was one with meat and range.   He accepted,
but on the condition that Whale would get Basil Dean to attend the performance.   Dean was one of Europe's foremost
producers for the stage, and Olivier was up for the title role
in Dean's upcoming production of Beau Geste.   Whale agreed,
and the rest of the cast was then selected.   Sherriff was invited to the first read-through of the play, in a shabby up-
stairs room over a shop on Charing Cross Road.   It was a
cold November morning and the cast huddled around a long,

bare table in overcoats and mufflers.  As work began, Sherriff was shocked to see the actor engaged to play Mason
walk in late and toss his script on the table:  he announced
that he had gotten a part that promised a longer run than the
two days Journey's End could, and left.  Unperturbed, Whale
turned to his assistant and said, "Ring up Alex and tell him
to come along as soon as he can. "  He then introduced Sherriff to the assembled cast and commenced the first reading.

Wrote Sherriff, "The men sat round the table hunched
in their overcoats:  some with mufflers around their necks,
some with their hats on--as unlike war-strained soldiers in a
front line dugout as they could possibly be.   They sat with
their eyes glued to their scripts, puffing cigarettes, never
making an attempt to emphasize or dramatize their lines; but
as the reading went on it came over beyond a shadow of a
doubt that the team had been perfectly chosen.   None had any
need to act the parts--they were the men--they merely had
to be themselves.   And luckily no famous star was there to
overwhelm the others. "

After the reading, Sherriff went back with Whale to
his rooms and worked through the script; the cuts and
changes proved to be small indeed.   It passed as first written and the cast was complete:

| | |
|---|---|
| Captain Hardy | David Horne |
| Lieutenant Osborne | George Zucco |
| Private Mason | Alexander Field |
| Second Lieutenant Raleigh | Maurice Evans |
| Captain Stanhope | Laurence Olivier |
| Second Lieutenant Trotter | Melville Cooper |
| Second Lieutenant Hibbert | Robert Speaight |
| The Company Sergeant-Major | Percy Walsh |
| The Colonel | H. G. Stoker |
| A German Soldier | Geoffrey Wincott |

Money was tight:   the actors would receive nothing
but exposure.   Whale got a mere £10 and the cost of building the set was £80.   Time was also tight.   With the casting problems, they barely had two weeks to rehearse, and
since the Apollo Theatre, where the performance would be,
had another play in residence, it was necessary to rehearse
in rooms with the dugout boundaries marked on the floor
with chalk.   It would be a race to erect the set and prepare
the lights after Saturday night's performance for a dress rehearsal.   With the sounds of war coming from whistles and

drums behind the stage, it successfully ended just minutes before the audience started to take their seats.

Author Sherriff had lent Olivier his own tunic and Sam Browne belt, revolver, and holster for the performance. As the audience filed in, he nervously paced and became drenched in perspiration. Whale went backstage to see the actors, and powerless to do any more, retired to the rear to concentrate on the proceedings.

"Sometimes I met Whale," Sherriff said, "who seemed to be as restless as myself. I'd whisper to him, 'How d'you think it's going?' and he'd nod and walk away. He wanted to be alone. His work was done, and nothing remained to do but watch and hope."

Sherriff knew the many things that could possibly go wrong, from a missed entrance to forgotten lines, or perhaps the precarious dugout steps collapsing under the weight of the Sergeant-Major and the wounded Raleigh toward the climax. As the end approached, he could no longer stand it, and darted into the cold night air while Whale stood his ground.

> ... I heard people clapping, and from the back of the pit I saw that the curtain was already down, and that people were putting on their coats. The curtain went up and down several times as the actors came forward to make a bow, but there didn't seem to be much applause. It sounded polite and formal, and when the house lights went up I saw a lot of people hurrying out to catch their trains or buses home. I was strung up and maybe oversensitive, but as I watched them hurrying off I had a feeling they were glad to get away.

Sherriff got his hat and coat and quickly left the area; Whale spoke with a few of the patrons, and discussed the performance with members of the cast--there would be a rehearsal the next morning to help correct some minor lighting and sound effect problems. The play had gone fine; beyond his expectations, having been involved as an actor in many Sunday situations himself. The actors were excellent, and the stage manager had done an A-1 job. But the Stage Society audiences were difficult. They were intellectual, not given to exuberant demonstration. The ones he had spoken with liked it, but felt it was too sad and depressing for the general public tastes. Barry Jackson and several other man-

agers had been there also; they concurred with its honest,
sincere picture of life in the trenches, but denied any commercial potential.    Basil Dean, who attended with Madeleine
Carroll in tow, liked it well enough to want to do it himself,
but knew he couldn't get the backing that would be needed.
In short, everyone liked Journey's End--but felt that no one
else would.

The Monday afternoon performance was poorly attended; the theatre was barely half-full, with gaps of empty
seats on either side.    The Monday shows were principally
for the reviewers and the Society members who preferred
matinees.    Members of the general public might also attend,
although good (or bad) notices would not appear until the
Tuesday or Wednesday papers hit the stands.

Alan Napier had run into Whale over the week-end and
was tendered an invitation to see the new masterpiece.    "I
was simply staggered, " he said.    "The thing that Olivier's
always been able to do is to etch certain lines that ring in
your head until the day you die.    In the second act, his sec-
ond-in-command has just been killed, and the new young
officer comes in and lies down.    Stanhope's keeping it in.
His curtain line is, 'And must you lie on Osborne's bed?'
A simple line, but it displayed the whole agony of war in the
trenches and your best friend dying before your eyes--I can
hear it to this day. "

The critics ranged their comments from good to excellent.    The Times felt it not so much drama as a histor-
ical document that could only lose its effectiveness with the
passing years; some noted women crying at the end, stifling
the applause.    Hannen Swaffer of the Daily Express headlined
his:    "THE GREATEST OF ALL WAR PLAYS. "    ("... All
London should flock to see it. ")

Whale read them all, and was properly delighted when
Sherriff rang up mid-day to make an appointment for afternoon tea at his rooms.    "Something's bound to happen now?"
he asked.

"I don't know, " Whale replied guardedly, "but let's
hope so. "

Sherriff later wrote,

They were modest rooms, very much like the

quarters of a man who lived for the theatre.
Framed around the walls were colored sketches of
stage sets that he had designed for various productions: his bookcase was full of printed plays, his
table piled high with manuscripts. On a sideboard
stood the model of the dugout for Journey's End.
  He said he had had several phone calls from
friends congratulating him on the good press the
play had received, but nothing from anyone con-
nected with a management. Theatre managers, he
went on, were suspicious about the enthusiastic reviews so frequently given to productions by the private theatre clubs. Critics went out of their way
to encourage the clubs that worked for the love of
the theatre rather than for the profit from it.
They had recently written glowing notices for an
obscure Greek tragedy that nobody in their senses
would expect the public at large to fork out a pen-
ny to see, and they frequently enthused over plays
by highbrow foreign dramatists that excited the in-
tellectuals but were obviously above the heads of
the people who bought the stalls and the dress cir-
cle seats that kept the theatres going. Managers
read these notices with their tongues in their
cheeks. Most of them at one time or another had
felt the urge to do something for art's sake and
been badly bitten for it. They were businessmen
who had to make their business pay. It might even
have been better, said Whale, if the critics had
condemned Journey's End instead of praising it.
If they condemned a production by a highbrow Sunday club it was more likely to attract the managers
and lead them to believe that by an error of judgment the society had produced a play with money
in it.

  Nonetheless, Journey's End was the most solid property James Whale had yet sunk his directorial teeth into. He
would definitely run with it.

# CHAPTER TWO

R. C. Sherriff's agent, Curtis Brown, had read and politely rejected previous works before agreeing to take on Journey's End. He charged no reading fees, which appealed to the author, and found his war play "very fine. "

They would do everything possible to secure a manager, but the West End managers showed no interest and offering it to prominent actors accomplished nothing. It had taken several months to attain the two Stage Society performances, and despite the exceptional reviews, there were no other takers.

James Whale's success with the property insured him the director's position if anyone could be interested, and aside from the slight fee he would get for his actual time invested, there would be good money from his percentage of the take should the play be a big hit. Consequently, he found himself rejecting further work--as either actor or director--in favor of it, as did most of the cast members.

James Agate of the Sunday Times had a popular weekly radio program that he gave over entirely that week to Journey's End.

"I have never been so deeply moved, so enthralled, so exalted, " he raved, "... but you will never see this play. I have spoken with several managers, urging them to give you the opportunity of judging it for yourselves, but they are adamant in their belief that war plays have no audience in the theatre. "

Whale heard the whole thing.   "It was tremendous.
I've never heard Agate talk like that before.   If it doesn't
do the trick, then nothing will. "

Nothing happened.

"They're businessmen all wanting to make money, "
Agate later told Sherriff.   "I knew there was a fortune lying
on their doorsteps, and they wouldn't go outside and pick it
up. "

At last a man called Maurice Browne called the Curtis Brown offices and asked to read Journey's End.   Browne
wasn't a manager; he had never produced a play in the West
End.   But Browne was evidently attracted to the play's "highbrow" reputation:   he had spent several years in America
presenting classic drama to the masses and had returned to
England with nothing but the clothes he wore.

Sherriff knew his play wasn't highbrow, and didn't
honestly feel it would be to Mr. Browne's liking.   Whale
was wary of such a man and his ability to do anything about
the play's impasse with the theatrical establishment, but
there was certainly nothing to lose in allowing him to read
it.   Sherriff dutifully delivered his copy to a shabby address
at Earls Court and waited.

The next day after work, he came home to a tele-
gram:

> Journey's End magnificent.   Will gladly produce it.
> Returning to London Monday afternoon.   Shall look
> forward to meeting you without delay.   My profound
> congratulations upon a splendid play.
>
> Maurice Browne

Sherriff and Whale were guarded.   This man would
need at least £5,000 to mount a proper production.   Nonetheless, a meeting was arranged and everything settled.
Browne had some wealthy friends who had promised to under-
write a worthy play when he decided he had found one.
Browne advanced Sherriff £200 and agreed to retain both the
cast and the director.   Much to Whale's amazement, he was
back to work at the Savoy.

The arrangements went smoothly, although Olivier had
won the part of Beau Geste and was scheduled to open at His

Majesty's Theatre on January 30th.   So the big problem fac-
ing them was to find a Stanhope.   Some of the name actors
who had rejected the part found themselves available, but
Whale was against them.   The earlier formula had worked
well:   no big, high-powered names.   They had a cast that
was letter-perfect--they couldn't afford a thoughtless move
that would queer the chemistry of the cast.

     Dozens of actors were interviewed; none were accept-
able.   They were all too careful, too smooth--not one displayed that rough, jagged edge apparent in Olivier's performance.   Whale despaired of ever finding another Stanhope.
One night, Browne received a call from Jeanne de Casalis,
a prominent actress who suggested trying the man to whom
she was then engaged, Colin Clive.   No one had heard of
him--he wasn't in Spotlight and his most impressive credit
was the part of Steve in Show Boat.   They were, however,
willing to talk to anyone.   Sherriff recalled,

     ... The moment I saw him I knew he was our
     man.   Whale also knew.   He had no doubt providing
     he understood the part and read it well.
        Clive didn't read it well.   He had a rough,
     husky voice and kept on misreading the words, but
     his bad reading made him the more appealing.
     Stanhope would have read it badly himself.   He was
     far and away the best man we had seen, but Mau-
     rice Browne and his manager were doubtful.   His
     lack of experience made him a dangerous risk.
        They were in favor of another actor named Colin--
     Colin Keith-Johnston:   a young and handsome actor
     who had made a name for himself on the stage and
     had won a military Cross in the war.   He had not
     only proved himself as an actor, but had played the
     part of Stanhope in reality, in the trenches.
        Both actors were asked to a final reading.
     Keith-Johnston read the part beautifully.   He had a
     fine, expressive voice; he had command and gave
     meaning to every word.   Clive's reading was worse
     than the first attempt:   blundering over the words,
     puffing a cigarette, shuffling his feet.
        When it was over it seemed that Keith-Johnston
     had romped home the winner.   Maurice Browne and
     his manager had no doubts.   Whale was thoughtful;
     something was worrying him, but he didn't know
     what it was.   Maurice Evans, who was to play Ra-
     leigh as he had done for the Stage Society, happened

Colin Clive

to be there and had heard both the readings.    His
part was tied so closely to Stanhope, he had so
many vital scenes with him, that his opinion was
even more important than ours.    He was asked
which actor he thought most suited the part.    He
didn't answer at once.    Then he said:    "Keith-
Johnston's got it here" (pointing to his forehead)--
"but Clive's got it here" (pointing to his heart).

Colin Clive, upon considerable gamble, got the part.
Journey's End was announced by Maurice Browne on New
Year's Day, 1929.    It would open at the Savoy Theatre on
Monday, January 21st.

The tall, grey-eyed, black-haired son of Colonel
Colin Clive-Greig was born in St. Malo,   France in January
of 1900.    He was educated at Stonyhurst College and the
Royal Military College before studying at the Royal Academy
of Dramatic Arts in London.    He was a fine actor with a
good background, who lacked confidence in himself and was
a chronic worrier.    He had been working on the stage since
playing a small part in The Eclipse at the Garrick Theatre
in 1919.    Jeanne de Casalis and he had met while doing The
Yellow Streak in September 1928.

"It was difficult for Clive to work his way into a word-
perfect company," wrote Sherriff.    "He alone was stumbling
over his lines, drying up and being prompted.    He was highly
strung and temperamental, and one day after a bad rehearsal
he went to Whale and offered to give up the part.    Whale
tried to reassure him, but everybody was worried.    Stanhope
the Company Commander was the rock upon which the whole
play stood:    if he failed, the play was doomed."

The rehearsals continued going badly.    Clive got no
better, but it was still obvious to both Whale and Sherriff
that he possessed the right qualities for the role--quali-
ties he was unable to unleash.    One night, Sherriff took
him aside and suggested a good stiff whiskey before the
afternoon rehearsal.    Clive was doubtful; drinking before
work was a cardinal sin for an actor.    Just once, Sherriff urged.    Finally, Clive agreed.    At lunch, he went
off to a small public house and consumed several whiskeys.
He returned a new man.    Said Sherriff,

He no longer stumbled over his words and dried
up halfway through his long speeches.    The words

were already photographed perfectly in his mind
through long nights of study, and only the inhibitions of anxiety had prevented them from flowing
freely.    The whiskey at lunch had freed him from
his inhibitions, and the words flowed out without
restraint.

Whale was astonished and delighted; he had always known what a fine performance lay in Clive's
power if only it could be released.    Now Clive had
found himself.    He didn't need the whiskey for sub-
sequent rehearsals.    His performance gained in
stature with every day that passed, and Maurice
Browne, who had resigned himself to the unhappy
conviction that he had put his money on a loser,
doubled the money set aside for advertisement.

When rehearsals moved to the Savoy, and the dugout
was again erected, a new, disastrous, and totally unforesee-
able problem arose.    One of the main strengths of James
Whale's staging of Journey's End was the remarkably authentic background noises--the sounds of war--that punctuated the
dialogue.    They were developed at the Apollo Theatre with
painstaking hours of trial and error.    A sniper's shot was
nothing more than a wooden box and a low whistle.    Machine
gun raps were sharp blows to a commandeered chair cushion,
and various drum-like contraptions supplemented small ex-
plosive charges in a large iron tank.    They were makeshift
but wonderfully effective with the Apollo acoustics.

Two performances at the Stage Society were one thing;
a generous run at the Savoy was quite another.    Whale sought
to improve upon the atmosphere of sounds they had created
so haphazardly before.    The devices were more permanent
and complex.    And the acoustics were a whole new matter.

Whale wanted Sherriff on hand as the whole process
came down to the wire, but with his Sun Insurance job he
was lucky for whatever time he could afford.    It all fell on
the director's shoulders.

Young Woodley had enjoyed a long run at the Savoy
that ended on the Saturday evening before the Monday opening
of Journey's End.    It was like the mad Stage Society scram-
ble a month before to get things in shape for a Sunday afternoon dress rehearsal, where the demoralizing effects of the
new surroundings first became apparent:    the space between
the stage and the back wall was narrower, effectively ruining
the careful realism of the sounds.

The rehearsal, which had started at five, dragged on toward midnight with no end in sight. Each new attempt at a solution brought another problem. Whale, ever calm and patient, ordered a lighting and effects rehearsal for ten o'clock the following morning and a final dress that afternoon.

R. C. Sherriff arrived at the theatre around eight o'clock the following evening. To his surprise, the cancellation signs were nowhere to be seen. Whale had sent a series of customary "good luck" telegrams to him, Browne, and the cast members before donning rented evening clothes and a white carnation.

"We did a lot of work this morning," he said, "and I think everything's all right now. Are you going round to see the company? I think they'd like you to look in. I'd leave Clive alone if I were you. He's all right--but I wouldn't disturb him."

Whale stationed himself with the stage manager, as Sherriff quietly obeyed and then slipped into a box to sweat it out.

It was a near-perfect evening.

When the curtain fell the auditorium remained in darkness while the cast assembled behind the curtain to take their bow. The effect was eerie and unreal, for there wasn't a sound from the thousand people who sat out there in the darkness. It was as if, by some magic spell, they had been spirited away, and the theatre was empty. When at last the curtain rose upon a line of soldiers and steel helmets and mud-spattered uniforms, with the smoke and the dust of the shattered dugout partly veiling them, the audience still sat in silence, and the curtain fell again without a sound. Standing at the back of my box I had the aching dread that the play had so bored them that they had all gone fast asleep. Was it possible to put the curtain up again? By all the rules of the theatre the curtain was only raised at the end of a play by the clamorous demand of the audience, but not a single one of them had clapped his hands together. Then out of the darkness came a solitary "Bravo!" The curtain rose again, as if to acknowledge the salute of the one remaining member of the audience who hadn't

dozed off.   This time it was for the small part
actors who by custom took their bow together.   The
audience began to applaud, slowly, almost reluctantly, like an engine that had stood over-long in the
cold.   When the curtain rose again upon the actors
of the larger parts the applause spread and
strengthened until it sounded like a hail storm on
the iron roof of a barn.   Maurice Evans, who
played Raleigh, George Zucco, and finally Colin
Clive took their bows alone, and with each the reception grew more clamorous.

Men stood up and cheered:   a paper the next
morning said, "Even the critics cheered. "

James Whale was the director of a tremendous hit.
The box office queues grew as slowly as the first night's
applause, but when the business did start to roll in, it was
strong and constant.   Maurice Browne sensed something unusual happening and enjoyed his first position of strength
against the all-powerful ticket agencies.

He soon effected the biggest deal for a straight play
in the history of the West End:   a three-month guarantee of
more than £1,000 a week.   Whale was ecstatic.   In just
three weeks, they were doing the theatre's £2,539 limit, a
position that would be retained well past the initial three
months.

The position Whale was now put in was a proper ad-
vance for his ten years of knocking around English theatres.
He began to receive a number of scripts to read and, with
his weekly check from Journey's End, he could afford to take
his time in selecting a follow-up.

Browne had a £50 option on the American rights to
the play, and great interest had been expressed.   After carefully weighing the contenders, he went with Gilbert Miller,
the only major producer that would gamble on an English
cast.   The terms were stiff.   60 percent of the net profits
and no share of the motion picture rights.   It was like
doubling the domestic earnings.

Of course, Browne, Miller, and Sherriff wanted Whale
to direct the U.S. version.   Sherriff was especially skeptical
at the acceptance his play might earn across the Atlantic; it
was most certainly too British, he felt.   The chance was
there, though--one he hadn't even counted on.   The money

would be like finding it, and would include a trip to America.
Whale wasn't terribly interested. In thinking of his own future in London, Journey's End would not necessarily serve
to establish him in itself. Surely his foot was now in the
door, but it would take another couple of reasonable successes
to put him in a comfortable position. He would be doing
what he loved best, where he loved doing it. Staging the
New York production would mean more money, but in terms
of that all-important niche he wished to carve for himself,
it would mean next to nothing.

On the other hand, they argued, a New York triumph
would not only extend his reputation but would open the door
to more of Broadway. Miller was interested in him beyond
Journey's End and his plan was to cast and rehearse it in
London. They would try it out for a week at the Arts Theatre, and then move everything to the United States. The
time factor would not be that great, but if all worked out,
the gain would be substantial. Sherriff, to help seal his decision, offered Whale a small percentage of the author's
foreign royalties if he would do it: he was the only one,
they were convinced, who could bring it off again. Whale
finally consented.

Gilbert Miller was keen on the casting process for
the new company. Whale worked closely with him, for he
accepted Miller's contention that there were certain visions
that most Americans held of Englishmen they did not want to
present in Journey's End. Stereotypes were deadly and had
to be avoided at all costs. Carefully chosen, the new cast
went together well. Rehearsals commenced as an exact
duplicate of the claustrophobic set was built with an eye toward packing it for shipping to the U.S. Evelyn Roberts
(Hardy), Leon Quartermaine (Osborne), Victor Stanley (Mason), Derek Williams (Raleigh), Henry Wenman (Trotter),
Jack Hawkins (Hibbert), Sidney Seaward (Sergeant-Major),
Eric Stanley, and Sol Dowday were hired, while the Stanhope
role quite properly went to Colin Keith-Johnston. The easy
atmosphere and lack of problems--after the nightmares of
the London company--were welcome, and after a week at the
Arts, they packed for the voyage.

Before boarding the Aquitania, Whale posed for photog-
raphers with Sherriff, Miller, Browne, Keith-Johnston, Colin
Clive, George Zucco, and the others. Sherriff quit his job
with the Sun Insurance office to make the trip, and had agreed
to sell Browne his share of the movie rights for £2,000 in

order to have some cash put away.    The money was not paid
until later, however, and the sale was a record one for
Britain.    Sherriff regretted the agreement, though only oral
in nature.    The new talking screen had made a film version
quite possible, and Browne held all the cards.

During the crossing, Miller and Whale rehearsed
lightly in the former's cabin with small groups of the cast
members.    They worked on the toning-down of their accents
for American ears, as the schedule was tight:    a dress rehearsal on the night of docking, an out-of-town preview the
following day, and the Broadway premiere on the third.

"If they're one hundred percent English, " Miller said,
"that's fine.    But if they're a hundred and five percent
English, they'll go down the drain. "

At the docking there was ample press coverage, but
it was all aimed at Sherriff and the cast.    Whale was to
share a suite with him at the hotel, but there was little time
to waste.    He slipped unnoticed past the reporters and caught
a cab to The Henry Miller Theatre on 43rd Street--east of
Broadway--where Journey's End would open in two days.
Whale supervised the erection of the set and enjoyed a small
dinner before the cast arrived.    There was a nagging dread
in the back of his mind of another possible acoustical problem,
though the fears proved to be unfounded.

The rehearsal went without a hitch; the next afternoon
they traveled by train to the Great Neck Playhouse, where
Miller had arranged the preview.    The reception that night
was, according to Sherriff, "formal and polite. "    Gilbert
Miller, overall, was pleased but guarded.    It was a tough
audience that would decide nothing.    Whale wasn't as bothered
because he didn't have as much riding on the American success of Journey's End as the others.    He was satisfied with
his end of the job:    he had made the play as acceptable as
it was going to get.    If it failed, it would not be a reflection of the quality of the thing--it would be a simple matter
of trans-Atlantic tastes.

The next day was spent at the theatre, as the dugout
was re-installed for that evening's performance.    Whale's
mind concerned itself with everything that bore upon what the
audience would see.    His nerves became more strained as
the day wore on, although he did his best not to let it show.
He busied himself with small details, to keep the nervous

energies in check.   It also made him feel better to dig into
the small things, because it meant that the play was otherwise in pretty good shape.   The American crew was coopera-
tive and friendly, but he and they worked with different
terminologies and accents.   He had trouble communicating
clearly with them, which made the experience all the more
fatiguing.   He was pale and tired when he returned to the
hotel to rest, and Sherriff rang down for some coffee and
sandwiches.

"I'd give anything for a whiskey and soda, " said
Whale.

Sherriff relished the night.

> The play was beautifully performed.   The art
> of the actors, the skill of the technicians, the in-
> finite care of the director--all they had to give was
> blended into a perfect harmony.   The quiet passages
> were timed and modulated to flow like meditative
> interludes in a robust symphony; anger would flare
> out like a burst of flame; and the drama had been
> polished and sharpened to an edge of steel.   Watch-
> ing it from a dark corner behind the stalls it was
> hard to link it with those thumb-soiled sheets of
> pencilled dialogue I had toiled over at home, or
> with the unsteady draft I had laboriously typed out
> with the first finger of each hand.   The small "f"
> had come off my typewriter.   I wasn't mechanical-
> ly minded enough to fix it back, and I had to go
> over the script afterwards, putting in all the "f"s
> with a pen.

The public and critics were as enthused as their British counterparts:   the play was a hit all over again.

## CHAPTER THREE

I was an actor in New York [recalled David Lewis],
and I had a health problem.  I had had a tonsillec-
tomy and developed some terrible sort of bronchial
condition.  Previously, I had done some reading
work for the New York office of Paramount and
knew some people there; Walter Wanger was kind
of interested in me.  So, I came to Hollywood without a job, but with certain contacts.  I knew Irene
Mayer and she got me to David Selznick--they
weren't married yet--and he talked to Bud Lighton,
who gave me a job as his assistant.
    (B. P.) Schulberg was in Europe at the time.
He had always said, "No assistants to producers.
We've had that and it doesn't work. "  Lighton hired
me anyway, and I did a lot of reading for him.  I
went to the set, watched the development of things,
and just generally assisted in any way I could.  For
someone who thought he knew everything and didn't
know very much, it was quite a job.
    But it didn't last long.  Schulberg got back and
wanted to fire me--he said I couldn't work that way.
Meanwhile, a man named Eddie Montagne had come
over from the story department and said that I had
done the best synopses he had ever seen and had
the best story mind that you could ever imagine.
So I became his assistant, but without reading.
    He said, "I want you to go on every set.  I
want you to watch every film.  I want you to read
every word--from the time it starts until the time
it finishes. "  And that I did.  I began to see how

35

stories were formed and what the essence of story was.

Mary Alice Scully, a literary agent, was a friend of David Lewis. One day in the latter half of June 1929, she gave him a call.

"We're bringing out a director from London, " she said. "He's just done Journey's End. I wonder if you would be nice to him and take him to lunch?"

Lewis agreed and she brought James Whale to his office about 11:30. With the coming of sound in the motion picture industry, the studio heads worried about the people they had who were used to making silent pictures. Most proved to be quite adept at making talkies. Some did not, and new talent had to be mined. Where else to look but to the Broadway stage? And what was more popular there than Journey's End?

This was a period when directors with experience in dialogue were used to supplement directors with experience in film production. George Cukor came out about this time, and through his association with Gilbert Miller, so did Whale. He signed a contract with Paramount in New York--at $500 a week--and came west to commence the education in film direction he would need to do Journey's End for the screen. His acquisition as a "dialogue expert" was heralded as a major coup to the press. "He produced about forty plays during his directorial days at the Oxford Playhouse in England, " the studio press release enthused.

Lewis took him to meet Bud Lighton, who was producing The Virginian with Victor Fleming. "Lighton was a sweet man who took his name to be Grover Whalen--and you couldn't convince him that it wasn't. As for lunch, there weren't many places to go. Either you ate at the commissary or you ate at a French restaurant called Madame Helene's, which was the best. Or you could go to Oblath's, which was a counter place across the street; they served terrible food, but the commissary was worse. So we went to Madame Helene's. "

They sat at a little side table and exchanged small talk; Whale didn't say much. He would be forty soon, and despite the white that salted his red hair, didn't look it. He staunchly refused to fly, and was groggy from the long rail

David Lewis, circa 1929

journey.  (He later told David Lewis, "The only way that I
would fly is if you were deathly ill on the other side of the
country.  I wouldn't fly for my own mother. ")

      The Englishman made a nice impression, but that was
all.  He was polite, but terribly reserved.

      "I thought he was very gullible, " Lewis, who would
be twenty-six in December, recalled.  "By that time I was
a great sophisticate--I had been in Hollywood at least a few
months.  I didn't pay much attention to him because I knew
a hell of a lot of people and my life was going in a hundred
different directions.

      "The only thing I said to him was, 'Save your money, '
and he said, 'You don't have to worry about that. ' "

      The two parted company a little after 1:00 and Whale
took a taxi to the Villa Carlotta, where Scully had found an
apartment for him.

      The Journey's End snowball had been phenomenal.  It
moved from the Savoy to the Prince of Wales Theatre in London with business more incredible than ever.  Companies in
more than twenty languages were being prepared for similar
experiences elsewhere.  It was the talk of Broadway, and
people were knocking down Maurice Browne's door for the
film rights.  Michael Balcon wanted them badly, but was up
against stiff competition from other British producers and
several American.  Balcon wrote,

> One thing in our favor was the determination of
> Bob Sherriff and Maurice Browne to preserve the
> spirit of the play by having the film made by Brit-
> ish people who understood the hearts and minds of
> the characters.
> Eventually the competition narrowed down to
> Tommy Welsh, of Welsh-Pearson Ltd. , and myself
> (representing Gainsborough Pictures) and, being
> very good friends, we decided to join forces and
> make the film as a co-production venture.  Our
> decision was a wise one as we had to commit our-
> selves to a payment of £15, 000 for the film rights.
> This sum of money today represents no more than
> the petty cash in an American sponsored British
> film (and today there are practically no others) but
> in 1929 it was an unprecedented sum for a British

company to pay for film rights and both Tommy
and I had some explaining to do to our respective
colleagues.

I had very little money available and I imagine
Welsh-Pearson had less, but we managed somehow
and at last came into possession of these most valuable film rights. There was one big snag, however. Welsh-Pearson had no studio, and therefore
no means of making a sound film; we had a studio
that was not equipped for sound. Both Welsh-Pearson and ourselves were desperately anxious for a
success after the financial bashing received by our
most recent silent films. It was absolutely impera-
tive for both of us to make the break into the new
medium without delay. "

Balcon assigned a writer-director at the Gainsborough
Studio, V. Gareth Gundrey, to begin preparing the property
and then sailed for New York to strike a deal with a small
American producer who could solve the equipment problem.
The man he dealt with was Phil Goldstone of Tiffany-Stahl,
and the final terms called for his company to produce Journey's End in the United States under "very stringent conditions." They would put up the production capital, and retain 50 percent interest in the finished product. [1] Gainsborough and Welsh-Pearson would remain equal partners in the
other 50 percent, and Balcon would retain artistic control.
Goldstone had seen the New York production, and was very
enthusiastic about this important new feather in the studio's
otherwise small and undistinguished cap. One provision was
insisted upon though: Gundrey as director was unacceptable;
it had to be James Whale.

So, while the screenplay was being readied in London,
Whale had come west to Hollywood. Journey's End would be
shot toward the end of the year at the RCA Studio in New
York, utilizing Colin Keith-Johnston and the New York cast.

Whale found Paramount a fascinating place. There
were motion picture studios in England, but not nearly as
advanced ones as in California. Basically, there were three
class levels in the studio system, the top level containing
the big, major studios: Metro-Goldwyn-Mayer, Warner Bros.,
Fox, and Paramount. Next came Columbia and Universal,
and the independent facilities of major figures and rental
stages like Metropolitan, Chaplin, United Artists (Pickford/
Fairbanks, later Goldwyn). FBO ("Film Booking Office") had

developed into RKO (Radio-Keith-Orpheum), straddling the
middle-ground between the majors and the minors.   Lastly
came the low-money independents, of which there were many,
collectively known as "Poverty Row. "   These companies included World Wide, Mascot, and Tiffany-Stahl, which entertained daydreams of moving up the ladder with director John
M. Stahl and such films as Mae Murray's sound remake of
Peacock Alley and Journey's End.

Whale's first assignment came quickly.   A well-
established member of the Paramount star roster was Richard Dix, who had recently completed his first talkie.   Dix
had signed a new contract with RKO, to take effect after one
final Paramount.   The studio seemed to think of him mainly
in light comedy, and had gradually lost interest in him with
the coming of sound.   The Dix career needed a shot in the
arm, on the order of Cimmaron, in which RKO starred him
a year later.   For the moment he was slipping, as dissatis-
fied with Paramount as they were with him.

The Dix vehicle to mark their parting was The Boom-
erang, a 1915 three-act farce by Winchell Smith and Victor
Mapes worked into a screenplay by Guy Bolton and J. Walter
Ruben called The Love Doctor.   Dix played Dr. Gerald Sum-
ner, a dedicated bachelor with an admiring nurse, who
treated young Morgan Farley for love sickness.   Miriam
Seegar, the object of his interest, was infatuated with the
Dix character, and more aggressive than the nurse.

It was pretty silly stuff, too cute and obvious for
Whale's tastes.   But unimpressed as he was, he was glad
for the experience.   Melville Brown was the director and
Henry Hathaway, having just finished with Fleming on The
Virginian, was his assistant.   Brown was easy enough to
work with; Whale's job was "Dialogue Director, " which called
for him to rehearse the actors with their lines before reporting to Brown for filming.   It wasn't the most demanding
task he had yet faced, and certainly not worth the $500 a
week he drew.   Whale lived conservatively, waiting for the
studio to catch onto him.

The Love Doctor, like most Paramount programmers,
was shot with three cameras in two weeks during July 1929.
Howard Hughes then sought him out for a seemingly similar
position on his infamous Hell's Angels.

Hughes, the boy wonder among millionaires, had en-

tered film production at the age of twenty with a bomb called
Swell Hogan and the more successful Everybody's Acting.
Encouraged, he poured $500,000 into his Caddo Company,
making Two Arabian Knights with Lewis Milestone directing.
It did better than Everybody's Acting and eventually won the
Academy Award for comedy.  Next came The Racket, a popular gangster picture, and Hell's Angels, which would glorify
the flying heroes of the great World War (and indulge Hughes'
love for planes).  He set to work with Marshall Neilan on an
awful script meant to justify the spectacular flying sequences
he planned, and brought fellow air enthusiast Luther Reed
over from Paramount to direct it.  Hughes knew exactly what
he wanted; when it was apparent the two could agree upon
very little, Reed was released from his contract and Hughes
declared he would direct the film himself.

     After several months of preparation, Hughes had a
script prepared by Howard Estabrook and Harry Behn.  Shooting commenced on October 31, 1927, and continued into early
1929.  In it were Ben Lyon, James Hall, Greta Nissen, and
87 airplanes, which alone cost the young producer almost
$600,000.  Shooting was mainly devoted to the aviation scenes,
which Hughes directed and flew in himself.  One hundred
thirty-seven pilots were employed, 1700 extras in an infantry
sequence, 35 cameramen, and 12 cutters.  Three men were
killed, and after more than two million dollars had been put
into it, Hell's Angels was considered unreleasable by its
maker.  In 1929, it was one of the most costly motion pictures ever made.  It was also completely silent.

     Howard Hughes determined that his masterpiece would
be obsolete before it was ever released; it would have to be
re-made with a soundtrack.  The trick would be to preserve
the excellent action footage--which contained no dialogue any-
way--and to re-shoot the ground story accordingly.  In dealing with actors who would have to talk as well as move,
Hughes realized that he was in over his head.  He needed
someone to act as director of the dialogue material, prefer-
ably British and with some experience in dealing with wartime drama.  The success of Journey's End prompted him to
investigate James Whale, and after conferring with Paramount,
arranged for his loan to Caddo for Hell's Angels.

     Whale liked Hughes because he was a rich and slightly
bizarre fellow.  He looked forward to watching him in action,
although Whale made it clearly understood he wanted nothing
to do with the air sequences--as if Hughes would allow anyone else to direct them anyway.

Paramount had next assigned Whale to Barrie's The Old Lady Shows Her Medals, but replaced him when Hughes' interest made it possible for them to loan him at a substantial profit. As Old Lady entered production--retitled Seven Days' Leave--and Hughes fiddled with a new script revision, Whale departed for the East Coast to direct the Chicago company of Journey's End and A Hundred Years Old, a Quintero play, both for Gilbert Miller.

A Hundred Years Old was another Granville-Barker translation, as slight and as pleasant as any of the Quintero plays, though with a less-than-usual complement of the strange characters that especially appealed to Whale. There was an excellent cast, headed by Otis Skinner as Papa Juan, celebrating his one-hundredth birthday with three succeeding, feuding generations gathered around him. Said The Commonweal,

> The onward emotional range of the play is slight. But that is not the point. Outward intensity, particularly in many modern plays, is merely a cover for absence of inner understanding. This play, by its very theme and the treatment of that theme, tries to cut into the exact centre of why we live and love--but in terms so fragile, so delicately human and humane that you might easily mistake it, as at least one newspaper critic seems to have done, for a mere human interest portrait of Spanish village types.
>
> If you do make such a mistake, please lay the fault to your own overstrained nerves and the brash influence of the many recent plays you have seen, but do not fail at least in retrospect, to think of the moments when A Hundred Years Old has laid bare, though always in beauty, some of the springs of your own existence and of those who will come after you.

After finishing A Hundred Years Old, Whale hurried back to Hollywood to start Hell's Angels at the Metropolitan studios. Hughes, he found, had borrowed Joseph Moncure March, author of The Wild Party and The Set-Up, from M-G-M to rework the script. Ultimately, he put March under contract for a three-year period.

> The first thing I had to do [wrote March] was to screen the silent version. With the exception of

the air sequences and the final dramatic scene in
which Jimmy Hall shoots his brother, Ben Lyon,
to keep him from telling all to the Hun, I thought
the film depressingly bad.  I had to contrive a
story better than the one Hughes had, but still
manage to have it logically embrace the sequences
that were good enough to keep. ...   Whale gave me
the advice and encouragement I needed and let me
work it out the way I wanted.   I completed a first
draft of the script in ten days and, although some
revisions and elaborations were subsequently made,
the screenplay stayed essentially the way it was
from then on.   Hughes and Whale liked the result,
and I was asked to stay and work with them. ...

The tale March brewed was necessarily a wildly frag-
mented story of two brothers, Oxford student Roy Rutledge
(the James Hall part), and Monte (Ben Lyon), weak and reck-
less, and their adventures in the R. F. C.   At best, the script
would act only as a frame for the action stuff, and it soon
became apparent to Whale that he was in on an artistically
lost cause.   Hughes was fickle and erratic, always in evidence in one way or another, although as production proceeded his contributions amounted often to little more than
buzzing the studio in one of his planes.

Production re-opened in early September with no replacement for the Swedish Greta Nissen, whose accent killed
her chance to play Helen, the British tart who seduces Monte
and is the mandatory sex interest.   Whale didn't care who
played it, as long as she could remember her lines and pho-
tograph acceptably.   Hughes' attitudes managed to kill much
of his sympathies for the film, and he simply plowed through
it, anxious to wash his hands of the affair.   Hughes delighted
in playing with the casting of the part, and Whale patiently
advised him to little effect.   At his suggestion, June Collyer
from The Love Doctor was considered, but she wasn't right
for Hughes.   Ann Harding and Carole Lombard (Carol Peters
at the time) were rejected, and things progressed at a tur-
tle's pace.

Arthur Landau, the agent who represented both Ben
Lyon and Nissen, tried, at Whale's urging, to get Warner
Bros. to loan Dorothy Mackaill, to no avail.   In desperation,
he dug Jean Harlow out of obscurity and pumped heavily for
her.   March recalled,

Ben Lyon, Jean Harlow, and James Hall in <u>Hell's Angels</u>
(1930).

We had been working all day on a scene in the
mess hall of an RAF squadron headquarters somewhere in France.... Come five-thirty, everybody
was exhausted. The actors scattered for their
dressing rooms, the lights were turned off, and the
camera crews began to remove the film they had
exposed. At this point, Tony Gaudio, the head
cameraman, was reminded that he was supposed to
shoot a test of some young lady. She was waiting
... it didn't take long to decide to shoot this girl's
test right there.... Two cameras were set up,
Tony yelled for lights, and the girl entered, framed
in the doorway.

She had almost albino hair, a puffy, somewhat
sulky little face, and she was dressed in what appeared to be an evening gown that fitted her tightly
in the bodice and hips.   Eyeing her flaring hips
and narrow waist the writer was moved to make a
disparaging remark to the director.   He said, 'My
God, she's got the shape of a dustpan. '
After Hughes had decided to give Harlow the
part, it was up to James Whale to get a performance out of her, and this took all the skill and patience he had. . . .

Whale didn't particularly like Harlow and she,  it developed,  didn't care much for him,  either.   She blew her
lines with great frequency and was subject to both insecurity
and defensiveness.   The trouble he had with her,  as well as
the problems Hughes created,  served to help wear down his
normally well-composed exterior.   During the latter stages
of production,  he was also involved evenings in preparing
and rehearsing Journey's End at the newly updated Tiffany
Studios  on  Sunset  Boulevard.

"Harlow was quite aware of her deficiencies, " March
noted,  "and a lot of it must have seemed like a nightmare to
her.   Even her ability to be seductive was questioned,  and in
one scene which demanded considerable allure,  she could not
seem to please Mr. Whale.   'Tell me, ' she said,  with desperate earnestness,  'tell me exactly how you want me to do
it. '

"Mr. Whale,  his patience sorely tried,  said,  'My
dear girl,  I can tell you how to be an actress but I cannot
tell you how to be a woman. ' "

Whale did eventually detect an improvement in her
performance--so much so that he had some of her earlier
material re-shot with finer results.

Nonetheless,  the Hell's Angels mess was exceedingly
irritating when the film version of Journey's End increasingly
required his attention.   Whale could do nothing but honor his
contractual commitment to Hughes and count the days to his
freedom.

*     *     *

Whale's studio portrait, Tiffany, 1929.

"There cannot be anyone better known in British filmmaking than George Pearson, " wrote Michael Balcon. "In
1912, at the age of thirty-seven, [he] gave up a promising
career in education in order to join the British branch of the
Pathé company as a film writer and director. For almost
thirty years he continued this work with Samuelson, Gaumont,
and his own company, Welsh-Pearson. The enthusiasm and
devotion he brought to British filmmaking did much to help
establish and maintain production in this country during the
difficult period 1910-1930, and he trained many famous stars
and studio technicians during that time. "

Pearson had hit a deep low in his professional life
when Journey's End came along in 1929. The silent picture,
he could see, would soon be dead; his future was uncertain
and his company floundering. British silents were doing exceedingly poor business, and while his partners, Thomas
Welsh and the recently included T. C. Elder, presided over
what looked to be the end of Welsh-Pearson-Elder, Ltd. ,
Pearson retired to a small room outside London to sort
things out and ponder what might be done. Meanwhile, Welsh
pursued Journey's End; it was the greatest domestic property
available and a guaranteed success. He didn't quite know
what he would do with it when he got it, but the trick was
simply to get it. Gainsborough, via Balcon, sought to remedy
their situation in a similar plan. When the two joined forces
and got the rights, no one was more taken by surprise than
Pearson himself.

In September, he was called back to London to assume control of the Journey's End project, of which he knew
nothing. Passage was booked for him to leave for Hollywood
in two days, to supervise and aid James Whale in a critical
hour for the entire English industry. The interests involved
in the picture's making were split seriously; Whale had read
V. Gareth Gundrey's script and had rejected it completely.
Maurice Browne, by then in New York, had backed him.

Agreeable to all parties, Pearson was prevailed upon
to mediate. He met with Balcon and his man Gundrey and
then boarded the Aquitania bound for America. Pearson assumed Balcon's creative control proviso and was prepared
for anything.

Armed with the Gundrey script, Pearson used the crossing time to read and note in detail his impressions of it. He
then compared it to the play it was his mission to preserve.

Wrote Pearson in Flashback, his 1957 autobiography,

> Gundrey's script had excellent points; technically
> it was well made, but I felt it over-elaborated much
> that only needed the utter simplicity of the play.
> To my mind, the stark realism of Journey's End
> was due to Sherriff's observation of life, rather
> than its dissection.  But my mission was not to
> write another script, but to find a writer to meet
> the wishes of Whale and Browne.

When he landed in New York, Pearson met straight-
away with Maurice Browne and tendered his notes for exam-
ination.  The following day, Browne happily endorsed them
and indicated he had "no further anxiety about anything. "  Re-
lieved, Pearson cabled London the good news and on October
1, began his trip to California aboard the Chief.

Currently embroiled in the making of Hell's Angels,
Whale welcomed George Pearson with open arms.  His help
during the daylight hours that Whale had to spend at Metropolitan was essential, and Whale was delighted to find a man
who was committed to the project in the same spirit as he.
Pearson established an office on the Tiffany lot and began the
laborious process of reviewing prospective cast members and
their agents, the most promising of which returned for evening consultations with the director.

Whale had not seen David Lewis since the day he had
first arrived in California, other than bumping into him at a
Paramount screening room before leaving for New York to
do the Miller plays.  Lewis could talk a good game, had an
exceptional story mind, and Whale thought him very bright
indeed.  As Journey's End neared its starting date, the two
began occasionally having dinner together to discuss the problems at hand.  They quickly became fast friends, the steak
dinner at the Brown Derby on Vine Street a nightly ritual.
"Jimmy loved steak, " Lewis recalled.  "It was very difficult
to get a good steak in England.  When he discovered what
we could get out here, he had it every night. "

The nightly dinner, which cost $5. 00, was a relaxing
interlude in the midst of a great deal of pressure.  Realistically, the end of the Hughes picture was nowhere in sight--
although he was scheduled to finish with it on Thursday, October 31st, and start on Journey's End the next day.  Whatever
happened thereafter was, mercifully, none of his concern.

As expected, the casting process was progressing slowly; toward the end of October, only two members were definite: Ian MacLaren as Osborne and Charles Gerrard as Mason. Many different avenues of casting were considered; the actors would ultimately make or break the film. Of course, the last-ditch solution--if all else failed--would be to draw upon the stage casts Whale had directed. "I should like to have the London, New York, or Chicago cast of Journey's End in the entirety of either for our screen version ... ," he told an interviewer, but there would be Hell to pay if this happened at the last minute.

As time got short, David Lewis saw Whale at Paramount, where he was reviewing the cutting and post-production aspects of Hell's Angels. Among others, he shot a test of Lewis for the role of Hibbert, the coward. "He kept pushing me to let go, which was hard for me because I was always a very controlled actor. I think there must be control to be any good, and the test was terrible. Jimmy always said that he liked it, but I never believed him. "

Aside from Stanhope, the part of the young Second Lieutenant was the most critical. In frustration, Whale toyed with the idea of requesting London's Raleigh. He then encountered David Manners, a twenty-eight-year-old Nova Scotian actor who had recently enjoyed a forty-five-week run in Dancing Mothers on Broadway. Manners was en route to Honolulu for his health when the two met at a party.

> He was responsible for my career in Hollywood, [said Manners of Whale]. We met at a lunch somewhere and he asked me if I would care to take a test for Raleigh in Journey's End. I had nothing to lose and gladly took it. He liked the test enough to hire me rather than send to England for Maurice Evans....

Slowly, the pieces fell into place. But the manner of the script was still unsettled and Tiffany, not noted for its vast reserves of production capital, was reviewing the budget with a fine-toothed comb. George Pearson pressed on admirably, and several writers were considered and rejected. Whale liked Joseph Moncure March and Pearson was agreeable. The three met, and March designated a fee of $7, 500 if Howard Hughes, who had him under personal contract, would allow him to do it. It was a stiff price by British terms, but they were in Hollywood now, and a Hollywood fee

Whale with actor David Manners at the Tiffany commissary,
1929.

would be asked.    Pearson approved, but several days later
word came that Hughes would not allow it.    At Pearson's
urging,  Tiffany General Manager Grant Cook had lunch with
Hughes and arranged a meeting.

     Hughes agreed to a compromise:   he would trade
March's services for four more days of filming with Whale.
There was no contract; simply a handshake.    Pearson reduced the fee to $1000 a day; March had four days to write
a complete screenplay.   He set to work at once, Whale and
Pearson joining him each evening to discuss questions of plot
and dialogue.   The question was not so much one of adaptation but one of expansion.   What to show in the film that
couldn't be shown in the play?   The question of actually showing Stanhope's girl--Raleigh's sister--was debated.    Whale
told a reporter, ''If we showed you a picture of a blonde, then

you might say, 'Oh, I thought she was a brunette.'"
The idea was to let the audience form a picture to their
own tastes, not Stanhope's.  She thereby becomes more
interesting than any actress could be.  Whale felt it was
also dangerous to tamper with the all-male flavor of the
piece.

> ... Lieutenant Raleigh [Whale continued] says to
> Osborne, "The Germans are quite decent, aren't
> they?  I mean outside the newspapers?"  And Os-
> borne then tells of an incident at "Wipers" when an
> English soldier was shot when he was out on patrol.
> His comrades couldn't get him in that night.  He
> lay out there groaning all day.  "Next night, three
> or four of our men crawled out to get him in, "
> continues Osborne.  "It was so near the German
> trenches that they could have shot our fellows one
> by one.  But when our men began dragging the
> wounded man back over the rough ground a big
> German officer stood up in the trenches and called
> out, 'Carry him, ' and our fellows stood up and
> carried the man back, and the German officer fired
> some lights for them to see by. "
> An incident of this kind could not be very well
> shown on the stage.  But on the screen--what pos-
> sibilities does it suggest to you?
> And then the incident of the daylight patrol, in
> which Osborne perished and Raleigh brought in a
> German prisoner, as he had been told to do.  Here
> was a raid that spelled certain death, as Trotter
> explained to Osborne in telling of a previous one
> "just south of 'ere the other night. "  Trench mor-
> tars were used to tear away the German barbed
> wire.  The Germans tied pieces of red rag on each
> side of the opening thus made.  And Trotter con-
> tinues:  "And even then our fellers 'ad to make the
> raid.  It was murder. "
> There you are.  Trotter tells Osborne of red
> rags.  Osborne is hearing a story similar to his
> own patrol in which he is destined to die.  This
> patrol is so close to the action of Sherriff's play
> that I believe it could be shown in the picture ver-
> sion.

March did a fine job.  On November 4, Whale finally
bid Hell's Angels good-bye, looking forward to working on
Journey's End in the daylight.  Hughes, in appreciation of

Whale's work, awarded him a $5,000 bonus. Whale promptly
bought an elaborate Chrysler and told friends that Hughes had
given him the car.

It was two weeks into November when the final cast,
still minus an acceptable Stanhope, was complete. Added to
MacLaren, Gerrard, and Manners were Billy Bevan, formerly
of Sennett, as Trotter; Anthony Bushell as Hibbert; Robert
Adair, Jack Pitcairn, Tom Whiteley, and Warner Klinger.
Devoid of another course of action, Pearson appealed to London for the loan of Colin Clive to get things moving. Whale
was very much in favor of using him, but knew the request
would encounter substantial opposition, as Clive was an important factor in the show's staying power and Maurice
Browne would not favor removing him. People were coming
and returning to see him as much as they were Journey's
End itself. "... So far as London was concerned," R. C.
Sherriff wrote, "Colin Clive was Journey's End. "

Clive was enjoying his new position of stardom, and
expanding himself. With Jeanne de Casalis he wrote Let's
Leave It at That, a pleasant little comedy--slightly auto-
biographical--about a squabbling couple (he an actor; she a
journalist) who had lived together for two years before finally
getting married. It was performed as a Journey's End family affair of sorts; at a Sunday Play Society presentation at
the Prince of Wales Theatre, Clive, de Casalis, Melville
Cooper, and George Zucco performed to the latter's direction
with considerable success.

Conversely, Pearson also discussed the possibility
of getting Laurence Olivier from New York, but Whale felt
that Olivier was slicker than Colin Clive and, lacking that
ragged edge, was not as good. They decided to wait for
word from England, and commence rehearsals with Whiteley
(the Sergeant-Major) reading for Stanhope.

In Britain, R. C. Sherriff got wind of Browne's decision to allow Colin Clive a temporary leave and begged him
to rescind. Browne didn't consider the matter a serious one--
due to the terms he specified--and for the first time since it
had caught on, Journey's End began playing to empty seats.

"Grant Cook, Michael Balcon, and Tommy Welsh had
fought for us, " said Pearson, "and won. Maurice Browne,
in London, had agreed to loan us his most valuable player
on the absolute guarantee that he would be gone only eight

weeks.   On January 13, 1930, he must be back in his role
at the Prince of Wales Theatre.   The financial terms were
heavy, but truly worth the hazard. "

Unfortunately, Clive's voice test was a disaster; three
days were lost correcting the R. C. A. Photophone malfunc-
tions.   Sound equipment for the talking screen was changing
daily, and still dangerously new to many of the people charged
with its correct operation.   Whale was unconcerned with such
problems; he had encountered too many similar situations at
Metropolitan and Paramount.   What was of concern was the
short time the star of the film would be available; speed was
of the essence.   Luckily, the cinematographer, Benjamin
Kline, was adept at working at a rapid pace; later he would
become Jules White's number one cameraman in the short
subjects department at Columbia.

> Whale's direction was impressive, [said Pear-
> son].   He had a habit of sitting with one foot tucked
> under him, perfectly still, eyes intent, ears alert
> for any error in emphasis or inflection.   These
> were really stage rehearsals, unimpeded by camera
> technique, in order that the players would be word
> and action perfect when the filming began, and a
> translation of a play to the screen called for new
> conventions.   The moment arrived after three days
> of stage rehearsals.
>      Filming started.   Whale was as determined as
> myself that nothing should go wrong.   In that inten-
> tion we discussed the vital element of camera mobil-
> ity, and the film's peculiar ability to condense time
> whereby stage minutes might become screen seconds.
> He was already aware of these essentials through
> his experience in Hell's Angels, and so, because of
> our mutual confidence in each other, all went well.
> With all the purely technical points agreed, we sat
> together during filming.   When he was satisfied
> that he had obtained what he wanted by rehearsal,
> the camera "take" was made, and during this I re-
> tired to the sound-booth to check speech clarity.
> In this friendly fashion the film was made.

Shooting progressed by working six days a week, generally into the evening hours.   After the initial few days, a
steady confidence embellished the efforts of all concerned.
Things went the way they should.   Breaking only for Christmas Day, Colin Clive finished on December 29 and left for
New York the following day.

All that remained to be done were several evenings of exteriors on a battlefield in Culver City.  Plagued by rain, these precious few remaining minutes of film took the company a full three weeks to secure, and it was February before Journey's End was complete.

Editing Journey's End took over a month, although editor Claude Berkeley had been at work on it since the first feet had come up from the lab in December.  Working closely with George Pearson and James Whale, it was a slow, careful process that was also lengthened by the realization that the soundtrack and the picture were not always in perfect synchronization.  Tediously, tiny adjustments were made to the picture negative, and it was March 9 before the film was ready for presentation.

Journey's End successfully previewed in Glendale, California, on March 13, 1930.  Within a month's time it was in release in both the United States and Britain.  In New York, Variety reported,

> Picture opens with a night scene, force of British Tommies moving up through a shell torn town toward the first line of trenches, stumbling in the half light over a shell torn road, the only sounds the crash of artillery and the creak and the rattle of troops moving.  First rate bit of pictorial atmosphere and it gets the action moving quickly.
>
> Thereafter the story slows down for a time during the 75 minutes up to intermission.  The second-half at the Gaiety runs 50 minutes and is fast and absorbing, with a striking bit of stage trickery for the curtain.
>
> Young Raleigh, the schoolboy Lieutenant, has been brought back to the dugout mortally wounded and he dies before his school-mate captain just as he is about to go up to his command, hard pressed by the attack.  Just as the captain disappears through the entrance a shell crashes the flimsy doorway in an avalanche of earth and timber.  Everything goes dark except a faint point of light in the last candle on the table, which flickers for five seconds perhaps, the last thing on a blank screen, and then goes out.
>
> Two Englishmen made this talker on the coast--

[Opposite:]  Ian MacLaren (left) and Colin Clive in Journey's End (1930).

James Whale and George Pearson, former directing
and Pearson supervising.   One might say that if the
English would leave their talker making to these
two men England would have talkers for worldwide
distribution.   Each has performed his job perfectly.

The paper's man in London added,

If one regards this as a British film, it is hardly too much to say that it comes near to, if it is
not actually, the best that has ever been done.   It
is a pity that it was not made here; but it is a
still greater pity that it could not have been made
here.   For it is foolish to delude ourselves that
so much sheer technical excellence as this film has
from the first foot to the last could have been ob-
tained in a British studio.   Maybe this should read
"would," not "could," because of the attempt that
has been made there, the production executives
would, as is their habit, have known so much better than the technicians what should have been done
that the film would have missed out in the way that
most of the high-cost productions here do miss.

New   York   concluded,

For Tiffany, other than the money possibility,
it's a great picture.   Tiffany is an independent producer.   When an independent can turn out a picture
like this, there's no limit that any indie can aim for.

The response was excellent, and Journey's End made
many of the "Ten Best" lists compiled at year's end, although its glory was somewhat overshadowed by the same
month's release of All Quiet on the Western Front, Universal's bigger-budgeted ($1,200,000) filming of Erich Maria
Remarque's pacifist best-seller, directed by Lewis Milestone.
It was an all-American production--so to speak--although
told from the German standpoint, and grabbed the year's
Academy Awards for Best Picture and Best Director.   Journey's End was not even nominated.

Late in May of 1930, Hell's Angels was finally pre-
miered at Grauman's Chinese Theatre in Hollywood.   The
budget peaked-out at over $4 million and although Whale re-
ceived the screen credit "Production Staged by James Whale"
the idea that Howard Hughes had written and directed the
thing himself was not widely discouraged.   The film certainly

attracted much attention, audiences being anxious to see just
what took almost three years and all that money to make.
The general consensus seemed to be that the elaborate action
sequences were well worth the price of admission.   The film
ultimately cleared a profit, although it took many years to do
so.   The earth-bound scenes were not as enthusiastically received and, for the most part, were considered downright dull.
The high point of the entire picture centered on John Dar-
row's character, Karl, the German school buddy of the Rutledge brothers, in a zeppelin bound to demolish Trafalgar
Square.   The scene is at night, and Karl holds as much al-
legiance to England, the country of his education, as to his
homeland.   When he is lowered down outside the ship cabin
in a car to watch for the target and phone up when the bombs
should be dropped, he stalls until the craft is over a body of
water in Hyde Park.   The zeppelin's crash after an enemy
attack was truly spectacular, but it was all material directed
by Hughes--$460,000 worth--not Whale.   Joseph Moncure
March recalled,

> The air sequences had been shot silent.   After
> a great deal of discussion, it was decided to "dub"
> sound into them.   When the scenes aboard the zep-
> pelin had been shot for the silent version ... the
> actors had ad-libbed in German ... and nobody at
> this point seemed to be able to remember what
> they had said.
> Undaunted by this complex problem, we brought
> in a German by the name of Julius Schroeder.   He
> and I sat down at a Moviola and ran the zeppelin
> sequences till our eyes dropped out....   Schroeder
> tried to determine from the lip movement just what
> each man had said.   I would then decide what he
> ought to be saying to make sense, and Schroeder
> would try to find a way of saying it in German that
> would fit the lip movement of the actors....

Wrote playwright Robert E. Sherwood in his syndicated
column The Moving Picture Album, "With his four million
dollars, Mr. Hughes acquired about five cents' worth of plot,
approximately thirty-eight cents' worth of acting, and a huge
amount of dialogue, the total value of which may be estimated
by the following specimen.   Boy: 'What do you think of my
new uniform?'   Girl: 'Oh, it's ripping!'   Boy: (nervously)
'Where?' "

Probably the most significant contribution Hell's

Angels made to film history was the resultant popularity and
stardom of Jean Harlow.    At the time of her death (in 1937),
it was reissued with her name prominently billed first.    It,
like Saratoga, did excellent business.

        With his credit displayed on two of the year's most
notable pictures, Whale was now in a position to enjoy regular employment as a motion picture director, although he
was still interested in working on the stage and dividing his
time between the two.    Needing an agent, he was signed up
by S. George Ullman, a dark little man who had been Ru-
dolph Valentino's agent.    Ullman flattered Whale into a nego-
tiation scheme that called for him to leave Hollywood immediately after Journey's End while Ullman roamed the various
studios in search of the best deal possible.    Tiffany had offered a two-picture agreement at $20,000 apiece (the same
money he got for Journey's End), but knowing how small-
time Tiffany was and how much the other companies could
pay, the offer was flatly rejected.    For Tiffany, $20,000
for a director was magnificent; for M-G-M, it was chicken-
feed.

        James Whale returned to the East Coast by rail, ar-
riving in New York on April 7.    He stayed a week, taking
in some Broadway attractions and arranging to direct another
cast of Journey's End for Gilbert Miller, then set sail for
Europe, where he would renew his passport after two exten-
sions and direct R. C. Sherriff's new play, Badger's Green.

        In London, Journey's End had been slowly winding-
down since Colin Clive's loan to the cinema.    His return on
the play's first anniversary was highly touted, but the damage
had been done.    Forecasts indicated another six months before a replacement would be needed, and Sherriff started to
re-work an older property he had.

            The last play I had written for the boat club
            was about a country village that became the target
            for a development company, and the project split
            a previously happy community into two hostile
            camps.    It was the best story I had come upon in
            those early days because, unlike the others, it had
            a genuine human conflict in it.

        He dug it out of mothballs and added a cricket game
around which the action would revolve.

... It was exactly the sort of story I was looking for to make a clean break from Journey's End.
The conflicts of the characters in their rural setting,
the atmosphere of the countryside and the rivalries
of a local cricket match were so far removed from
a dugout on the Western Front that there could be
no conceivable comparison between the two plays.

I called the village Badger's Green, and that was
the name I gave to the play.

Whale had agreed to direct it from only a brief outline sent to him while still in America.  He liked the idea
of a complete departure from the war--after almost two years
of Journey's End and Hell's Angels, he wanted to establish
that he could handle other subjects with equal success.  The
fact that it was a comedy made it even more attractive.
Again, Maurice Browne would produce; Badger's Green would
follow Journey's End into the Prince of Wales Theatre.

There was no problem casting this time [Sher-
riff said].  "Everybody who was free was glad to
play in it.  We offered the leading part of the village doctor to Horace Hodges, the best character
actor of his day, and he willingly accepted it.  Fe-
lix Aylmer took the part of the company promoter.
None of the other parts demanded stars, but there
were first-class actors and actresses for them all.
Whale had an instinct for finding the right people,
and after the first reading I could say to him, as
I did after the first reading of Journey's End, that
he'd got together a perfect team.

Rehearsals were conducted at the theatre in front of
the dugout set, and on the last night of Journey's End there
was a sentimental curtain speech by Colin Clive, and a party
afterward.

James Whale was staying with me in the house
I had now bought in Esher.  We drove home together,
but neither of us had much to say.  We had been
through the thing together from the start, and
shared all its anxieties, hopes and triumphs.  We
were both feeling the emptiness it had left behind--
far more than we had expected, far more than we
allowed ourselves to admit.

"We mustn't let it get us down," he said.
"There's Badger's Green next week, and we've got

to put our backs into it. It's quite a different
thing, but if we give it the best we've got then it's
going to surprise people, and I guarantee that in
its own way it'll be as big a hit as Journey's End. "

Opening night came on June 12, 1930. The ad in The
Times read:

PRINCE OF WALES.                    Gerrard 7482.
  proprietor:  Tonie Bruce.  Lessee:  Andre Charlot.

EVENINGS, AT 8. 30.
MAURICE BROWNE
presents

"BADGER'S GREEN. "

A New Play by R. C. Sherriff.
with
HORACE HODGES.

The Play Produced by James Whale.
Mats. , TUESDAY and THURSDAY, at 2. 30.

Whale's direction credit was the only one of its type in the
theatre directory.

Sherriff wrote,

The first act went beautifully. It was, in a
sense, a struggle for power between the village doctor and a retired major who sought to dominate
Badger's Green, and the struggle took place round
a little table at which they were holding a committee meeting. It was superbly acted by Horace
Hodges and Louis Goodrich. The audience loved
it--they took up every point and never missed a
laugh. In those days, if a play was going well,
the actors took a curtain after the first act, and
when it went up after the first act of Badger's
Green the audience gave a great burst of applause,
and there were shouts of "Bravo!"
I kept my fingers crossed. Anything could go
wrong to take the gilt off. But every scene went
splendidly; the cast excelled themselves, and when
it was over they got the applause they deserved.
There weren't the same excited demonstrations that

we had had on the final curtain of Journey's End,
but we weren't expecting that, and didn't want it.
It was a totally different sort of play, and I was
delighted that the audience had recognized it.

Unfortunately, the critics who had been so kind to
Journey's End were expecting another one.   When they got instead a folksy comedy about cricket, they had trouble rear-
ranging their tastes.   The reviews, ignoring the good time
the audience had, all joined in repeating the comment, "It's
not another Journey's End. "   It wasn't, but that line was all
the ticket-buying public seemed to need to make a judgment.
Within a few weeks, the play was dead.

Sherriff and Browne were bitterly disappointed.   Whale
was sorry for the whole affair, but he had done his best with
it and liked it still.   He assured his friends that the next
one they did would, once and for all, prove that Journey's
End was not a fluke; that they would survive to collaborate
again.

Badger's Green was not a bad play, and became a
favorite for revival in later years.   In England, it even inspired two film versions--one in 1934 with Bruce Lister and
Valerie Hobson, and one in 1949 with Barbara Murray.

Whale returned to New York, where he directed a new
cast for Journey's End headed by Richard Bird as Stanhope,
Maury Tuckerman as Raleigh, and William Bauter as Osborne.   It was an effective revival after the original Broadway cast had disbanded, but there wasn't much business left
in it.   It went on for little more than a month, and then
dropped.   To replace it, Whale then prepared two one-acts
for Gilbert Miller:  The Violet and One, Two, Three!, both
by Molnar.

The first was a comedy of young, aspiring stage actresses who tend to offer themselves to harried stage producers, thinking they will get plum parts in return.   The
producer, in this case, was A. P. Kaye, and the actress,
one Ilona Stobri, was Ruth Gordon.

The second was a feverish farce starring Arthur Byron
as Mr. Nordson, the Napoleonic director in charge of a grand
Central European organization.   As he is on the point of leaving for a vacation, he learns that a young American woman
who is visiting his family has done a horrible thing: she has

married a taxi driver. Within an hour, her rich and powerful parents, who expect great things of her, are due to arrive and learn the shocking news. Nordson's task is to trans-
form uncouth Anton Schuh (John Williams) into a son of Count
von Dubois-Schottenburg (Reginald Mason) before the unwit-
ting family arrives.

The plays worked well but the notices were lukewarm
at best and they weren't great successes. Years later, Billy
Wilder molded One, Two, Three! into a Cold War comedy
with James Cagney as the head of West Germany's Coca-Cola
plant.

Back in Hollywood, George Ullman had come up with
nothing. Ullman wasn't the town's best agent, and although
most everyone who mattered had seen Journey's End and admired it, there were no takers for its director. David
Lewis did some inquiring and spoke with Paul Bern, a producer at Metro-Goldwyn-Mayer. He, in effect, crystalized
the industry position: Journey's End was a filmed stage play.
It was good, but it wouldn't tell them enough to risk a high-
money contract. Whale would still have to prove himself.

Of course, the Tiffany offer still stood. Whale finally
called Grant Cook personally and accepted. In October, he
returned to California and established an office on the Tiffany
lot.

The studio was experiencing turbulent times. The association with John M. Stahl had collapsed earlier in the
year, at which time Stahl signed a contract with M-G-M.
After only a few months, he moved to Universal, where he
would enjoy great success. Money was tight; the major productions of the past year were simply not generating needed
capital: Zeppelin, Mr. Antonio with Leo Carrillo, and notably Peacock Alley, which was released while Journey's End
was in production.

With David Lewis, Whale shared a house on top of the
Hollywoodland area of Los Angeles. It was an old rustic cot-
tage with four bedrooms, plenty of grass and trees, and a
fine view overlooking the city. The rent amounted to $150
a month and Whale paid two thirds of it. He also made a
$200 down payment on an old Ford for Lewis.

The situation at Tiffany was bleak. They spoke of
big things, but the money wasn't there. The studio owned

nothing of interest, property-wise, for Whale to make, and couldn't afford to buy anything.    There was little he could do--they would move on nothing and they weren't paying him either.

In late November, the studio announced the new Whale picture would be an original newspaper story called X Marks the Spot by Jack Natteford and Edward T. Lowe, Jr.   Whale half-heartedly went to work on the script with Lowe, but inwardly he expected little to happen.

As 1930 ended, things around the Tiffany studio were dead.    Two other directors, William Nigh and Bert Glennon, were also in preparation, but well into March, only a Ken Maynard western (they were produced separately) was shooting.

Whale grew restless.    He was desperate to work.


NOTE

1.   Woman to Woman (1929) was filmed in America under a similar arrangement.

CHAPTER FOUR

In 1931, Universal was an interesting place. It was
the largest of the motion picture lots in Southern California,
presided over by Carl Laemmle, a middle-class Jew from
the south of Germany, born in 1867 and in the film business
since opening a nickelodeon in Chicago called "The White
House" in 1906. From there he got into distribution and
produced his first film, Hiawatha, in 1909. His company
became The Universal Film Manufacturing Company and went
west in 1914. After a short time in Hollywood at Sunset and
Gower, Laemmle acquired 230 acres in the San Fernando
Valley, roughly ten miles north of Los Angeles, and, in
March 1915, Universal City was opened on the site.

Laemmle was an engaging promoter who knew little of
the production side of motion pictures but held a rich instinct
for talent and was a shrewd businessman. His name was on
everything from the films Universal made to the keep-off-the-
grass signs, and his employees were expected to think of
him as "Uncle Carl." In 1918, he hired young Irving Thalberg as an assistant's secretary in New York, later made
him his own secretary and, eventually, General Manager of
the studio. During the twenties, Universal made Outside the
Law, The Hunchback of Notre Dame, and The Phantom of the
Opera with Lon Chaney; Erich von Stroheim's Blind Husbands
and Foolish Wives; The Cat and the Canary; scores of cheap
westerns; and the popular Reginald Denny comedies.

Uncle Carl begat a daughter, Rosabelle, and a son,
Carl, Jr. (born Julius), who was expected to carry on the
tradition. "Junior" Laemmle, as he came to be known, was

64

born in April 1908 and finished school at the age of 15.
When 16, he was producing Collegian shorts for his father;
he was made an associate producer in 1928.   Rosabelle married an agent named Stanley Bergerman, who promptly went
to work for Universal.   For his 21st birthday, Junior was
placed in charge of production.

Universal had been doing nicely on a steady diet of
programmers, with an occasional "class" production thrown
in.   Junior announced a new policy of important, attention-
getting features costing considerably more, and his father
proudly backed him.   Under the policy, the all-star, all-
talking, all-color King of Jazz was made, as was All Quiet
on the Western Front, only half-kiddingly known around the
studio as Junior's End.   Both were great successes; soon
Carl Laemmle, Jr. was well-known throughout the industry.

"His office, " wrote an interviewer in late 1930, "done
in regal reds and dark mahogany, is a veritable throne room.
He looks such a babe sitting in his big chair behind his great
desk.   Like his dad, he is only about 5 feet tall, and is
very slender and youthful.   Universal Pictures are his whole
life.   Next year, he says, they will only put out twenty first-
class pictures instead of the usual forty, of which a percentage were of indifferent value. "

One of those intended twenty was Robert Emmet Sherwood's two-act play Waterloo Bridge, which was snapped up
after a somewhat disappointing run on Broadway early in the
year.   It wasn't Sherwood's best work, being predictable and
not overly popular.   The story was inspired by an American
prostitute Sherwood had met briefly in Trafalgar Square at
the end of the world war.   In the wild celebration, he found
himself confronting a pretty woman who told him she had
come over from America in the chorus of The Pink Lady and
gotten stuck.   They said little to each other, never met
again, but Sherwood expanded the incident into a play of a
young American wounded in France while fighting in the
Royal Canadian Regiment, like himself.   The character, Roy
Cronin, meets Myra the whore on Waterloo Bridge and falls
in love with her.

"... Would you like to go out with me?" he asks.
"I mean to shows and things like that?"

"Why, yes--sure--of course I would.   But you can find
lots better things to do than that. "

The Laemmles, Senior and Junior


        Myra is incapable of a lasting relationship; the two
part in the last scene--he to go back to the war, she to possibly be killed in a raid some night.

        The problem at Universal was to find a director who
could handle it properly.    John M. Stahl, the studio ace,
was finishing with Seed and preparing to direct Preston
Sturges' play Strictly Dishonorable.    Junior didn't think anyone else under contract could do the job correctly and was
open to outside suggestions.    Mary Alice Scully, aware of
Whale's impasse with Tiffany, suggested him for the task;
he was English, and had already brought two wartime stories
to the screen with considerable success.    Junior Laemmle
had seen and liked Journey's End.

        Scully arranged for Whale to meet with Laemmle, and
the two hit it off well.    "He spoke so simply and frankly, "
Laemmle recalled.    An agreement between Whale and Uni-

versal was soon reached. But Tiffany--on the verge of a
major reorganization--pointed out that he was still con-
tractually bound to make two pictures for them. Moving to
Universal would require a cash settlement that Whale was
loath to pay. Tiffany insisted they would soon proclaim a
full slate of features, but to Whale waiting was out of the
question. He'd be damned if he'd make X Marks the Spot
in lieu of Waterloo Bridge. In mid-March, Universal announced that he would direct it, starring Rose Hobart and
Kent Douglass. Tiffany stubbornly maintained that he would
soon start their picture also.

Whale retained attorney Walter C. Burke to help find
a loophole in the Tiffany pact. Burke suggested he sue Tiffany for back salary: originally, he had agreed to do Journey's End for $20,000, although his contract broke that
figure down to $1333 per week for 15 weeks, with like re-
muneration for each additional week. Whale was paid for
the 15 weeks, but, counting preparation and post-production,
the figure would rightly be for 21 weeks. In May, Whale
went to court seeking $12,998 in damages, and the studio
admitted he had them. An out-of-court settlement was ef-
fected--Whale dropped the suit and they dropped the contract.

His deal with Universal was for five years--forty
weeks a year--starting at $2,500 a week. Filming began in
late May with Columbia Pictures contractee Mae Clarke selected for the role of Myra. "I think Whale saw something
I know I had then," she ventured, "and that is a basic con-
fusion and insecurity I didn't mind projecting and putting into my work. It would give a little timidity to a scene that
would normally have a lot of bite in it, and I think that
might be what he saw in me."

Clearly, Whale also saw a tremendous talent, as he
and Clarke evolved one of the great unsung performances of
the early sound period.

He wanted to see what you thought of it [she
said of his approach to a scene]. He'd say, "Now
this is where you're trying to pass the time before
he comes to visit you. You know he's coming and
you don't know what you're going to say to him.
He's going to try to take you out and you don't
want this thing to go any farther--still you'd like
it to--and so you're in a general snit. So to over-

Robert Emmet Sherwood visited the Waterloo Bridge set and
posed for stills with Mae Clarke and Whale.   He inscribed
this shot, "for Mae Clarke--who did right by 'Waterloo
Bridge.'"

come it you're going to sit here and you're going
to knit.    You're not a knitter, but you want him to
catch you knitting.    It's also going to give you
something to do when he comes in.    Beyond that,
all you can think about is that HE is coming to
that door any minute ... but you can't get out of
here; you've got to open it and he's going to come
into here.    And what you're going to say to each
other you don't know.    You're just breathless and
caught.    Now let's see what you want to do. "
       He wouldn't say how to do it, he would tell you
what was happening.

Mae Clarke and Kent Douglass in <u>Waterloo Bridge</u> (1931).

      <u>Waterloo Bridge</u> was not as adaptable to screenplay
form as <u>Journey's End</u>.   Benn Levy expanded the story,
changed much of the dialogue, and made it a much better
piece of work (both Whale and Sherwood felt so).

      Whale opened the film with Myra's introduction back-
stage at a musical comedy, and took her and Roy to the latter's home in the English country, where it was possible to
use two fine character actors, Enid Bennett and Fredrick
Kerr, as his mother and father.   Robert Sherwood, who had
come to California to do screenplays himself, visited the set
one day and complimented Levy on the quality of his work.
He watched at a rehearsal, and later commented that he had
"a hard time choking back the tears" when he saw Kent
Douglass in his Canadian uniform.   Whale worked efficiently,
confidently, and brought the film in within its 26-day schedule,
more than $25,000 under its $252,000 estimate.   Working
with editor Clarence Kolster, the film was ready for preview-
ing in late July and received its premiere at the R. K. O. -
Orpheum Theatre in Los Angeles in early September.

"It's the nearest thing to that first-night thrill on the stage," Mae Clarke enthused to a reporter, "and I love it. Why, to satisfy my ego, I'd even fly to New York for the opening if I had time off." Clarke had started on the vaudeville stage and was making good money performing with her husband, Lew Brice, before testing for Fox's Big Time in 1929.

After the deal was made for Waterloo Bridge, Whale signed with Myron Selznick, the most powerful talent agent in Hollywood. Selznick seemed to hold a personal grudge against the industry he believed drove his father, mogul Louis J. Selznick, into bankruptcy in 1923, and moved to the representation field in 1926 by striking a fabulous deal with Howard Hughes for the services of Lewis Milestone. By 1931, he represented a high percentage of the industry's top talent--writers, directors, and actors--and was a ruthless negotiator. Whale liked him, but the jobs he got while under his representation were generally of his own doing.

Junior Laemmle was delighted with Waterloo Bridge, and developing an immense respect for his new directorial property. While still filming in late June, talk of Whale's next picture began. Laemmle, in effect, offered him anything Universal owned--which amounted to some thirty properties--with special emphasis toward Frankenstein. It was felt that this particular title held great financial promise, based upon the exceptional performance of Dracula earlier that year.

Frankenstein had enjoyed a long and varied history. The original novel, entitled Frankenstein; or The Modern Prometheus was written in 1816-17 by Mary Wollstonecraft Godwin, the daughter of Mary Wollstonecraft and William Godwin, who, at its inception, was living with poet Percy Bysshe Shelley near Geneva. She was 18, and on wet evenings would read German ghost stories with friends for amusement. At the suggestion of Lord Byron, one of the party, they agreed to each devise a ghost story of their own; ultimately only Mary's was completed, the next year at Marlow in England. It was the most horrifying of tales--the story of a man of science who endeavors to endow a body made from random corpses with life. Mary later wrote of the period,

> Many and long were the conversations between
> Lord Byron and Shelley to which I was a devout but
> nearly silent listener. During one of these, various

philosophical doctrines were discussed, and among
others the nature of the principle of life, and
whether there was any probability of its ever being
discovered and communicated.   They talked of the
experiments of Dr. Darwin, (I speak not of what
the Doctor really did, or said that he did, but, as
more to my purpose, of what was then spoken of
as having been done by him, ) who preserved a
piece of vermicelli in a glass case, till by some
extraordinary means it began to move with volun-
tary motion.   Not thus, after all, would life be
given.   Perhaps a corpse would be re-animated;
galvanism had given token of such things; perhaps
the component parts of a creature might be manu-
factured, brought together, and endued with vital
warmth.

She thought all night of the idea at hand, and began
to write the next day.   The book that was finally published--
anonymously--in three volumes in March 1818 was told in
letter and manuscript form by one Robert Walton to his sister, Margaret.   He was the captain of a ship bound to the
North Pole who encountered Victor Frankenstein, worn and
near death, drifting on a large fragment of ice.   Walton took
him aboard, and in the ensuing days was told the story of
Frankenstein's creation:

It was a dreary night of November, that I be-
held the accomplishment of my toils.   With an
anxiety that almost amounted to agony, I collected
the instruments of life around me, that I might in-
fuse a spark of being into the lifeless thing that
lay at my feet.   It was already one in the morning;
the rain pattered dismally against the panes, and
my candle was nearly burnt out, when, by the glim-
mer of the half-extinguished light, I saw the dull
yellow eye of the creature open; it breathed hard,
and a convulsive motion agitated its limbs.
How can I describe my emotions at this catas-
trophe, or how delineate the wretch whom with
such infinite pains and care I had endeavoured to
form?   His limbs were in proportion, and I had
selected his features as beautiful.   Beautiful!--
Great God!   His yellow skin scarcely covered the
work of muscles and arteries beneath; his hair was
of a lustrous black, and flowing; his teeth of a
pearly whiteness; but these luxuriances only formed

a more horrid contrast with his watery eyes, that
seemed almost the same colour as the dun white
sockets in which they were set, his shrivelled com-
plexion and straight black lips.

Within Frankenstein's telling the Captain of his story
was the Monster's account to its maker of its own existence.
He was an innocent, benevolent thing of chance--rejected by
Frankenstein and his world, moved to beg for a mate like
himself.   He became literate, but in Victor's all-consuming
repulsion of him, the second, half-formed creature was destroyed.   The demon was moved to evil; to bring death to
Frankenstein and the people he held dear.   One by one, they
died.

Frankenstein's ultimate quest was to destroy the creature,  though he died of exhaustion and remorse aboard the
ship--to which the creature came to end his charge and then
sail to burn to death by its own hand.

It was certainly not a tale easily transformed to
drama, but done it was.   The book was immediately popular
and the first play based upon it appeared in 1823, entitled
Presumption; or The Fate of Frankenstein by Richard Brins-
ley Peake.   It prompted a second edition of the book, rear-
ranged in two volumes, and a somewhat revised third edition
in 1831.   Unhindered by copyright restrictions, many versions
of the story hit the stages of the world; it must surely rank
as one of the most dramatized novels of all time.

A brief motion picture version appeared in 1910, produced by Edison, and its basic theme became familiar to
the world cinema long before there was talk of such a thing
at Universal.

It was Richard L. Schayer, the head of Universal's
story department, who had gotten the Frankenstein project
in motion in early 1931 via discussions with a friend, French
writer-director Robert Florey, who was not working there at
the time.   The idea was to develop an acceptable follow-up
to Dracula for Bela Lugosi, and Florey discussed Poe's
Murders in the Rue Morgue and The Invisible Man with Schayer,
as well as the Shelley novel.   An informal agreement was
reached between the two, and Florey prepared a five-page
outline of Frankenstein in March, which he would work into
a complete screenplay in exchange for a contract to direct if
Carl Laemmle, Jr. was agreeable.   A contract was signed,

and Florey went to work on a script with writer Garrett Fort
(Applause and Dracula) in mid-May.

     The story Florey put to paper had little to do with the
novel.   Geographically, the book covered a lot of ground, and
has never been faithfully dramatized. [1]  The concept of a man
built with dead tissue and endowed with life formed the basis
for both, but any similarity ended there.  Dr. Frankenstein's
assistant, Fritz, carelessly stole a criminal brain from Dr.
Waldman's laboratory to account for the murdering beast created; the goal not being to present a monster of sympathetic
value.  The creature was mute; he growled.  He did not
speak fluently and pitifully, as he did in the book and most
of the plays.  Florey's contribution to the dialogue could only
be limited; he depended greatly upon Fort.

> I had little to do with it, [Florey said] except
> to suggest in a rudimentary way--being French--
> what the actors might or might not say.  During
> the early days of sound, the producers wanted "a
> lot of talk."  I preferred the actors to talk when
> necessary, and more action, contrarily to the di-
> rectors coming from the theatre who liked much
> dialogue and a minimum of movement.  We con-
> tinually argued about this.  Garrett Fort insisted
> on too much repetitious text.

     The script took four weeks to write, and Florey and
Fort clashed on an ending.  Florey continued,

> I had typed the many cuts of the final chase,
> ending with the Monster cornered on the mill's bal-
> cony and seeing the peasants piling their burning
> torches around the base of the mill, getting ignited,
> the flames commencing to lick up the sides.  Fort
> came up with the idea that the Monster should pick
> up Frankenstein (slumped down in a heap on the
> balcony at the time), and hurl him down over the
> rail at the peasants, the Baron, and Victor, killing
> him instantly.
>     Thinking of a follow-up in case of success, I
> was against the idea, but Dick Schayer, taken as
> a referee, decided that, for the time being, "let's
> end the picture with the double death of the Monster
> and its creator, and a short sequence in the village
> church written by Garrett.

The script completed, it was necessary to get Junior Laemmle's approval.  Recalled Florey,

> In order to be admitted to his chamber at Universal one had to ask charming Buddy Daggett (his secretary) for an audience, way ahead, and then wait for an hour--or two--or three--and perhaps return the following day--in the antechamber till the door would open and the young Boss could be seen having a manicure while talking on the phone ... Harry Zehner standing behind him, and some characters from the race track--bookmakers and others--hanging around the room, the phone ringing constantly.
>
> Schayer had suggested reading it to him (he never had time to read himself).  Junior listened impatiently--playing with the carnation in his lapel-- to my first two lines before talking to some girl for fifteen minutes on the phone--then gone out for half an hour, returning to say, "Well, go on ... " and as I was saying, "... the Monster ... " he interrupted me with, "What monster?  Who is the monster?" before placing a bet on a race.
>
> It had been a conversation as fruitful as I have had with other producers of the same ilk.  Schayer decided to leave him with a copy, adding that he would try to catch him early in the morning, or some time when not as busy.  In any case, we went along.

Laemmle subsequently approved the filming of the creation scene on a Dracula set, with Lugosi, Edward Van Sloan, Dwight Frye, and actors to represent Henry and Victor, as a test.  It took three days to make, and ran almost twenty minutes when edited.  Florey directed, and Paul Ivano was the cinematographer.  When Junior saw it in late June, he rather liked it, but maintained the script "wasn't very good, " and left the film in mid-air.

"How could he decide or remember ... if my script was not very good, " asked Florey, "if at the time he couldn't even find three minutes to listen to a resume of the adaptation?"

Carl Laemmle, Jr. was always fickle in dealing with his people.  Unlike his father, he didn't have a great eye for talent, and frankly didn't care sometimes.  "I didn't like working as hard as I had to, " he said simply.

Bette Davis was once under contract to Universal, and had a small part in Waterloo Bridge. She was signed in New York, and Junior had always thought it a mistake. ("That girl has nothing," he told Robert Florey after viewing a test he had shot with her for Murders in the Rue Morgue. "Let her go...." She was replaced with Sydney Fox.) Preston Sturges, several times over, petitioned Laemmle for a chance to direct one of his own screenplays. It took him almost two years to get Junior's permission to make A Cup of Coffee, which itself was not made until several years later at Paramount (as Christmas in July). Thanks to Uncle Carl, there were many Laemmle relatives on the studio payroll that had to be kept busy: William Wyler was a second cousin to Junior; Ernst Laemmle, who directed German versions of Universal pictures, was the son of Sigfried Laemmle and a cousin. Director Eddie Laemmle was the son of Joseph Laemmle; Alfred Stem, the son of Junior's aunt, was an assistant director at age twenty.

For his "class" pictures, Junior Laemmle required special talent, and he had two directors under long-term contract whom he considered worthy: John M. Stahl, and, after Waterloo Bridge, James Whale. Others came and went, such as Lewis Milestone and Tod Browning, but Stahl and Whale were part of the Universal family.

Often, Junior was given to say one thing, and do another. So it was with Robert Florey and Frankenstein. "I simply felt that James Whale could do a better job of it," Laemmle reasoned.

Whale was unimpressed with the stories Universal had made available to him, and was not terribly enthused with Frankenstein, either. It just seemed to be the best of a bad lot, and was--mercifully--not about the war. "He came home one day," David Lewis remembered, "and asked me to read the book. I did, and found it interesting, but, my God, it was so weird. I didn't know what to say."

At Junior's urgings, Whale agreed to do Frankenstein, and set about to see what had been done with the story up to that point. Robert Florey was left hanging.

> My only direct contact with the Universal management was Dick Schayer, who hired me in the first place. He suggested that I should prepare an adaptation of Murders in the Rue Morgue, one of the stories we had previously discussed for Lugosi.

I wanted to know what had happened to Frankenstein, and he answered that one of the big New York
directors had shown some interest in it, and that I
might do another film.

Later, Dick told me that James Whale had seen
the edited two-reeler I had directed with Lugosi,
and that he had shown some interest in making the
film when, up to that point, he had refused several
other stories.

"If he wants to do it, you might as well forget
about it, " said Schayer.

Florey's name was on the script he had prepared with
Fort as both adaptor and co-author.   It was also on the test,
but this was of no concern to Whale; dealing with Universal's
directors was Junior's problem.   Junior had asked him to
do the film, and it was then his responsibility to make the
best of it.   Seeing the test told him one valuable thing though:
Bela Lugosi was wrong for the part of the creature.   The
studio make-up artist, Jack Pierce, had apparently referred
to the original text for an idea of how the Monster should
look, and followed suit with what the stage make-ups and the
Edison monster had in common:   a large clump of hair.
"His head was about four times normal size, " recalled Edward Van Sloan of the Lugosi character, "with a broad wig
on it.   He had a polished, claylike skin. "   Traditionally, the
monster was ratty-looking, but relatively human in appearance.

The novel Frankenstein was, of course, in the public
domain in 1931, but Universal had purchased an American-
ized version of the latest of the plays, written by Peggy
Webling and performed in London in 1930.   The adaptation
was commissioned from John L. Balderston, a Philadelphia-
born Londoner who became a well-known journalist and part-
time playwright in the twenties before achieving considerable
success with Berkeley Square in 1929.   Balderston had
worked with the macabre before, in co-authoring (with Hamilton Deane) a version of Deane's play of Dracula, from which
Universal's screenplay by Garrett Fort and Dudley Murphy
was written.   Balderston's name added a certain prestige to
the picture; he and Webling were paid $20, 000 and one per-
cent of the gross earnings for their efforts; Florey, for one,
never read it.

To hammer out the final shooting script, Francis Ed-
wards Faragoh, a seasoned studio veteran, replaced Florey

as Fort's collaborator.  The Webling play had starred Hamilton Deane as the Monster and his character was of a more sympathetic sort than in the initial scenario, something that Whale felt vital to the story; he wanted the audience pulling for the monster as well as Henry (the names of Henry and Victor were switched in the play, for some unknown reason, and remained so in the film).

It was announced to the press that James Whale would direct Frankenstein around the first of July, and that Robert Florey was being shifted to Murders in the Rue Morgue.  In consulting his contract with the studio, the specification was that Florey would direct a film, not necessarily Frankenstein. Two weeks later, Dela Lugosi was released from the Monster's role, and the publicity department diplomatically noted that he was unhappy with a non-speaking part, and had requested a release.  Lugosi was also assigned to Rue Morgue, though through no doing of Florey's.  "After seeing Max Schreck in Murnau's Nosferatu, I had not been particularly impressed by Lugosi in Dracula, " he noted.

In casting Frankenstein, who else, in Whale's mind, to play the tormented Henry than Colin Clive?  Elizabeth's role was a rather thankless one, but Whale liked Mae Clarke and requested her.  Edward Van Sloan was a natural for Dr. Waldman, as Dwight Frye was for Fritz.

"I chose Colin Clive, " said Whale, "... because he had exactly the right kind of tenacity to go through with anything, together with the kind of romantic quality which makes strong men leave civilization to shoot big game.  There is also a level-headedness about Clive which keeps him in full control of himself even in his craziest moments in the picture. "

But with Lugosi gone, the big question was who would play the Monster?  Said David Lewis,

> Jimmy was absolutely bewildered, although I didn't realize they needed a monster as badly as they did until he told me one day.  I had seen Boris Karloff in The Criminal Code and he was so good, I cannot tell you.  His face-- the way he moved--everything about him stuck in my mind.  He was powerful, and you had to have a powerful monster.  "Have you thought of Boris Karloff?" I asked.

Jimmy said, "Boris--who?"  He hadn't even
heard of him.
I said, "Check out Boris Karloff.  He's just
what you're looking for. "  And he did.

Karloff, as chance would have it, was working on the
Universal lot in Graft--another gangster picture--and Whale
met with him in the studio commissary during his lunch
break.   He was asked to shoot a test.

"For what?"  Karloff asked.

"For a damned awful monster!"  Whale replied.

The actor's gaunt, beautifully rendered face fascinated
Whale.   "... I made drawings of his head, added sharp, bony
ridges where I imagined the skull might have been joined.
His physique was weaker than I could wish, but that queer,
penetrating personality of his I felt was more important than
his shape, which could easily be altered. "

Whale's pencil sketches were used by Jack Pierce as
a guide for moving in a new direction from the monster he
had fashioned for the Florey test.   "We had to surmise, "
Karloff later explained, "that brain after brain had been tried
in that poor skull, inserted and taken out again.   That is
why we built up the forehead to convey the impression of
demoniacal surgery.   Then we found the eyes were too bright,
seemed too understanding, where dumb bewilderment was so
essential.   So I waxed my eyes to make them heavy, half-
seeing.   We built up my height with huge soles to my shoes.
We showed where the first hand grafted probably died and another had to be substituted. "

"Jack Pierce was a genius, " recalled Mae Clarke,
who enjoyed watching the film develop before shooting actually
began.   "I remember him working with the still man, taking
pictures of each step as the make-up was applied.   He would
add here, and change there, and then ask Whale's opinion.
White nose putty used on the face was toned down to a corpse-
grey.   Then there was a sudden inspiration to give the face a
green tint. "

Meanwhile, the completed script--in basic dialogue
form--was turned over to Thomas Reed, the continuity writer,
who broke it down into scenes and shots, adding camera nota-
tions and other information that Whale would disregard, but

that was needed for budgeting and scheduling purposes. Reed's job was to mold the work into a tangible tool for gauging production needs, rather than to make any creative contributions.

At Universal, Whale screened several examples of the type of film he was after; he was an avid movie-goer in Hollywood. Germany's The Cabinet of Dr. Caligari was especially fascinating, due to its famous expressionistic design. Walls and walkways were angled, elongated, and shortened; the bulk of the film was the contrivance of a madman. Paul Leni's The Cat and the Canary, an old haunted house thriller made by Universal four years earlier was another. Charles D. "Danny" Hall, the studio art director, was in charge of the physical look of the picture. He and Whale communicated well, working out sketches of various sets in water colors, referring at times to hasty pencil examples of what Whale wanted. Some standing sets had to be used, but their adaptation was effortless. There was a definite Germanic influence.

After some delays (notably the lack of an actor for the Monster), shooting finally began on August 24, 1931. In charge of camera was Arthur Edeson, who had done Waterloo Bridge; as had the editor, Clarence Kolster; Joe McDonough, the assistant director; and Mae Clarke. Once Whale found someone he could work well with, he endeavored to use them again. That made things more comfortable for him--and the more comfortable he was with a situation, the happier he was.

> I consider the creation of the Monster to be the high spot of the film [Whale said] because if the audience did not believe the thing had really been made, they would not be bothered with what it was supposed to do afterward. To build this up, I showed Frankenstein collecting his material bit by bit. He proves to the audience through his conversation with Professor Waldman that he actually did know something about science, and particularly the ultra-violet ray, from which he was expecting the miracle to happen. He deliberately tells his plan of action. By this time, the audience must at least believe something is going to happen; it might be disaster, but at least they will settle down to see the show. Frankenstein puts his spectators [John Boles, Clarke, and Van Sloan] in their positions, he gives the final orders to Fritz, he turns the levers and sends the diabolic machine soaring up-

ward toward the roof, into the storm.   He is now
in a state of feverish excitement calculated to carry both the spectators in the windmill and the spectators in the theatre with him.   The lightning
flashes.   The Monster begins to move.   Frankenstein merely has to believe what he sees, which is
all we ask the audience to do.

The creation scene was a masterpiece of construction:
the great table rising to the storm, and cuts of the spectators.   Whale emphasized the faces.   The faces told the story;
he had little use for master shots and rarely made them.
The great noise and flash of the electrical equipment, fashioned by Kenneth Strickfaden, was the music to which was
added Colin Clive's performance of unrestrained euphoria.
"It's alive ..., " he began quietly, "It's Alive! ... It's
ALIVE! ... IT'S ALIVE!!"

"The whole thing hung on Colin, " said Mae Clarke,
"and he was masterful.   Jimmy said in my presence, 'Colin
is like a beautiful pipe organ:   all I have to do is pull out
the stops and out comes this glorious music.'  He knew
which stops to pull, which words to say to bring him to his
own realization of what to do. "

To play Baron Frankenstein, Clive's father, who
simply wants to know when his son's wedding will be, Whale
again employed old Fredrick Kerr.   "... Kerr is an asset
to any picture, " Whale affirmed, "and I wanted him because
he is conventionally well-bred enough not to interfere with
the personal liberty of any son over 18 years old. "

The date for the marriage of Henry and Elizabeth is
set, and the little village around which the story is set gives
over to a grand celebration.   "Having created the Monster,
the problem presented itself, what to do with the thing?   The
transition from the slow-thinking, stupid monster into a developed criminal had to be done quickly. "

The creature's first few days of life are spent wander-
ing about the darkened old tower where Henry has established
his lab.   His introduction in the film is through a doorway,
as he enters a room occupied by Dr. Waldman and Frankenstein.   Slowly, he opens the door and backs in, turning toward the camera.   Here is the classic Whale introduction:
brief cuts of the face, each slightly different, to examine and
emphasize the features and state of mind.   Clive speaks to

him as he would a child, leads him to a chair where he is
exposed, for the first time, to the rays of the sun through
a skylight.   Instinctively, his arms raise toward the light.
Mae Clarke remembered,

> Whale had perfect control over everything.   The
> shadows, the camera shots, the scenery:   he'd say,
> "I want that shadow there. "   He knew exactly.   And
> sound:   he had to hear what it sounded like.   He
> worked like a conductor; he could hear everything
> blended together.
>    He and Boris got on well together after the first
> couple of scenes were done and they knew they had
> something.   They were so at ease they would just
> whisper and agree.   I remember all the gestures
> the monster did were Whale's; I saw him do them.
> When he first said, "Sit down, " Whale mapped it
> all out.   He said, "Now you don't know what sit
> down means, but you know because his hands are
> going that way he means back.   So you go.   What
> am I doing?   Hands.   Where do I go?   You hit
> the chair, you go down. "

The Monster is bewildered, but has no cause to be
violent--until Fritz, the hunchback assistant, takes to teasing
him with a lighted torch.   Fire hurts and frightens the creature.   Fritz persists.   "Fritz's cruelty in torturing him begat cruelty in the Monster, " Whale reasoned, "and the rest
was merely devising the types of murders and how to com-
mit them. "

Naturally, Fritz is the first to die, the Monster acting in self-defense.   Dr. Waldman then convinces Henry that
it should be destroyed and assumes that responsibility himself as the creator returns to the village to be wed.   Heavily
drugged, the Monster wakes on the dissection table and over-
powers Waldman.   He then leaves the building to investigate
the outside world, coming upon Maria, a little peasant girl
who is playing alongside a lake.   This sequence, inspired
by a somewhat similar one in the Webling play, was destined
to become one of the best remembered in motion picture history.

"Here is this beautiful direction by Whale, " Mae
Clarke remarked.   "He told little Marilyn Harris, 'Here is
Mr. Karloff in a funny costume who's just being friendly.
You just look up at him and say, 'I'm Maria. ' "

Colin Clive and Boris Karloff in <u>Frankenstein</u> (1931).


"Would you like one of my flowers?" she offers as
they sit at the water's edge.    Clumsily, he accepts some
daisies as she shows him how they float on the water.    "I
can make a boat, " she says.

The progression of the scene called for Karloff's
flowers to run out, and then for him to reach for Maria and
throw her in after them, thinking, of course, that she too
would float; the game was great fun--why stop with the flowers?    The scene was shot on a hot afternoon in late September of 1931.    Underneath the heavy make-up and padding,
Boris Karloff was less than comfortable.    Whale, at first,
wanted to shoot the actual picking-up and throwing in one

Whale and Karloff enjoy a smoke between shots on <u>Franken-</u>
<u>stein</u> (1931).

shot, but the poor Monster was hard-pressed to even lift her,
let alone to toss her eight or ten feet.    He struggled with effort for an action the Monster should have found effortless.
Harris' mother, standing off-camera, was as distasteful a
stage-mother as Whale had encountered; the child responded
accordingly.    "Throw her in again, " the mother hollered.
"Farther!"

    After due consideration of the problem, Whale decided
to film her landing again, tossed by two grips, one taking her
feet and the other her hands.    Once thrown, however, she
didn't surface and Whale, who couldn't swim, sent two men
in after her.    There were several tense moments before the
girl appeared from a clump of plants a few yards away.
"Here I am!" she called as Mother fumed.

    "The close-up of Karloff's reaction when the girl sank
was one of the most heartbreaking and poignant moments in
the movies, " Clarke said.    "The way Whale directed Karloff
and the way Karloff reacted was pure art.    It was a classic.
The Monster bent over and dug into the water.    Where did
she go?    He slapped the water like a child as if to say,
'Bad water.'    Then he got up and left in slow, dumb confu-
sion.    Too soon after these first joys of smiling, playing
games, sharing and a new friend, there was the new experience of disappointment and loss. "

    The discovery of the child's body called for the forma-
tion of search parties, cattails alight, to search out the
"fiend" responsible for the crime.    "The villagers were
thrown in for nothing, " Whale said, "merely as a background
for the bloodhounds, whose yowls formed such a delightful
background to the pagan sport of a mountain manhunt. "

    Mae Clarke remarked,

        Here's a scene that could have been funny.    I'm
    in my room dressed in my bridal gown and Henry
    and I are discussing our future plans and the Mon-
    ster.    Suddenly we hear the Monster but Henry isn't
    quite sure where he is.    First he's upstairs.    Then
    he's in the cellar.    Henry just isn't tuned in.    Then
    he foolishly locks me in for safekeeping while he
    and the others search for the Monster.    Doesn't he
    know the Monster could get in through the window?
        Just before filming the confrontation scene be-
    tween the Monster and myself, Whale said, "Now

we've all read it, let's do the mechanics. " He
really directed from inspiration. As the Monster
advances toward me, my attention is drawn away
every time I am about to turn and see him. Whale
milked it carefully. The scene had to be peaked
and cut off at just the right moment.

Between Karloff's perfect performance and my
throwing myself so thoroughly into the role, I
feared I would drop dead. I asked Boris if he knew
any tricks that would help me. "Remember, " he
said, "when I am coming at you keep your eye on
my up-camera little finger. I'll keep wiggling it.
Then you'll know it's only Boris underneath all this
make-up. "

There was no time for socializing on the set,
particularly with him. He would arrive at 4:00
a. m. and spend four hours in make-up. He didn't
have lunch with us in the studio commissary because it was easier for him to eat alone in his
dressing room where he could remove some of his
body padding. Then a couple of hours would be
spent removing his make-up at the end of the day
and he would require a rub-down after stomping
around all day with those weights in his shoes which
gave him that stilted walk and allowed him to lean
forward.

In mid-afternoon, there was always a tea-break.
Though the film ran five days over schedule--and some
$30,000 over budget--the air was congenial; Frankenstein's
problems didn't start until after it was finished.

### NOTE

1. Terror of Frankenstein (1975), a Swedish/Irish
co-production, probably comes closest.

## CHAPTER FIVE

In November of 1931, Carl Laemmle, Jr. arranged to preview a work print of Frankenstein in Santa Barbara, a small resort community about two hours north of Los Angeles. Whale picked David Lewis up at Paramount, and they drove there together. "Up came the first shot in the grave yard," Lewis recalled, "and you could hear the whole audience gasp." The normally blasé Variety reviewer wrote,

> Picture starts out with a wallop. Midnight funeral services are in progress on a blasted moor, with the figure of the scientist and his grotesque dwarf assistant hiding at the edge of the cemetery to steal the newly-buried body. Sequence climaxes with the gravedigger sending down the clumping earth upon the newly-laid coffin. Shudder No. 1.
> Shudder No. 2, hard on its heels, is when Frankenstein cuts down his second dead subject from the gallows, these details being presented with plenty of realism.

David Lewis added,

> The film has been imitated so much that today, those scenes don't bother people. But in 1931, this was awfully strong stuff. As it progressed, people got up, walked out, came back in, walked out again. It was an alarming thing.
> After the showing, we all went over to the Santa Barbara Biltmore. Junior was scared to death. He said, "Jesus, God, we've got to do something!

This thing's a disaster!" He thought no one was going to come to see it.

Whale was alarmed, to say the least. He thought much of Frankenstein was a masterpiece, but Laemmle was too worked-up to listen to reason. Would an audience come to a film that would upset them so?

"I didn't know enough at the time to say anything," said David Lewis, "but I was Eddie Montagne's assistant at Paramount, and he used to be at Universal. I talked to him the next day. He said, 'My God, they're got the hit of all time. When you can stir an audience like that, you've really got them.'

"I told Jimmy, and Jimmy got Junior to call me-- they were taking things out--and he said, 'Have Eddie Montagne call me.'

"Eddie called him and said, 'I didn't see it, but from what David tells me, you've got the hit of the year.'"

"They were walking out," Junior protested.

"You're insane," Montagne insisted. "If we had a picture like that, we'd clean up."

Laemmle regressed. He greatly respected Montagne's judgment, and decided to let the picture alone, promote it for its shock value, and hope for the best. Universal was in very shaky condition--financially speaking--and Frankenstein had cost them $291,000. Good or bad, it was best not to dilute whatever power it had. By general consensus, it was agreed to remove the actual throwing of Maria into the lake. Karloff, who hadn't seen the completed film, was against her being thrown in, and suggested that the Monster should gently set her on the water's surface. Whale felt he should toss her, as he had the flowers; it had more shock value while keeping the character just as consistent as Karloff's version. He had used the first shot, reluctantly, when the stagehands' toss hadn't matched the rest of the sequence well enough. He wasn't terribly happy with it, and thought the same impression would be conveyed with it cut--leaving the action to the viewer's imagination.

The ending at the old windmill, in which Colin Clive dislocated a shoulder, had been shot two different ways.

When the Monster threw his maker to the ground, the scene faded on the burning structure and the audience couldn't tell whether Clive was dead or alive.  In the preview, he died in an epilogue, but that was replaced with an alternate shot of Fredrick Kerr outside his recovering son's room for the general release.

A brief prologue was shot to underscore the film's reputation, and tacked on before the opening credits, something that was popular with Universal under the Laemmles. Similar hypes were added to Dracula, The Old Dark House, and Once in a Lifetime.  Edward Van Sloan appears in the introduction:

> How do you do?  Mr. Carl Laemmle feels that it would be a little unkind to present this picture without just a word of friendly warning.
> We are about to unfold the story of Frankenstein. A man of science, who sought to create a man after his own image--without reckoning upon God.  It is one of the strangest tales ever told.  It deals with the two great mysteries of Creation:  Life and Death.
> I think it will thrill you.  It may shock you. It might even horrify you.
> So ... if you feel that you do not care to subject your nerves to such a strain, now's your chance to--
> Well ... we warned you. ... "

The audience was scared even before the titles appeared.

Frankenstein opened at the Mayfair Theatre in New York in the first week of December to incredible business. Junior Laemmle was ecstatic.  It opened in Los Angeles at the Orpheum on New Year's Day of 1932 with continuous showings from 9:00 a.m.  Lines stretched around the block, and the usual newsreels and intermissions were dispensed with.  They ground it out all day without a stop.  It did a quick $5,000,000 in its first release, which was unheard of for a film of such modest origins.

"No man has ever seen its like ...," the ads screamed.  "No woman's kiss ever touched its lips!"  "No children's prices!"  "No one seated during the final reel!"

Whale gave out more interviews than he had for Journey's End. Karloff, overnight, was a sensation. Whale enjoyed adjusting the facts of his life for recording in the public press. He was 42 at the time, but professed to be 35. Karloff was 44 and made no secret of it. He told reporters he had been in films since 1919, and drove a truck when work was light. Whale discussed the "private tutors" he enjoyed in his youth, and presented himself in that British upper-crust he so admired--regardless of what really had happened. "I never intended this picture for children, " he drolled to one interviewer, "but I would like to make a children's version. It is an adult subject and I tried to make it as real as it was possible. "

Junior Laemmle, meanwhile, was watching the money pour in and considering a sequel. Robert Florey had prepared a seven-page treatment on speculation entitled The New Adventures of Frankenstein--The Monster Lives !, but Dick Schayer didn't read it until December 20th, and Ardel Wray, of the scenario department, a month later. Florey thought it was more faithful to the novel than the first adaptation had been, but it was returned to him in February 1932 and nothing further came of it. Florey was announced as preparing The Invisible Man and The Wolf Man for Karloff, but having been burnt by Laemmle's fickleness once, he refused to proceed without an iron-clad contract and the matter was dropped.

After the success of Frankenstein, any assignment would seem commercially anticlimactic, but Whale wished to keep busy and earn his salary. He gave due consideration to anything the studio needed done, and his next project, The Impatient Maiden, needed doing.

The story came from a book they had bought cheaply called The Impatient Virgin, and it had retained that title in a screenplay fashioned by Francis Edward Faragoh in 1930. Impatient Virgin was thought to be hot material for Clara Bow when it was purchased, but her career took a fatal nosedive before the film could be launched. Universal lost interest in her, assigned the film to director Cyril Gardner, and then shelved it completely in May 1931.

When shooting on Frankenstein was finished, Junior Laemmle made plans to leave for two weeks' vacation at Lake Arrowhead. Before he left he asked Whale to assume control of Impatient Maiden (as it was then known) for the latest of the studio's Lew Ayres vehicles. Ayres was the personable young man who had become well-known for his

leading part in All Quiet on the Western Front. Although
they were paying him over $1,700 a week, the studio didn't
quite seem to know what to do with him as a saleable name.
They tried and tried to fit him into different kinds of starring
roles without success; they simply weren't a star-making kind
of company.

Whale agreed to do the film, but entertained no delusions about the quality of the poor script Dick Schayer and
Winnifred Dunn had written after Faragoh.   He did, however,
put Mae Clarke into it, and filmed it as efficiently as he
could.   Little preparation was needed; he simply took the
script as written and began filming during the first week of
December.

Ultimately, the film was significant as Ayres' first
medical role.   Later he became M-G-M's Dr. Kildare in a
popular series of films.   For The Impatient Maiden, he
played a young ambulance surgeon in love with the erratic
Mae Clarke.

> I don't think he and I really hit it off [Lew
> Ayres said of Whale], without there being any kind
> of clash.   Perhaps he thought he couldn't communi-
> cate well with me, and I don't think he could.   In
> many ways, I was not on his level.
> He was cold--very cold--and he never seemed
> to make any comments.   He would watch a scene,
> always wiggling a foot--nervously kicking--as one
> does when one's leg is crossed.   He would watch
> and look impatient, and you would think, "Oh, I
> must be boring him."   When the scene was over,
> he would simply say, "Clip," and get up and walk
> away.   You were left thinking, "Well, I guess I
> just squeezed by and he figured that was about the
> best he could get."   No encouragement from him
> whatsoever.

The two men harbored no hostility; Whale was somewhat bored with his given task, and related more to people
like Colin Clive and Fredrick Kerr.   Ayres was used to
tough, strong, but easy-going directors like Lewis Milestone;
"fatherly," as he said.   "Whale was recessive and introverted
and cool and critical, in a sense.   He never came near you--
you felt he just didn't bother with you."

Whale brought the film in under schedule and under

Lew Ayres, Mae Clarke, and Una Merkel in Impatient Maiden (1932).

budget; when it opened in New York in March 1932, the reception was poor. It was quickly forgotten.

After completing Impatient Maiden, Whale checked off the lot for a few weeks and returned to England to visit his family. He particularly enjoyed returning after a great success like Frankenstein to soak up the attention, as if to say, "England, here I am!"

Universal was again faced with a dilemma. Junior Laemmle had taken some time off during Impatient Maiden, and had landed in the hospital with hayfever. He spent two weeks' convalescence in Palm Springs, then returned to try and make a durable star of Boris Karloff. Karloff was easier to deal with than Lew Ayres. Ayres had made his big hit in an expensive war picture, but he was young and handsome, and they couldn't keep putting him into more war pictures. Karloff, on the other hand, was an accidental

sensation in a horror picture.    He was an excellent character actor, and the story department could pump material for
him for years.    Bela Lugosi, who pre-dated him, was lost
in his dust.

Once the impact of Frankenstein was known, the
Laemmles signed Karloff to a contract and then loaned him
to Paramount for a remake of Lon Chaney's early success,
The Miracle Man (though he didn't play the Chaney part).
Upon returning, he was a guest star in The Cohens and the
Kellys in Hollywood (along with Lew Ayres and Tom Mix),
and then starred with Ayres and Mae Clarke in Night World.
What was needed was a good "horror" picture, but it ap-
peared that Invisible Man--the first great Karloff vehicle--
would not be ready for some time.

Whale petitioned Laemmle to buy J. B. Priestley's Benighted.    Marketed in America as a straight thriller under the
title The Old Dark House, it was a delightfully creaky tale,
replete with an assortment of weird characters that Whale
found fascinating.    Most important, there was a part for
Karloff--that of the dumb, drunken butler of the piece, Morgan.    Laemmle was happy with the thought of another Kar-
loff-Whale combination; Benn Levy went to work on a script.

Concurrently in the works was the sequel to All Quiet
on the Western Front, Remarque's The Road Back, where it
was hoped that lightning would strike twice.    This time,
Whale would direct and R. C. Sherriff, who had declined an
offer to work on All Quiet, would be brought out to write the
screenplay.

For Old Dark House, Levy efficiently removed any
hint of underlying seriousness present in the novel, which
dealt with the post-war madness of an entire family.    The
picture would be a study of bizarre people in an old, dark
house encountering relatively normal people taking refuge
from a violent thunderstorm in Wales.    There was great
fun in assembling the cast, an all-star one by any standard.
First to arrive at the house were Philip Waverton (Raymond
Massey), and his wife Margaret (Gloria Stuart), along with
Melvyn Douglas as Roger Penderel.    Soon thereafter came
Charles Laughton (Sir William Porterhouse), traveling with
a chorus girl played by Lillian Bond.    The household consisted of Horace Femm, played by Ernest Thesiger, whom
Whale brought over from Britain for a part that he was born
to play.    His sister, a hard-of-hearing religious fanatic

Whale poses with his friend Benn Levy on the Universal lot, 1932.

named Rebecca, was Eva Moore in her American film debut.
And, of course, there was Boris Karloff.

Charles Laughton had signed a contract with Paramount
in London, and had come to Hollywood to appear in The Devil
and the Deep with Tallulah Bankhead.  The picture was held
up for several weeks, however, and during the interim,
Whale borrowed him for Old Dark House.  Wrote Elsa Lanchester,

> Charles was very pleased to get the camera ex-
> perience.  He knew he had to bridge a large tech-
> nical gap in one giant stride.  On stage you have
> to enlarge everything a dozen times so that it will
> reach to the back of the gallery and at the same
> time will not lead the front row of the stalls to
> think that you are a "ham" actor.  On the screen,
> you always have to understate, if anything, and
> bear in mind that you are playing right up against
> the audience and that everybody is even nearer than
> the front row of the stalls.  Charles was quick to
> grasp this difference, but at first suffered agonies
> in controlling his gestures.
> The Old Dark House centered around an English
> household, so a lot of English actors were in the
> film:  Ernest Thesiger, Brember Wills, Eva Moore,
> and others.  About two weeks after we had been in
> Hollywood all these people turned up.  The Old
> Dark House was a horror picture.  Boris Karloff
> played the part of a servant who was mad.  The
> house harbored quite a large family of very jumpy
> old people who secreted some even more ancient
> relatives in the top stories.  All that I can remem-
> ber clearly is that each horror seemed to have
> more hair on than the last; the play dealt chiefly
> in hairy horrors.

Bob Sherriff arrived from England to start work on
The Road Back.  The studio took a suite for him at Chateau
Elysee, and assigned a small office on the lot, with which
he was impressed.  He recalled,

> The star of the cowboy pictures used to arrive
> at the studio in an all-white Rolls-Royce, dressed
> to match in an all-white cowboy rig-out with golden
> spurs.
> The studio was laid out in streets of huts and

bungalows, with the big stages looming out like air-
craft hangars.   The important people had bungalows
with thick lawns and flower-beds round them, and
their offices sported thick carpets and carved oak
desks, but for the rest it was rough and ready, with
dry brown desert grass round their huts still waiting to be cleared away.

Sherriff set to work, observing much on the set of
Old Dark House (which began production in mid-April) and
contributing bits of dialogue to the Levy script.   "This is
my first job in a studio, " he told an interviewer.   "I am
only doing the adaptation of Remarque's book, you know; not
the 'shooting script. '   It is so admirably written, so visual
in style, that in itemizing the incidents I find there is little
for me to change. "

Gloria Stuart said,

The first few days on the set were very formal.
He called me "Miss Stuart, " and I called him "Mr.
Whale"; there wasn't an instant first-name basis.
Once initial familiarities developed, the atmosphere
became an easy, good one, although always very
serious.   There was a great deal of rehearsal, and
whatever directions he gave the actors were offered
then.
Whale was meticulous, quiet, at some time sar-
castic.   I've worked for some directors who just
said, "OK kids, believe it!" or "Once around the
strawberry bush, " or "Let's shoot!"--deep direction
like that.   James had the whole thing laid out.   He
would say how he felt the scene, we'd play it, and
then he'd start to work individually.   Very politely,
very thoroughly, very tactfully, but there was no
kidding around.
Once in a while, if someone angered him or opposed him--said "Yes, " and then did it their own
way--he was very swift to notice and point it out,
sometimes with an unkind word.   There was never
any yelling though; simply an intellectual report.
I was very snobbish about film at the time, as
I had been on the stage and one tended to look down
upon such things.   But working with Whale and the
caliber of actors he had assembled changed my
mind.   It soon got through to me that I was in top
company.   The English were very respectful of

James and did precisely what he wanted them to--
there were no last-minute instructions before shooting a scene.

Whale liked Gloria Stuart personally, and was her es-
cort to L. A. 's Biltmore Theatre on several occasions during
the period.

With such an outstanding cast, it came as no small
surprise to find that Old Dark House was Ernest Thesiger's
film whenever he was on the screen.    Except to Whale, of
course.    Thesiger's Horace was in full command.    He was
a very hollow, aloof character, seemingly off into another
world somewhere.    His lines were curt announcements of
fact, piped into the atmosphere with perfect timing.    "We
make our own electricity here, " he explained to Gloria Stuart as the lights dimmed, "but we're not very good at it. "

The Old Dark House is done a disservice when classi-
fied as a "horror" film.    In reality, it could just as easily

Boris Karloff and Eva Moore in The Old Dark House (1932).

be considered a black comedy--James Whale style.  Here,
he took a classic situation--innocent travelers thrust by natural elements into a strange old house--and displayed a most
perverse sense of humor in what they encountered.  Unlike
Frankenstein, where his intention was to make a genuinely
frightening motion picture, and where there was relatively
little humor, The Old Dark House was frequently hilarious.
It was carefully made, however, to work on both levels;
realistically, it was going to be sold as a chiller starring
Karloff, and viewers looking for such a thing could easily
take the various peculiarities with great seriousness.   In
1932, it wasn't the shocker that Frankenstein was, and many
people took its humor as a weakness, rather than a strength.
Whale's attitude toward the film is possibly best exemplified
by the casting of a woman to play the part of the Femm's
102-year-old father.  "Jimmy couldn't find a male actor who
looked old enough to suit him, " said David Lewis.  "So he
finally used an old stage actress he knew called Elspeth
Dudgeon.  She looked a thousand. "

     Unconcerned about anyone noticing, Whale billed her
in the credits as "John Dudgeon. "

     After production on The Old Dark House was finished
in May 1932, Whale's year was occupied with the preparation
of The Road Back, which, after much work, was finally
scrapped.  Bob Sherriff had fashioned a fine screenplay--fol-
lowing the novel closely--but Junior would not move on the
project, saying the script needed work.  He was, more likely, put off by the money it would cost to make.

     The Old Dark House was Universal's Halloween attrac-
tion and Boris Karloff's first starring picture.  Junior liked
it, but it was too specialized a work to be as popular (or
understandable) as Frankenstein.  The studio moved forward
with other Karloff projects.  Cagliostro, based on the life of
the Italian adventurer, written by Nina Wilcox Putnam, was
announced in May.  Imhotep, based upon a story by Putnam
and Dick Schayer, was being prepared by John Dalderston.
It began filming in late September as The Mummy with cinematographer Karl Freund directing for the first time.

     Whale had known H. G. Wells in England and greatly
admired The Invisible Man, which had long been hung up in
script, direction, and technical problems.  After Robert
Florey had dissociated himself with the project, director
Cyril Gardner was assigned to it, and John Balderston joined

Garrett Fort on the script.   When Whale finally became involved in September,  Preston Sturges was the writer,  and he
had set the story in Russia.   Paul Lukas joined the cast in
November,  then the film was indefinitely shelved next to The
Road Back, which was supposed to begin in early 1933.

In addition,  Balderston was tinkering with a play entitled Red Planet by J. E.  Hoare,  about a civilization on
Mars.   There seemed to be an endless preoccupation with
the development of Karloff material.   Also discussed during
the year were Stevenson's The Suicide Club,  Robinson Cru-
soe,  and remakes of The Wizard and The Hunchback of Notre
Dame.   Aside from the Whale picture though,  the best the
studio could do was to loan him to M-G-M for The Mask of
Fu Manchu.

Karloff's handling of such success was amusing to
Whale.   They had had a good time making Frankenstein, but
after the critical praise Karloff received--and the new con-
tract--he began to take himself very seriously.   Just after
it was agreed that Whale would direct him in The Invisible
Man, a messenger presented himself at Whale's office bunga-
low and announced that Mr. Karloff was in the make-up department, and would like to have Mr. Whale view his latest
make-up, the one that he would be seen with in his new film.

Whale obediently followed as he was led up stairs,
down corridors, and through doors where, with great cere-
mony, he was ushered into a small room in which Jack Pierce
was standing proudly behind a throne-like barber's chair, its
occupant seated under a concealing sheet of red velvet.   Slowly, the cloth was removed to reveal Karloff with, as Whale
later described it, a "pail of garbage" dumped over him.
He deduced that all this must relate to Freund's Imhotep,
which was about an Egyptian mummy returned to life.

"I think this is the most marvelous thing, " Karloff
enthused, "ever to be seen upon the silver sheet. "

Ultimately, both The Road Back and The Invisible Man
were stalled in favor of The Kiss Before the Mirror, another
studio property Whale was asked to do, rather than one he
had developed.   It was taken from a Hungarian play; Junior
hoped to get Charles Laughton on a loan from Paramount for
it.   Whale found the story an appealing one, very European
in flavor, and deliciously ironic.   It was the story of an attorney defending a friend for murdering his unfaithful wife,

and seeing the same circumstances developing within his own
marriage.   Hence, his efforts in the courtroom became ra-
tionalizations of his own murderous emotions.

Whale wanted Laughton as the lawyer, but he returned
to England instead to do The Private Life of Henry VIII.   He
settled for Nancy Carroll as the attorney's wife.   Her husband
would be Frank Morgan, just prior to his long association
with M-G-M.   Paul Lukas was cast as the hapless defendant,
and Whale wanted Gloria Stuart as the victim.

"James said, 'This is a very small part, Gloria, but
I would appreciate it if you would do it.   You're exactly what
I want.'   Well, it was very flattering.   By that time, I was
a big leading lady and used to practically carrying a picture
by myself, but I was happy to do it."

There was little time for preparation, and some of
Whale's usual people were committed elsewhere.   Arthur
Edeson was working at California Tiffany Studios on Auction
in Souls (released as The Constant Woman) with director
Victor Schertzinger.   In his place, Whale asked his friend
Karl Freund to shoot Kiss Before the Mirror, although
Freund was now a director--having finished The Mummy--
and making plans to make Men Without Fear and possibly
Gulliver's Travels.   Joe McDonough, who usually functioned
as the assistant director, was on another picture, as was
editor Clarence Kolster, who was replaced by Ted Kent.

The film was made in sequential order in January of
1933.   The climax of the story amounted to a compelling
courtroom drama, with Frank Morgan delivering an impas-
sioned speech that wins acquittal for Lukas, and frightens his
wife with the knowledge that he knows of her infidelity and
would kill her if he could.

Whale lavished great care on the set-up for Kiss, the
opening sequence in which Gloria Stuart comes to meet her
lover, Walter Pidgeon.   He waltzes around in preparation
for her arrival, half-singing to himself in a musical comedy
flavor that puts the audience off guard for the murder that
takes place when she enters the bedroom--the appearance of
her husband and the gunshots through the window glass that
shatter the mood.   Stuart recalled,

> First day on the set, when I walked through the
> garden, Whale said to me, "I want you to walk

Frank Morgan and Nancy Carroll in The Kiss Before the
Mirror (1933).

through the garden knowing that you have a rendez-
vous--that you are the most beautiful woman in the
world.    Enjoy the air, the adventure.    Lean down
and smell the perfume of the flower.

He gave me a strong, vivid picture of how I
was to feel, which he was able to do so beautifully.
The feel of the scene was totally different from the
rest of the film.    The contrast was important.

Whale was initially distrustful of his new editor, Ted
Kent, as he strived to maintain a strong grip upon all phases
of production.   He liked working with people he knew, and
who knew what he wanted.   Kent had been aware of Whale
on the Universal lot, but they had never met.   For the first
couple of days of shooting--until the first footage came up
from the lab--Kent simply observed on the set.   Kent remembered,

Whale had taken the script and outlined exactly
what he wanted. Medium shot, couple of close-ups,
two-shot, medium shot; everything was laid out so
he himself was sure to be covered for continuity,
and also so it would be easier for the editor not to
make mistakes.

When we first started work, he began to tell me
how to cut a relatively simple sequence. I said,
"That's the scene I'm going to cut today. I'll line
it up, and we can take a look at it in a few days. "

Whale said, "But how will you know where to
cut?"

That stopped me cold. I'd been cutting since
1922, and no one had ever asked me that before.
"I've had a little experience, " I said. Of course,
later, when he saw what came out, he wouldn't
have anybody else.

The Kiss Before the Mirror was previewed at the Cri-
terion Theatre in Santa Monica on March 2, 1933, and was
warmly received.

"Subject matter necessarily stamps the picture as arty
which will react at the box office, " said Variety. "However,
Universal will probably class it as one of those pictures
necessary to give their program class, which it certainly
will. "

Whale tightened the film from 75 to 67 minutes, and
it opened at the massive Roxy Theatre in New York less than
two weeks later. As a by-product of its success, Paul Lukas
signed a two-year contract with Universal.

Whale was anxious to begin work on The Invisible Man.
He admired the Wells book as it was, and the problem with
the writing was a conflict in bringing the book to the screen
--with as horrific an approach as possible--to satisfy Boris
Karloff's many followers. Toward this end, the studio had
earlier bought The Murderer Invisible by Philip Wylie, to
combine with--and punch-up--the elements of The Invisible
Man. Whale wasn't out to make a "horror" film though; it
was the story of a man caught up in circumstances of his
own making which he could no longer control, not dissimilar
to Frankenstein. But there would be no grave-robbing or
gruesome monsters. In fact, Whale was dead-set against
using Karloff and felt confident of getting rid of him in one
way or another. Karloff, he felt, was simply wrong for the
part--and that was that.

"From the very start, " emphasized David Lewis, "Jimmy said that Claude Rains was the only man for the part. "

The problem with Rains, whom Whale knew well in England, was that he was totally unknown to American movie audiences. Junior Laemmle would not be receptive to the idea of using him in the leading role of such an important undertaking.

Whale was fascinated with the problems of developing the necessary special effects techniques. Again, here was something new and different he could throw at the world. He was confident of his abilities to bring it off, but bedeviled by the unsuccessful attempts to write a proper script. It had to be perfect; once shooting began, it would be difficult (and certainly expensive) to make changes.

With The Road Back scuttled, and Preston Sturges' work on Invisible Man unsatisfactory, Whale prevailed upon R. C. Sherriff to work on the script. After his treatment of the Remarque novel, Whale knew Sherriff would have respect enough for the original work to stay within it, although Whale wanted, as with Frankenstein, a sympathetic main character. Wells' scientist lacked that sympathy when he turned his invisibility toward crime. Whale and Sherriff decided to explain that the man Griffin was not a killer by choice, but that the drugs he had taken had affected his mind. The understanding for that inner drive of a man trying to escape his fate was important.

Sherriff went to work in Britain, and returned to California in June 1933 with a faithful adaptation of The Invisible Man. Whale was pleased. "He had sat up reading it most of the night, " Sherriff wrote, "and thought it magnificent. It was so simple and straightforward, so free from affectation; the characters sprang to life in the first words they spoke; the suspense was tremendous and breathlessly exciting. It knocked all those other adaptations into a cocked hat. They couldn't hold a candle to it, and he was delighted. "

Whale set about to sell Junior Laemmle on it. Laemmle had become discouraged with the Invisible Man script problems and liked instead the idea of a Frankenstein sequel.

"They're always like that, " Whale complained. "If they score a hit with a picture they always want to do it again. They've got a perfectly sound commercial reason.

Frankenstein was a gold-mine at the box office, and a sequel
is bound to win, however rotten it is.   They've had a script
made for a sequel, and it stinks to heaven.   In any case, I
squeezed the idea dry on the original picture, and I never
want to work on it again. "

He took the Sherriff screenplay to Laemmle, suggesting that he read it that evening after dinner, something
Laemmle hated to do.   He respected Whale as he did few
directors though, and spent that evening going over the script.
Whale knew the film would be more expensive than the others
he had done--a major undertaking.   In Universal's troubled
times, Junior would need to think the script exceptional to
give it a green light.

Money was a real problem.   Universal had reported a
net loss of $602,255 for the six-month period ending May 20,
almost double the loss for that previous year's term.   In his
all-consuming desire to cut back, Laemmle had asked Boris
Karloff to take a cut in pay.   Karloff had been at the studio
18 months, starting at $750 a week, with a specified $250
increase for every six-month option exercised.   He had
waved his first increase, which would have given him $1,000
a week, on the condition that he would receive $1,250 a
week when the next option came due on June 1.   Laemmle
pleaded fiscal crisis and Karloff walked out, leaving Whale
without a star for his film.

That suited Whale fine.   Unwittingly, Laemmle had
helped rid him of Karloff so that Whale could once again
push for Claude Rains.   Laemmle was against using Rains--
regardless of how fine an actor he was--so long as no one
had heard of him.   Rains had made a name for himself on
the New York stage--as well as in Europe--but this mattered
little on the West Coast.

"How about Colin Clive?" Whale finally inquired.
Clive, after Frankenstein, was most acceptable to them both.
Whale, however, prevailed upon Clive to decline the offer,
as he was returning to Britain anyway.   Clive would have
remained to play the part had Whale actually needed him,
but his plan was simply to create a demand for Rains.

Earlier, Rains himself had been in Hollywood, where
he had appeared in an unsuccessful test for RKO's A Bill of
Divorcement.   Whale had a test of him in The Invisible Man
made for Laemmle's benefit, and Laemmle, with the thought

of bolstering the cast with Gloria Stuart and new Universal
contractee Chester Morris, finally consented. Whale argued
that the public would flock to see the finished film for its
spectacular special effects, not for a combination of stars.
The fact that the film would be a compelling melodrama of
the first order would be an added bonus. Morris, however,
balked at sharing top billing with Rains in his film debut and
was promptly replaced with William Harrigan. Whale was as
happy as could be.

With a good script, and the cast he wanted, Whale
now set about to concern himself with the special effects.
"How the hell are we going to do this?" Laemmle asked the
morning after he had read the script. Whale assured him
that it could be done, just as John P. Fulton, the head of
Universal's special effects section, had assured Whale. Par-
ticulars had not been discussed.

Whale was convinced that the film would be hugely
popular. Crowds would flock to see the invisibility effects
and marvel at how they might have been done. It would make
a bundle, and Universal needed a hit badly. Junior was anxious to get it into production as soon as possible. Whale
had been preparing it since September, and if Fulton was
ready, so was he.

Whale delighted in assembling a fine cast of supporting actors to help create a definitely British atmosphere:
Forrester Harvey, E. E. Clive, Holmes Herbert, Dudley
Digges, and especially Una O'Connor as the innkeeper who
first encounters the mysterious stranger wrapped in bandages
who demands a room on a snowy night. She was a wonderful Irish actress who had come to Hollywood to appear in
Fox's Cavalcade with Clive Brook. Whale had known her on
the London stage; he liked her immensely, and was able to
borrow her from Fox for the part of Mrs. Hall. She appealed to his sense of humor as a typical, flighty, nosey old
bag, slightly exaggerated, with the world's greatest manner
of screaming--high-pitched, dripping with character.

Shooting began at the last of June in 1933, with Arthur
Edeson on camera again and Ted Kent in the cutting room.
As they were all treading virgin territory, things proceeded
slowly. John Fulton and Whale worked closely through long,
rewarding hours.

The scenes of total invisibility could obviously be han-

dled with wires.    "But, " wrote Fulton later in <u>American</u>
<u>Cinematographer</u>,

> the scenes in which our man is partially clothed,
> with all of his unclothed parts invisible, presented
> more of a problem.    The wire technique could not
> be used, for the clothes would look empty, and
> would hardly move naturally.    So we had recourse
> to multiple-printing--with variations.    Most of these
> scenes involved other, normal characters, so we
> photographed these scenes in the normal manner,
> but without any trace of the invisible man.    All of
> the action, of course, had to be carefully timed,
> as in any sort of double-exposure work.    This
> negative was then developed in the normal manner.
> Then the special-process work began.    We used
> a completely black set--walled and floored with
> black velvet, to be as nearly non-reflective as pos-
> sible.    Our actor was garbed from head to foot in
> black velvet tights, with black gloves, and a black
> headpiece rather like a driver's helmet.    Over
> this, he wore whatever clothes might be required.
> This gave us a picture of the unsupported clothes
> moving around on a dead black field.    From this

Una O'Connor and Claude Rains in <u>The Invisible Man</u> (1933).

negative, we made a print, and a duplicate negative,
which we intensified to serve as mattes for printing.
Then, with an ordinary printer, we proceeded to
make our composite:   first we printed from the
positive of the background and the normal action,
using the intensified, negative matte to mask off
the area where our invisible man's clothing was to
move.   Then we printed again, using the positive
matte to shield the already printed area, and printing in the moving clothes from our "trick" negative.
This printing operation made our duplicate, composite negative to be used in printing the final mas-
terprints of the picture.

Each scene required a great deal of preparation.   Fulton ran many tests, examining the footage from different
vantage points.   The editing was considerably more involved
also, as the footage took much longer than normal to come
up from the lab, and then not always perfect.   Fulton would
ask Ted Kent if he could fix certain problems, and a give-
and-take situation would result in yielding the desired effect.

Whenever the special material would be filmed, Whale
and Fulton formed an effective team on the set.   Fulton
would direct the scene from a technical advisor's standpoint.
The normal action material seemed easy in comparison, although just as smooth in style.   Whale loved dolly shots, and
would intensely rehearse them, riding the camera platform
like the engineer of a small train.

"It was a very serious set," said Gloria Stuart, "and
we put in long hours.   Claude Rains was an actor's actor.
I think all good actors are egotistical in nature, perhaps
women somewhat less than men.   Claude was a big ego.
One could sense a tenseness within him.   No jokes; very little relaxation."

Once the special effects work was started, a tight lid
was placed on what was being done--there would be no other
studio stealing away the picture's thunder with a hasty copy.
"They were very secretive," Stuart recalled, "and they
didn't tell me a thing.   I remember playing some scenes
with Claude against black velvet, and James was obviously
enjoying every second of the film's making."

Actual filming took two months, and with special work
required, The Invisible Man took four months to make.   John

Claude Rains and Gloria Stuart in The Invisible Man (1933).


Fulton supervised the retouching--by hand--of exposed material before it was sent to Ted Kent:  a slow, tedious process.
Fulton later estimated retouching approximately 64, 000 frames
of film.

        The finished film, when ready for viewing, was mag-
nificent.   Laemmle was justifiably proud and held several
special screenings before its release to show it off.   When
it opened in New York at the Roxy Theatre, it did a whopping
$45, 000 in one week.   After an extended run, it moved to
the Radio City Roxy and the RKO Palace to accommodate the
crowds.   Claude Rains' option was gladly picked up; with
The Man Who Reclaimed His Head, his motion picture career
was off to a flying start.

        Later, H. G. Wells complimented Whale highly on the
screen version of his novel, but objected most strenuously to
the device of making his scientist a helpless lunatic by way
of the drug he took.   Whale countered with his basic com-

plaint of much of Wells' work:  its lack of simple humanity, as in Things to Come.  "After all, " he reasoned, "in the minds of rational people,  only a lunatic would want to make himself invisible in the first place!"

# CHAPTER SIX

The next major project for James Whale was an original story based upon the idea of putting Boris Karloff on Mars. At various times, both John Balderston and Benn Levy were indicated as working on such a script, but the task eventually fell to R. C. Sherriff, who went to work after his return to England from The Invisible Man. Karloff, after his brief altercation with Universal, returned in mid-July with a new contract and was loaned, after an idle period, to RKO for John Ford's The Lost Patrol with the expectation that A Trip to Mars would soon be ready for him.

On a Sunday in September 1933, while Invisible Man was in post-production, Carl Laemmle, Jr. phoned Whale and asked him to assume the direction of Counsellor at Law, a big production in the sense that a sizeable amount of money was earmarked for the services of its star, John Barrymore. The schedule had been arranged to provide for finishing with Barrymore as soon as possible, leaving material that could be "shot around" him for later. Unfortunately, the director, William Wyler, was behind by a week with Barrymore's footage and Laemmle could see at least another week's work ahead. Laemmle felt Wyler was doing a poor, costly job, and wanted the efficient Whale to step in and finish. Whale cautiously asked to view what had been shot by Wyler already, and declined to become involved after the screening. "I couldn't do any better than this, " he told Laemmle. "It's excellent. "

Somewhat bolstered by a respected opinion, Laemmle resumed a careful watch on Wyler and allowed him to finish

the picture, which was released to great acclaim--although
Laemmle was never able to develop a liking for it.

Shortly after this incident, however, Whale was once
again asked to step in on a picture being directed by a Wyler
--Willie's brother, Robert.   This film was entitled By Candlelight, and Whale interrupted his work on A Trip to Mars to
take over shooting on September 25, several days after production had begun.   Candle Light was a light German comedy
in three acts that had been a success on the London stage in
the late twenties, and later on Broadway.   "I remember Bob
shot about four days in the dining car of a train before being
replaced, " said Robert Florey.

By Candlelight was the simple, yet elegant story of
the butler of an amorous prince who mistakes a personal
maid for a grande dame, as she mistakes him for his em-
ployer.   The script had been run through four different writers, but was nonetheless a good one, and Whale was able to
do a creditable job with very little preparation.   The cast
was headed by Elissa Landi as the maid and Paul Lukas as
the butler, with Nils Asther as the real prince.   On camera
when he took over was John J. Mescall, who had done some
post-production work on The Invisible Man.   He filmed well
and rapidly; Whale liked working with him.   Other than to
bring Ted Kent onto the picture as editor, Whale made no
other cast or crew modifications and resumed production almost immediately.

After two pictures together, Ted Kent and James
Whale had settled into a comfortable pattern of working.
Kent recalled,

> His scripts were built different from others,
> revealing his close association with the writer.
> Except for physical sequences--such as battles,
> fights, musical numbers, or, for instance, the cre-
> ation scenes, his scripts were purposely simplified.
> Places where he thought close-ups were necessary
> were clearly indicated in dialogue scenes, and in
> shooting, that formula was followed.   This, no
> doubt, not only helped him on the set, but saved
> film and time.   Later on in the editing, there were
> fewer decisions to make as to where to use the
> close-ups.   As a rule, a director would shoot an
> entire sequence in various angles, and it was up
> to the editor to construct it for value.   I did not

Paul Lukas and Lawrence Grant in By Candlelight (1934).

always agree with Whale's style, but one could not
help but admire his skill.

In The Invisible Man, for instance, when he
comes in the door, Whale had a full shot, then a
medium, and then a chest shot--boom, boom, boom.
I didn't like that. There is no such thing as a
right way to cut a scene, but to me an introduction
of a character in that manner is making the audience conscious of the film element; it reminds them
that they are watching a film. To me, the finest
compliment that could be paid an editor is if someone were asked, "How did you like the editing?"
and they replied, "I didn't notice it in particular."

James Whale's first pictures were not too far
removed from the silent days, and I believe he
didn't recognize the film editors as they are today.
He found it very difficult to trust anyone else with
a creative aspect, although later--when he became
more confident--he might say, "Ted, you know what
to do with that."

He never entered the cutting room, but we would
have a screening at night every week or so for dis-
cussion. His scenes would start out simply enough
--he didn't like to get things all jumbled-up at once
--and then we would build them as we went.   He
would say, "That two-shot plays too long.   I think
we'd better use some close-ups there, " and it
would get more complex.   By the time a scene was
finished with, there was very little film left in the
can; he would have used every angle he had shot.
He prided himself on using it all--he didn't waste
a thing.
      At those screenings, he would sit in the theatre
and bounce his crossed leg.   As long as the leg
kept bouncing, I knew things were going fine.   When
the leg stopped, I knew there was something wrong.
      He was a very private person, serious, business-
like, with no time for nonsense, firm but kind.   He
was easy to work with, and although his compli-
ments were few, he had a way of letting you know
if he was pleased.

By Candlelight was shooting well into October of 1933,
and work on A Trip to Mars was stalled further by the loan
of Boris Karloff to Twentieth Century for House of Rothchild.
In the face of Whale's continued refusal to have anything to
do with a Frankenstein sequel, Junior Laemmle put director
Kurt Neumann in charge of The Return of Frankenstein, and
brought it to the front of the studio's Karloff projects.

After the release of The Invisible Man in November,
there were rumors that Whale was unhappy at Universal.
Adding fuel to the fire was his opposition to Return of Frankenstein, and the set-backs incurred by Trip to Mars.   There
was also an understanding that Whale was to direct the recently acquired Little Man, What Now?, which was abruptly
given to Frank Borzage after plans for him to re-make
Show Boat had fallen through.   Whale had received several offers to work in England, both on the stage and
from Gaumont-British and Alexandar Korda, and was anxious
to gain a release from his contract, it was reported.   A
great cause of tension, of course, were the ever-present
money problems, even though The Invisible Man was cleaning
up.   The trade press, always smelling for such developments,
had overplayed the problem.   Whale needed a vacation, and
on December 2, began his twelve-week lay-off by leaving for
England to work with Sherriff on the Trip to Mars script and
to discuss a new property, John Galsworthy's Over the River.

Whale in his office at Universal, 1933.

        In Britain, Whale visited with his family in Dudley,
took in some West End theatre, worked with Sherriff, and
had some photographs made of buildings and locations that
might prove helpful in designing sets for Over the River.
Whale liked the novel--Galsworthy's last--which would give
him a chance to work with England as he knew and loved it.
One More River, as it was known in America, was the ninth
novel in The Forsyte Chronicles.  Established as popular
and enduring works of twentieth-century literature, The New
York Times once said of them: "A social satire of epic pro-
portions and one that does not suffer by comparison with
Thackeray's Vanity Fair ... the whole comedy of manners,
convincing both in its fidelity to life and as a work of art."

        As A Trip to Mars progressed, it evolved into a de-
lightful screenplay with Karloff as the leader of an under-
ground civilization on the Red Planet that captured spacemen

from the Earth.  Whale was very pleased with the script,
but soon after his return to California in February 1934, the
film was scrapped for good.  Laemmle didn't like the script,
and decided it would be too costly to film.  For Karloff, The
Return of Frankenstein was also floundering, and the new
idea was to team him with Bela Lugosi in a series of pictures, the first being The Black Cat.  As this was done,
Whale was given the go-ahead for One More River.

Each time Whale had gone abroad, David Lewis would
take a small apartment in Hollywood, as he could not afford
to pay for the rent and upkeep of a large home when Whale
was not there to contribute.  Early in 1934, Whale returned
to find Lewis in a small room at the Chateau Marmont,
above Sunset Boulevard, and they decided it was time to buy
a house.

Together, they found a large house in Pacific Pali-
sades--about one block south of Sunset--between Beverly Hills
and Malibu.  The address was 788 South Amalfi Drive, a
white, single-story home designed by architect Millard Sheets.
The purchase price was $22,500 and although Lewis planned
to make the purchase on time, Whale decided that they should
have the deed as long as they were planning to keep it.
Whale bought the home himself, with the understanding that
Lewis would repay him.  However, Whale would normally
send Lewis' checks back, and Whale ultimately accepted only
about $15,000 toward the purchase price.  He moved in while
preparing One More River, and lived there for the rest of
his life.

Whale had long wanted to do a story of traditional
England, but the story chosen proved to be a complex one
for Sherriff to handle.  It had been published only after the
author's death, and much of it had been written while he was
mortally ill; One More River was almost universally considered the weakest of the nine Forsyte works.  The last
three novels had branched off to form the chronicle of the related Charwell family, and Galsworthy had seen these as statements in support of England during the turbulent times of the
great depression and shortly before.  He referred to the
Charwells as an "... older type of family with more tradition
and sense of service than the Forsytes. "

There were two major plot lines in One More River;
one of Lady Clare Corven escaping from her cruel husband,
Sir Gerald Corven, and the second--and more important--a

tragic romance of her older sister, Dinny Charwell.   Dinny's
story formed the crux of the book, but Whale and Sherriff
agreed that, cinematically, it was a drama of the mind, and
the film would be better served by following Lady Clare and
placing her sister in the background.   This amounted, in effect, to doing away with 50 percent of the original tale.
Sherriff eliminated two characters entirely, because they
worked toward the development of Dinny's story, not Clare's.
Sherriff added much, condensed much, and came up with an
excellent script centered on Clare's romance with a naive
younger man, whom her husband had named in a divorce suit
as corespondent after she had refused to return to him because he had beaten her with a riding crop.

        In casting such a film, Whale had great fun.   Its star
was Diana Wynyard, and in supporting roles he was able to
use Colin Clive as Sir Gerald; C. Aubrey Smith as General
Charwell; Reginald Denny; Mrs. Patrick Campbell; and Henry
Stephenson, Alan Mowbray, Lionel Atwill, Kathleen Howard,
E. E. Clive, Tempe Piggott, and Gilbert Emery.   Frank
Lawton, soon to be seen as M-G-M's David Copperfield, was
cast as Clare's younger lover, Tony, and 22-year-old Jane
Wyatt made her film debut as Dinny.

E. E. Clive, Diana Wynyard, and Frank Lawton in One More
River (1934).

Young Jane Wyatt with Mrs. Patrick Campbell in One More
River.  "I planted that tree when I was five, " drolls Mrs.
Pat.  "I'd like to be buried under it, but I suppose I won't.
They'll probably do something stuffy. "

Shooting began in mid-May of 1934 and continued
through the first of July.  The sets looked appropriately authentic and Whale's flair for decorating his sets before shoot-
ing--simply by adding some cut flowers or the like--helped
to personalize them to his tastes.

Whale especially enjoyed the experience of working
with 69-year-old Mrs. Patrick Campbell, a legendary actress
and a notorious wit.  She had won world fame in Pinero's
The Second Mrs. Tanqueray in 1893, and had created the
role of Eliza Doolittle in Shaw's Pygmalion in 1912.

"I've just seen a film ..., " she said to Whale one
day.  "I know you can work miracles here.  I would like to
look like a woman called 'GARBO.'"

Later, upon seeing the first rushes, she relented.
"I look like a little chest of drawers, " she cooed.

Junior Laemmle was pleased with the results of One
More River, although it had run over budget and seemed too
British to be very successful in the United States; it was
more popular in England, where it played to great acclaim.
The domestic notices were excellent, and except for a scene
in which Diana Wynyard was beaten by Colin Clive, which had
to be cut after a preview, it was generally felt that the material was handled with the best of taste and style.

Wrote Mordaunt Hall in the New York Times,

> One might hazard that this film can boast of one
> of the finest courtroom episodes ever projected on
> a screen.   This comes at a climactic point of the
> pictorial narrative and is concerned with the pro-
> ceedings in the trial of a divorce suit instituted by
> Sir Gerald, with Tony Croom, who is desperately
> in love with Clare, named as corespondent.   It
> happens in London, and there are the bewigged
> judge, barristers and others in the court.   It is a
> remarkable sequence and one endowed with consid-
> erable vitality, truth and imagination.

Colin Clive had returned from England to appear in
The Key at Warner Bros.   After One More River, he performed Journey's End at the Hollywood Playhouse, then
stayed for Clive of India at Twentieth Century.   Beyond The
Right to Live, based on the Somerset Maugham play The
Sacred Flame, he planned to re-create his role of Henry
Frankenstein in The Return of Frankenstein, which Whale,
in an unguarded moment, had finally consented to make for
Universal.   He would, of course, exercise complete creative
freedom in its development, and the Laemmles didn't care
as long as they could sell it as a Karloff Frankenstein picture.

Throughout the motion picture industry, there were
weekly rumors as to the state of affairs at Universal City.
Every few months, Uncle Carl would issue a denial that he
was planning to sell out to any of a dozen or so potential investors.   Junior and he had been known to quarrel on occasion, most fiercely over the former's plans to, at one time,
marry actress Constance Cummings, who later married Benn
Levy.   Senior's objection was that she wasn't Jewish, and

his son finally backed down in the face of a threatened disin-
heritance, much to his later regret.   His costly production
policies were also under fire by the company's sales person-
nel, who felt that Universal just could not compete on an
equal footing with the big major studios like Paramount and
M-G-M.   The low-cost programmers on which Universal used
to survive quite nicely were easier to sell, they maintained,
although Senior stubbornly supported Junior and fired East
Coast sales manager Phil Reisner for his vocal opposition.
Toward the end of 1934 though, Junior did step down and was
replaced briefly by his brother-in-law, Stanley Bergerman.
"I didn't need to work so damned hard, " Laemmle rational-
ized   "It just wasn't worth it. "

        He was rumored to be engaged, for a time, to Florida
society debutante Virginia Yahlen, and his health was precarious at best, though his hypochondria was legendary.   His
father would soon be 68 years old, and most observers felt
it would just be a matter of time before something happened.
Junior announced he would personally produce only seven pictures for Universal in 1935, the first to be The Return of
Frankenstein, which he fully expected to make just as much
money as its predecessor.

        Needless to say, James Whale had no intention of
making a straight sequel to Frankenstein.   Writer William
Hurlburt did the spade work on a continuation of the Frankenstein story, as vaguely followed in the Shelley book, pertain-
ing to the Monster's need for a woman-creature--a "bride"--
although, in the novel, Frankenstein destroyed her before she
had been finished   In Whale's mind, the whole idea of a female Karloff-like monster was highly amusing.

        Whale set about to refine the Hurlburt screenplay with
John Balderston.   What they fashioned eventually became one
of the most unusual films ever made.   Ideally, it was a black
comedy; an outrageous exercise with a unique premise that
had been fully set up and explored in a previous feature,
milking it for all the "horror" it was worth.   What was left
was a rare opportunity--what, indeed, would happen to a man-
made creature, like the Frankenstein Monster, if he had lived
longer than the few days he was allowed to in the first film?
He supposedly died in the old burning windmill, and Whale
felt it would be unforgivably contrived to propose that he actually survived all that in order to return and do the same
thing all over again.   Suppose, like a child, he began to develop himself?   Could he learn to talk, as he did in the book,

The Monster not only talks in The Bride of Frankenstein, he
also drinks wine and learns to smoke cigars.


and grow closer to the human race--perhaps even become
more identifiable with the audience?

The Return of Frankenstein was approached by its director as a "hoot." In fact, he cast the film before the
screenplay was finished, and had the parts written expressly
for the people he wanted. Boris Karloff, of course, would
play the creature, and Colin Clive his maker. In addition,
Whale considered both Una O'Connor and Ernest Thesiger absolute necessities. For her, a character was created as a
servant in the Frankenstein household, and she was there to
scream, embody all the local townsfolk, and generally be the
character Whale found so vastly amusing.

Ernest Thesiger, on the other hand, was to be the
villain of the piece, and the cause of all the trouble that confronted Dr. Frankenstein after his creation supposedly had
been killed. Like O'Connor, he would play the character
Whale loved so--a strange, evil, eccentric old man, aloof
and hilarious.

The major problem of preparing the script was to establish the Monster's return to the director's satisfaction.
He honestly felt he had milked whatever "horror" there was
in the premise with the first film.    Half the effect,  in fact,
was the relative uniqueness of it, something that had been
considerably diminished in the three years since its release.
Frankenstein stood by itself, and Whale would not stoop to
remake it.    His way out, therefore, was ingenious.

Characteristically enough,  the screenplay began with
the camera moving in on a distant house amidst thunder and
lightning.    Inside the "richly furnished house of the period--
1816, " however,  the audience found Lord Byron,  Percy Shelley, and young Mary Godwin.    Spurred by the storm, Byron
recounts the events of the creature's creation, and his de-
struction in the burning mill.    "That wasn't the end at all, "
Mary teases.    " Would you like to hear what happened after
that?"

The two men come closer.

"I feel like telling it, " she continues.    "It's a perfect
night for mystery and horror--the air itself is filled with
monsters. "

"We're all ears!" crows Byron.    "While heaven blasts
the night without--open up your pits of Hell.... "    With that,
the scene once again reverts to the old mill.

Whale felt this scene to be the most important in the
entire film.    With it,  he was able to launch his sequel into
a different realm than the first film.    No longer was it the
stark reality of Frankenstein, but a fantasy world pouring
directly from the mind of the author to--in effect--entertain
some friends on a dreary evening.    He no longer felt bound
to any of the conventions of the sequel, and proceeded to
dump everything but the kitchen sink into it.

The Bride of Frankenstein, as it came to be known,
worked up to a starting date in the first week of January.
In addition to the previously set cast, Valerie Hobson, under
contract to Universal from England, was assigned the part of
Elizabeth, and from M-G-M, Elsa Lanchester was borrowed
for a dual role.    She wrote in Charles Laughton and I,

In one role I was the female monster with a
terrifying, sculptural sort of make-up; in the other

Karloff reportedly found The Bride of Frankenstein less
amusing than did Whale.

I was Mary Shelley who was sweet and docile.   The
film was a good show ground for me because there
was such variety in these two parts....   It was
[Whale] who insisted that I should play them both.
I thoroughly enjoyed working on the picture with
him and admired both his method of directing and
the pleasant atmosphere he created around him.
     The monster make-up took three hours for my
face alone.   My hair was stiffened into a topsy-
like mop and was made to stick out backwards on
a little cage.   I was then bound in yards and yards
of bandage, all most carefully done by a nurse.
This took one hour.   I used to get very tired in
this curious form of costume, because it was difficult to move and impossible to sit down or walk.
Boris Karloff ... had a five hour make-up, and as

there was only one expert who could do these difficult make-ups, there were not many hours left in
the working day.   It was simple when one of us
could be shot while the other was being made-up;
but we only had a very short time for our scenes
together, because Karloff only liked to be in the
studio for so many hours and then go home.   I do
not remember his daily limit; I think it was twelve
hours in all.   His make-up certainly was very un-
comfortable.   He walked about with a spike apparently sticking through his neck, great heavy boots
and a bright green skin.

Recalled Ted Kent,

The bride's make-up was Whale's conception.
He was very clever with his pencil and I saw several sketches he made showing how her hair should
look, etc.   In fact, the back pages of his scripts
were full of sketches he would draw for the art director or costumer to illustrate what he wanted--
the shape of arches, drapes, the style of dress, or
type of uniform.   In this area, I would say, at
least in the pictures I worked on, he had complete
control from beginning to end.   I don't believe he
could have worked any other way.

The Bride of Frankenstein was part of an ambitious
schedule for 1935, announced during the Christmas season by
Universal.   Beyond it were The Great Ziegfeld, The Good
Fairy, The Man Who Reclaimed His Head, Show Boat,
Magnificent Obsession, and Within This Present.   Whale was
not idealistic enough to think that his new picture would be
sold or treated any differently than the first.   It would be
advertised as a horror picture, and people who paid to see
it would be looking for a horror picture.   He would have fun
with this film, but at the same time, he had to be sure it
would work on two different levels:   his own sly fantasy, and,
naturally, as a horror film to please the fans of the first
who allowed Universal to make so much money from it.   To
be sure, then, Bride of Frankenstein would contain some
genuinely thrilling material.

Whale exercised much care in shooting the Shelley
opening, and in the editing of it.   It was rehearsed well, as
he was very serious about the delicate nature of the scene,
and the fact that if it were not successful, the rest of the

picture would decline in its wake.   Ultimately, the sequence
was shortened from its original text, and the dialogue ad-
justed to get around objections of Mary and Shelley openly
living together.   Ted Kent personally didn't like the scene
and suggested its removal.   "As far as I was concerned, "
he explained, "it was a horror picture, and I wanted to get
on to the Monster.   The Shelley sequence was unnecessary. "

In fact, few people clearly understood Whale's motives
behind the opening, and he recognized the importance of it
being both brief and effective.   He knew the audience who
came to see a horror film would stand for very little of it,
but its removal was out of the question.

Editorially, it was a complex and visually exciting
scene for a simple three-way dialogue.   Almost each line
was accorded a cut all its own, and much was photographed
in medium and close shots that emphasized the subtlety of
the faces.   It was lovingly handled.   Said Ted Kent,

> Whale shot only what he felt he needed, and
> sometimes he would get caught without enough foot-
> age; there were times when he wished he had more.
> Often, when I'd get stuck on something, I'd go to
> the set and tell him I had a situation that wouldn't
> match.   He'd think for a moment, and if he didn't
> have a quick answer, he'd say, "Do the best you
> can, " or "Go ahead and jump cut it--it'll only hurt
> for a moment. "
> Fortunately, I always had something I could cut
> to, if only for a split second--someone raising their
> eyebrow or the like.   He was never terribly con-
> cerned about matching shots, but had faith in my
> ability to always get him out of trouble.   Or so he
> thought.

Shooting on the Bride took forty-six working days to
finish and the script, in places, was well-pruned.   Originally,
the Monster committed more murders than in the final cut,
but they were gratuitous killings--unmotivated and inconsistent
with the careful elements of the first film.   In addition, the
inside humor of some of the scenes got a little out of hand,
and threatened to hurt the flow of the story.   Consequently,
the film ran more than $100,000 over budget, coming in at
just under $400,000.

Ernest Thesiger was able to accomplish the near im-

possible--to threaten to steal the picture away from Boris
Karloff's monster.   Karloff turned in a flawless performance,
and Thesiger matched him every step of the way.   Between
takes, he would busy himself in a corner of the stage with
needlepoint.   Occasionally, he would come to Amalfi Drive
for dinner.

"I thought he was the most loathsome man I ever
knew, " said David Lewis.   "He was very nasty to me.   He
treated me like some kind of servant in my own home.   He
was a terrible snob, but he was related to the aristocracy
and that's what Jimmy liked about him. "

Whale understood what some people took to be Thesiger's inherent nastiness, and was able to channel it into
the camera with just the precise amount of force.

The Bride of Frankenstein set was, as always, serious but easy.   "They were obviously having a good time, "
observed Gloria Stuart, who dropped by to watch one day.

A problem that did exist was the drinking that cinematographer John Mescall did.   It had become so serious
that the studio had daily to send a car for him, in order to
get him safely to the studio.   Mescall, however, was one of
those people who seemingly worked just as well drunk as
when stone sober.   He did an excellent job; Whale liked the
fact that he worked fast, as he rarely fussed with incidental
camera hardware and meticulous lighting conditions, as some
cameramen were given to do.   His work on The Bride of
Frankenstein ranks it as beautifully photographed a film as
has ever been made.

With the creation of the "Bride, " Whale had an opportunity to try a creation scene more lavish than in the first
picture.   He shot angles and movements aplenty, and Ted
Kent was able to construct a beautifully thrilling sequence.
Kent recalled,

> The Special Effects and Electrical Departments
> made up numerous meaningless gadgets, switches,
> indicators and the like, and Whale chose the most
> interesting.   In a sequence of this sort, where so

[Opposite:]   Whale and Ernest Thesiger take tea on the set
of Bride of Frankenstein (1935).

many cuts are required, the burden of constructing
it has to be the editor's.  Procedure is slow and
one has to feel his way through an abundance of
film.  The length of the cuts is important.  The
gadgets and paraphernalia interspersed with the subject must be interestingly used so as to avoid
repetition.  The effect is made to hold the audience's
attention to the extent that they forget that they are
watching nothing but film.  The director, of course,
can and does have a say in its overall length.  The
sound effects are an important factor, but in my
opinion, the most valuable contribution to this sequence was made by Franz Waxman for his imaginative musical score.

Waxman had come to Hollywood with Erich Pommer
to arrange the music for Jerome Kern's Music in the Air at
Fox in 1934.  Whale was delighted to have him available for
the Bride score, after having admired his work in Pommer's
Liliom, directed by Fritz Lang in 1934.  Waxman's haunting
main theme for Bride was very much like the music later
known as "Bali Ha'i" from South Pacific.  It won him a contract at Universal as Musical Director, where he scored a
dozen films before moving to M-G-M two years later.
Whale thought him a wonderful composer.

For as much fun and satisfaction as Whale got from
The Bride of Frankenstein, he had the ending written to ex-
clude, he hoped, the possibility of any more sequels.  He
had had quite enough of Frankenstein:  the Monster, rejected
by the new female, would blow up the entire laboratory with
everyone, including Henry, in it.

With the lightning and the thunder of the heavens
for accompaniment [the script read], the structure
that was the laboratory collapses into a burning
heap--the cloud of smoke and dust disperses a little and settles down over the scene--the thunders
of a jealous and triumphant Jehovah roll--for positively the FINAL FADE OUT.

A little thought given to the situation, however, per-
suaded him to allow Henry and Elizabeth to escape for a
semi-happy ending.  In reality, the Monster was the real
hero of the film, and as long as he was blown to bits, Whale
figured he wouldn't have to bother with another Frankenstein
sequel.

The Bride of Frankenstein was released in April 1935 to fine notices and good business, although it didn't come close to the gross of the original.  Junior Laemmle was delighted with it all the same.

For Elsa Lanchester and Charles Laughton, Whale arranged a preview screening of the completed Bride at Universal.  Laughton, who had been working hard on Les Miserables during its production, sat quietly through the showing, and offered only a singular comment when it was over. "Doesn't Elsa have the most beautiful shell-like ears?" he wondered.

The problem with the film was that it was a little too much toward Whale's own peculiar tastes to relate fully to the mass audiences of the period.  Some reviewers noted that the excess of humor interfered with the "horror," and others objected to the genre in general.  Whale had little use for them, and enjoyed telling of the time he took a group of friends to see The Bride of Frankenstein during a reissue in the late forties.  They stationed themselves toward the rear of the theatre and were chuckling quite audibly when a woman seated in front of them finally turned to Whale.  "If you don't like the show," she admonished, "you can damn well leave!"

Basking in the good favor of The Bride of Frankenstein, Whale began to prepare for filming the long-awaited remake of Show Boat, a musical budgeted at over $1,000,000. The studio planned it along with Diamond Jim (assigned to director Al Santell), and The Great Ziegfeld, to be directed by Eddie Sutherland; their total cost projections exceeded $2,225,000.

Show Boat was originally a dramatic novel of river life on the Mississippi in the latter part of the 1800's, published by Edna Ferber in 1926.  From that, composer Jerome Kern approached Ferber for the stage rights to her work.  However, she thought him crazy; the book was anything but proper material for a musical.  The story spanned some fifty years, concerned an unhappy marriage and miscegenation aboard the floating Cotton Blossom.  Kern took his subject matter to Oscar Hammerstein II, who wrote the book and lyrics, and to Florenz Ziegfeld, who agreed to produce it.  The musical Show Boat had its world premiere in Washington, D.C. on November 15th, 1927, and moved to New York shortly thereafter, where it became one of the great stage successes of all time.

Carl Laemmle, Sr. bought the moving picture rights to Show Boat shortly after its publication and filmed a part-talking version in 1928, directed by Harry Pollard, with Laura La Plante, Joseph Schildkraut, Otis Harlan, and Stepin Fetchit. In a prologue to the story, Uncle Carl and Ziegfeld paid tribute to the musical's stage success with members of the original cast--headed by Helen Morgan--singing selected numbers from it. The film was not a huge success, however, and a good, all-talking version of the greatest musical property a studio could own remained to be made.

To do it right, Show Boat would be a costly undertaking, and Universal had stalled plans to shoot it again since 1933, when director Frank Borzage was to make it with Irene Dunne, Russ Columbo, and Charles Winninger from a screenplay by Columbia's Jo Swerling. Junior Laemmle liked the idea, and one of the films he planned to produce in 1935 was Show Boat, directed by Whale, who seemed to be an odd choice on the surface. An Englishman? Certainly; if there was a director in Hollywood who could bring Show Boat to the screen with more unique a style and practical eye toward costs than Whale, Laemmle didn't know of him. His faith in his friend was unquestioned, and Whale was delighted to be able to do something entirely different from what he had done in the past. Three initial screenplays from playwright Zoe Akins were scrapped and, in late 1935, the final shooting script was completed by none other than Hammerstein himself. The company was in serious financial trouble, though, and as the year wore on, rumors of the studio's impending sale grew more frequent.

In the face of such problems, Show Boat was placed on a back burner while production was begun on John Stahl's Magnificent Obsession. Laemmle suggested that Whale do a smaller, less cumbersome picture in the interim. He happily obliged with The Hangover Murders, a comedy-mystery about a wild party waking up on the morning after to find a dead body that nobody can remember anything about. Whale had read it in novel form, liked it, and had asked the studio to buy it for him.

Shooting began in late July with a wonderful cast of character actors, including Constance Cummings, Robert Young, Sally Eilers, Robert Armstrong, Reginald Denny,

[Opposite:]  Filming Remember Last Night? (1935).

Gregory Ratoff, and Louise Henry as the partiers; Edward
Brophy as the detective who suggests at one point that inves-
tigating the case was like an Easter egg hunt as new bodies
turned up; Edward Arnold, who conducts a vigorous police
investigation; Gustav von Seyffertitz as a hypnotist who is
called in to help jog the memories of the potential witnesses,
only to be killed himself; and Arthur Treacher as Phelps the
butler.    It was a simple picture to make, and as with Bride
of Frankenstein, Whale had fun with it.    It emerged as a
masterpiece of style and grace, witty and elegant.

"Every picture ends with a kiss, " Whale told David
Lewis, in summing up his attitude toward the film.    "I'm
going to open with one. "   And so, the first shot of Hangover
Murders was a "The End" kiss between Constance Cummings
and Robert Young.    Cummings, by that time, was married
to Whale's friend Benn Levy, who was present during some
of the filming and helped contribute to the script.

Despite Whale's affection for the film (he later considered it--along with The Invisible Man--one of his personal
favorites), Junior Laemmle disliked it, the story, and the
title, which he changed--with Whale's approval--to Remember
Last Night?   In accordance with its director's own tastes, it
predictably drew mixed reactions from the press, and was
quickly relegated to a position of undeserved obscurity upon
its release in November 1935.

Meanwhile, reports of Universal's sale persisted,
fueled in late October by Uncle Carl's failure to deny them,
as he had always been quick to do in the past.    Potential
buyers included A. C. Blumenthal, who had attempted to acquire a share of the studio in 1934; Warner Bros. , which had
indicated interest in the spring of 1935; Myron and David
Selznick; Dr. A. H. Giannini; Phil Goldstone; Sol Lesser;
Charles R. Rogers and J. Cheever Cowdin, representing
Standard Capital of New York; Louis Laurie, with some San
Francisco financiers; and a British group headed by C. M.
Woolf, the former head of Gaumont-British Theatres, who
had made a very definite offer early in October.

Laemmle was still a long way from selling, though.
Within a few days, he confirmed a mere "assist" from Standard Capital ("... not in the picture business") of $750, 000.
Laemmle had $4, 500, 000 in unreleased negatives:   six films
in the can, and two underway.    The loan allowed for production money for Spinster Dinner (with Carole Lombard, directed

An early moment of Remember Last Night? (1935). Constance
Cummings and Robert Young take drunken aim at a passing
boat.

by Walter Lang; released as Love Before Breakfast), which
was scheduled to start within the week; Sutter's Gold, due to
begin on November 3; and Show Boat, which Whale was definitely intending to start on November 21.   John Stahl had
just completed 88 days of shooting on Magnificent Obsession.
Remember Last Night? was the first release under the new
loan.   In return, Laemmle gave Standard Capital, controlled
by J. Cheever Cowdin, his partner George Armsby, and
broker Lawrence W. Fox, Jr., an option on his stock until
February 1, 1936, gambling on the probability that they would
not be able to muster the money that would be required for a
purchase in that length of time.   Senior genuinely hoped to
move back into the black with his upcoming schedule of re-

leases, although Junior was in favor of selling due to his
father's age (69) and work load. He also liked the idea of
liquefying the Laemmle money; for the 53 weeks ending November 2, the company suffered a net loss of $474,053.

Even as Show Boat approached, Uncle Carl talked
briefly with Whale concerning a new contract when the old
one expired. Laemmle grew strangely distant when Whale
explained his higher salary requirements. "I'm not unrea-
sonable," he said, "but I'll want the going rate."

"Well, you shouldn't," Laemmle countered. "After
all, you've made more off of us than we have from you."

"That comment," said David Lewis, "really pulled
Jimmy away from the old man. After Frankenstein, how
could he possibly make a statement like that?"

How indeed? The matter was dropped, and Whale
watched the further developments with both interest and
amusement. At M-G-M, where David Lewis was then an
associate producer under Irving Thalberg, plans were being
made to film James Hilton's Good-Bye, Mr. Chips with
Whale and Charles Laughton in England. Lewis had discovered the book among the studio's forgotten purchases and
had sold Thalberg on the idea of making it.

"Irving was going to go to London with us," said Lewis, "and take a rest. I would produce the story--which they
had paid very little for--and Jimmy would direct. He loved
the novel, and was planning to go to Metro for at least that
one film when Show Boat was finished, no matter what happened at Universal."

The Show Boat cast was a good one. Irene Dunne
was a natural for Magnolia Hawks; she had played the role
on stage, and was a good name with which to head the cast.
There was talk with Paramount about borrowing W. C. Fields
for the part of her father, Captain Andy Hawks, but Charles
Winninger was a traditional second choice. The part of his
sour wife, Parthy, went to Helen Westley after Edna May
Oliver, who like Winninger had created the role on stage,
had rejected it. For the river gambler Gaylord, whom Magnolia would marry, John Boles and Walter Pidgeon were first
mentioned, although Irene Dunne favored Nelson Eddy. Jerome Kern opposed Eddy because he was a baritone, and Kern
wanted a tenor. Finally, Allan Jones was settled upon.

As was usually the case, Whale considered the supporting cast the more important, and he wasn't as concerned
about Magnolia and Gaylord as he was about acquiring Paul
Robeson for Joe, Helen Morgan for Julie, and Hattie Mc-
Daniel for Queenie (she and Whale became good friends).

Sutter's Gold was momentarily delayed in favor of
Show Boat, which was pushed into production on December 9,
1935, amid rumors that Junior Laemmle would leave Universal after its completion to become a producer at M-G-M.

Show Boat was in production for the rest of the year,
and well into 1936.  To direct the dance numbers with Whale,
Le Roy Prinz, a top dance specialist from Paramount, was
engaged.  Together, they worked out continuity problems between the dramatic scenes and the various musical numbers.
Whale sketched outlines of how the numbers should be photographed for cutting into the final product.

The film's most impressive number was the simple
but beautifully realized "Ol' Man River" sequence sung by
Paul Robeson.  It brought the flavor of the river environment vividly to life, and its design was pure Whale.  Seated
at the edge of a dock, Robeson leaned back and sang in his
deep, rich, magnificent voice as the camera made a 270°
pan around him, daringly moving into a tight close-up as the
picture dissolved to scenes of Joe acting out the lyrics to
the song against expressionistic, Caligari-like backgrounds.

Le Roy Prinz recalled his few weeks on the picture:

> There were Laemmles all over the place.
> Senior brought them all over from Germany, and
> they couldn't speak a word of English.  They had
> the backs built onto the false-front houses on the
> back lot so that they could live in them.
>    I remember explaining the "Ol' Man River" num-
> ber to a few background extras one day, and they
> wouldn't say a thing to me.  "This man is singing
> with his soul," I told them, "not his voice.  You
> don't notice him; you don't hear him.  Just keep
> on going.  Any questions?"

Prinz received no response from the people, and wondered if they understood him correctly.  "Do you folks understand?" he asked.

Nothing.

"Finally, an assistant told me that they spoke no English.   'Oh!' I said,  'Sprechen Sie Deutsch?' and they all
smiled and nodded.   It turned out that they were all Laemmle relatives--every last one of them. "  Prinz dubbed them
his "German Army, " and they followed him throughout the
duration of his work.

Whale depended greatly upon Prinz for coordinating
the musical numbers, something with which he had had no
personal experience.   He did have his own tastes and opinions
on the material used.   He loved "Ol' Man River, " and Helen
Morgan's torch song,  "My Bill, " but detested "You Are Love, "
as did its composer, Jerome Kern.   Their dislike of it, however, was about the only thing on which they found themselves
in agreement.   Kern was present throughout the filming of
Show Boat; his interjections into the staging of his baby
threatened to drive Whale crazy.   Kern was very decisive in
his views and when overruled, he pouted.

Furthermore, when not contending with Kern, Whale
had to deal with the drinking of Helen Morgan.   "Every morning I was on the picture, " Le Roy Prinz recalled, "Helen
Morgan was dead drunk.   We had to stick her under a cold
shower and get some coffee into her before we could even
think of shooting. "

Jack Pierce, the make-up man, and John Mescall
were able to work wonders with her and Morgan's performance became one of the film's great assets.   In addition to
the ones selected from the show, several new numbers were
written for the film.   "Gallivantin' Around" was a song-and-
dance routine for Irene Dunne in blackface; "I Have the Room
Above Her, " a love song for Allan Jones; and "Ah Still Suits
Me, " an amusing song for Hattie McDaniel and Paul Robeson,
who was excellent in the picture but dismayed by the fact
that he could play only "nigger" roles in Hollywood.   Whale
and he became good friends during the filming; Whale was a
man of absolutely no racial prejudice whatsoever, and he expected the same attitude from everyone else.

"Robeson felt he should be able to do a lot better, "
said Prinz, "and he was right.   He had one of the world's
finest voices, and was a good actor beside. "

Oscar Hammerstein's script was a good one, but for

all the money and size of <u>Show Boat</u>, Whale wasn't totally
happy with the adaptation, and things were shot that he never
intended to use.   The chief liability, he felt, was the extension of the story from the 1880's period through to the 1930's,
maintaining all the cast members in perfect health--especially
Charles Winninger and Helen Westley, who would each have
been over 100 years old if allowed to age naturally.   After
Dunne marries river gambler Jones, they move away to the
big city, where Jones goes broke and leaves her.   Once
again, she enters show business to become a big star.

In the final cut of the film, there was a rather abrupt
passage of time between Magnolia's career beginnings and
headlines announcing her retirement (with white hair).   In
between, Whale removed a lavish Harlem hot-spot version of
"Gallivantin' Around, " the Jazz Age, the great World War,
and Irene Dunne's favorite number, "Why Do I Love You?"
sung while on the road in an early automobile.

<u>Show Boat</u> was a vast undertaking, and through the

Paul Robeson and Whale on the set of <u>Show Boat</u> in late 1935.

many problems and complications, those involved remember
it fondly. "I can say James Whale was a perfect gentleman, "
Irene Dunne who questioned Whale's choice as director, later
wrote. "We had no problem on the set. "

By January of 1936, it was a generally acknowledged
conclusion that Universal would be sold, although the elder
Laemmle held on despite Junior's persuasive lobbying.   All
assumed that the Standard Capital option would be exercised,
although J. Cheever Cowdin found it necessary to deny a New
York Times report that it wouldn't.   The delay, he explained,
was due to delays in the final reports on studio assets.   Universal was doing better, however, than it had ever done before; the second week of January 1936 generated more reve-
nue for the company than in any other week in its history.
Senior Laemmle held firm and hoped that Standard would not
be able to come up with the $10 million it would need by the
end of the month.

Then, on January 13, 1936, it was confirmed that the
deal would not go through.   Cowdin admitted defeat in obtain-
ing the money he would need:   $5, 500, 000 for the Laemmle
interests, $2, 000, 000 for current obligations, and the rest
for production.   It was then rumored that Herbert J. Yates
of Republic Pictures might be interested in merging his studio with Universal, as Laemmle owed Yates an estimated
$900, 000.

Charles R. Rogers, formerly of Paramount, who
stood to become head of production if the Cowdin deal went
through, tried unsuccessfully to shave the original terms of
the sale as February approached.   The down payment was to
be $1, 500, 000 on February 1, with yearly payments of
$500, 000 on that date for the next eight years.   Rogers pro-
posed that Laemmle agree to a $500, 000 down, and like pay-
ments for the next ten years, but received a flat turn-down.
Undaunted, he pushed for an extension of the deadline to
March 1, which was finally agreed to, and a third extension
after that date, as money from many different sources, including Eastman Kodak Company, Electrical Research Products, Inc. , and some British investors, was gathered.

[Opposite:]  Whale prepares a shot with cinematographer
John J. Mescall.

Helen Morgan, Hattie McDaniel, and Irene Dunne in <u>Show</u>
<u>Boat</u> (1936).

      Show Boat was completed on March 11 with over
300,000 feet of exposed film in the can.  Three days later,
on the morning of Saturday, March 14, 1936, Universal officially passed from the Laemmle family to J. Cheever Cowdin
and Charles R. Rogers.  The Cowdin interests acquired
Laemmle's holdings of 185,883 shares of common stock, and
16,972 of preferred.

      Thirteen days later, on Tuesday, March 24, 1936,
Carl Laemmle, Sr. left Universal for the last time, to attend the opening of <u>Sutter's Gold</u> in Sacramento.  A billboard
near the main gate read:  "My heartfelt thanks to all of you.

Continue to give the company all that is in you, as you have
always done.  With your united help, Universal will always
be a leader. "

　　Rogers announced an ambitious program of production
and physical expansion.  Talk was that Senior and Junior
would enter into an independent production agreement with
Paramount, although the latter was still on the lot finishing
with Show Boat, and preparing My Man Godfrey, which had
been delayed for over a year in awaiting the availability of
William Powell.  Rogers fully expected Laemmle to remain
at Universal, at least for a while, and was somewhat taken
by surprise when he abruptly decided to accompany his father
on a trip to Europe.  He resigned as producer of My Man
Godfrey after preparing the package that included Carole Lombard, Powell, and director Gregory La Cava.  Junior left the
lot on April 18, also a Saturday, and La Cava became pro-
ducer/director on the film which began shooting the following
Monday morning.  Senior and Junior boarded a train to attend the Kentucky Derby, and went from there to the East
Coast to sail for Europe.

　　Show Boat was released the following month to remarkable reviews and fantastic business.  Whale was highly praised
for his deft handling of a large and difficult project, and he
was personally very pleased in being able to bring off a musical so well.

　　"People wonder, " Whale said in a New York Post interview, "Why I, an Englishman, should have gotten such fine
results with a story so typically American.  I think as an
outsider I had a better appreciation of the situation, and, because I realized how much I really don't know about the Mississippi, I surrounded myself with people who knew everything. "

　　Whale was particularly pleased with the fine reception
the film got in England.  "When the film opened in London, "
Irene Dunne affirmed, "I happened to be there and he received great acclaim. "

　　Whale made plans to return to his homeland on the
crest of the wave.  He had completed one of the year's biggest and most popular pictures.  He was now free of his contract and could move in any direction he pleased.  He was,
however, wary of Hollywood and careful.  He knew all the

current glory could dissolve overnight; when you were hot, you were red-hot, and when you were cold, you couldn't be colder.

"That they should pay such fabulous salaries is beyond ordinary reasoning!" he exclaimed. "Who's worth it? But why not take it? And the architecture! And the furnishings! I can have modernistic designs one day and an antiquated home over night!

"All the world's made of plaster of Paris!"

## CHAPTER SEVEN

James Whale had helped end the Laemmle regime with a big hit; Show Boat was the last Universal Picture released with Carl Laemmle's name above the title. Charles Rogers wanted Whale to sign a new deal with them, but he was tired and wanted to take a brief vacation. He toyed with the idea of making a picture in Britain. He also intended to do Good-Bye, Mr. Chips for M-G-M there. He was in no mood to sign another long-term contract, at least for the moment.

While in England, he talked with producer Alexander Korda about making Knight Without Armor with Robert Donat and Marlene Dietrich. He also visited his family, and sat for a large portrait by Doris Zinkeisen. Upon his return, Whale conferred with Carl Laemmle, Jr. over two projects that they hoped to make independently: Rachel Field's Time Out of Mind and Barre Lyndon's The Amazing Dr. Clitter-house. He came to uneasy terms with Irving Thalberg over Mr. Chips. Whale wanted $75,000 a picture--which was fine --but he also wanted a time limit on each film to which Thalberg was reluctant to agree. Thalberg was famous for his post-production retakes and changes that could require a director to spend more than a year on one film, which Whale was not interested in doing. He also wanted the credit "A James Whale Production." Thalberg balked at that.

Whale loved Good-Bye Mr. Chips and the idea of working with Laughton, Thalberg, and Lewis helped transcend any technical differences between them. It was Charles R. Rogers who managed to queer the Chips deal with a phone call to Thalberg: he emphasized that Universal had only two top-

141

notch directors--John Stahl and James Whale--while M-G-M
had their choice of the rest of the field. He pleaded with
Thalberg to back off of the Whale contract until Universal had
had a chance to sign him up themselves. Reluctantly, this
he did.

"It was a code of the industry, " said David Lewis,
who found out later what had happened. "Irving knew Universal needed Jimmy, and there wasn't much he could--or
would--do. "

Shortly thereafter, on September 14, Thalberg died of
pneumonia. Plans for the film were put off while all attention was turned toward finishing the Thalberg productions
still in progress--Camille, A Day at the Races, Maytime,
and The Good Earth.

Whale signed a new contract with Universal in late
1936 calling for $75, 000 a picture, his production credit,
and the freedom to do outside projects. He also engaged a
man named George Lovett--Myron Selznick's accountant--to
manage his business affairs, and established The James
Whale Company to handle real estate investments. Whale
considered his new contract an unprecedented high in his
career, and almost immediately began preparation for the
making of The Road Back as his next film.

Pulling The Road Back out of mothballs seemed like a
logical thing for the "New Universal" (as they called themselves) to do. They already owned the property, had an excellent script, and an excellent director. It was a follow-up
to All Quiet on the Western Front, which had been a monster
hit for the Laemmles, and Rogers was certainly eager to
start his tenure as production chief with a hit.

Upon entering the project, all involved expected to
meet with widespread objection because of the strong, unrelenting anti-war theme it carried, but no serious concern
was expressed. Whale was assured that the studio felt no
intimidation from foreign markets, although it was fairly certain that the picture would find itself banned in most countries. The foreign gross accounted for a good 40 percent of
a film's earnings. Some countries, such as Sweden, objected
to "horror" pictures like The Bride of Frankenstein; others
including China, Spain, Mexico, and Italy censored films that
portrayed their nationals as villains or objects of fun. But
no one theme was as roundly objected to as the antimilitaristic

or anti-war message. Generally speaking, this sentiment was usually strong enough to keep such distasteful movies to a minimum, but the great financial rewards seen in the domestic issues of a few top-flight titles like All Quiet and Journey's End, plus the undeniable publicity value and prestige of such works, occasionally overrode their liabilities. Of course, the ever-present need to turn a profit on such ventures sometimes allowed foreign governments to dictate American film production policies. M-G-M was stopped from making Sinclair Lewis' anti-Fascist It Can't Happen Here by German objections, and The Forty Days of Musa Dagh was put aside after protests from the Turkish government influenced a threatened boycott in France. Often, foreign nations would enter into friendly agreements with each other to the extent that films found unacceptable to either would be banned by both. In this way, China's well-known disapproval of Paramount's The General Died at Dawn was also extended to Italy.

Universal's All Quiet had encountered opposition in 1930. It was banned in Germany, but still was a highly profitable movie to make. In seven years' time, however, the European situation had caught fire to the extent that German opinions carried more weight than ever before. Hollywood became a haven for artists fleeing the Nazi powers and America--although officially neutral--was strongly anti-Hitler. More than 100,000 Jews had gone into exile, but Germany carried powerful ties with many members of the foreign market who did not wish to offend or antagonize The Third Reich. Germany's expected opposition to The Road Back would keep it pretty much within American and British borders, but its domestic appeal would be, it was hoped, just that much greater.

As preparation progressed into 1937, Whale confidently selected a cast of fine character actors and opposed the inclusion of any big-name stars. "When 'All Quiet' came out," he told the L. A. Times' Lee Shipley, "the names of the actors were not publicized. It was the story itself that was advertised, and the success of the story made the actors famous. I think we should do the same thing with 'The Road Back,' not starring any of the fine actors who will be in it."

Whale saw himself as the director of several highly successful war pictures, who was going to put everything he knew into the making of the war picture of the decade.

"'The Road Back,'" Shipley concluded, "bids fair to
be the most important picture, in its influence on the world,
since 'All Quiet.'"

To play the lead in The Road Back, Whale selected
young John King, a former Cincinnati radio crooner who
starred in the Universal serials Ace Drummond and The Adventures of Frank Merriwell. Slim Summerville was carried
over from All Quiet, and Andy Devine, Richard Cromwell,
Barbara Reed, Louise Fazenda, Noah Beery, Jr., Lionel Atwill, Spring Byington, Samuel S. Hinds, Laura Hope Crews,
John Emery, Larry Blake, Maurice Murphy, Al Shean, and
Arthur Hohl were equally billed in parts ranging from major
to minor. In supplementary roles were E. E. Clive, Edward Van Sloan, Dwight Frye, Reginald Barlow, Tempe Pi-
gott, Francis Ford, Dorothy Granger, Tiny Sandford, and
many others.

Shooting was projected to begin in late January and
extend over the next nine weeks. The budget of $770,000
was significantly less than All Quiet's. The studio hinted
nonetheless that it was much more, prompting the inevitable
press comments that it promised to be a "Whale of a picture."

Although the studio readily accepted the film's ban in
Europe, it was not expected that the Nazis would actually
undertake to stop its production entirely, which they did when
it became clear that Universal was not sufficiently dissuaded
by the simple lack of their business. After filming began, a
meeting was arranged at the request of the German government between Whale, studio manager Val Paul, and Dr.
George Gyssling of the Deutsches Consulate in Los Angeles.
Gyssling made the extreme displeasure of the German nation
known to them both, and in return received assurances that
the protest would in no way affect their plans of proceeding
on schedule. Remarque, by this time, was in exile and his
writings were long unavailable in his homeland. The very
fact that he was the author of the story, the film makers
reasoned, made The Road Back unwelcome in Germany regardless of subject matter or political overtones.

Distressed at his lack of effectiveness, Gyssling then
proceeded to acquire a list of twenty of the actors engaged
to appear in The Road Back, and mailed each one, along
with Universal executives and the major production staff, a
mimeographed letter threatening a boycott of the future output of anyone involved in its making. Only slightly unnerved,

Whale peers into a view finder between set-ups on The Road
Back (1937).    Note the military greatcoat he sported throughout filming.    (Photo by Roman Freulich, Universal Pictures)

the studio ordered the letters kept secret, but news of their receipt soon filtered to the local press.  The Hays Office expressed little alarm, although both The Screen Actors Guild and The Hollywood Anti-Nazi League filed official protests with the State Department to no apparent avail.

Filming had begun with much ballyhoo, and as a promotional stunt for the wide-reaching press corps, Whale and his staff were dressed in German military uniforms, according to rank within the unit.  Whale liked the warmth and durability of the gabardine against the cold night air and subsequently sported the greatcoat and boots through the rest of production.

The story opened on the night before the Armistice (November 10, 1918) and the early phase of the shooting, which began February 1, 1937, was given over to the staging of the battle scenes, working every night from 8:00 p. m. through 6:00 a. m. the next morning.  Progress was slow as filming moved through an especially wet California winter.  Costs were cut considerably by digging the battlefield trenches on the studio backlot--as opposed to staging half the film at the Irvine ranch some sixty miles to the south, as had been done for All Quiet seven years earlier.  Still, the heavy rains quickly put the picture a full seven days behind schedule.  Whale himself contracted the flu, forcing a complete three-day shutdown.  That pushed the budget estimate to the $800,-000 mark before ten usable minutes had been shot.  Wrote Douglas W. Churchill, a visitor to the set during the initial few weeks,

> The no-man's land of "Road Back" is a 150-foot square on the studio's back lot.  Around three sides is a backdrop of a sky and along the forth runs the track for the huge traveling camera crane.  All trenches, roads, barbed wire entanglements and buildings are built in perspective, so that at 150 feet they may appear to be miles away.
> The action ... moves across a field from right to left.  Each night, but one segment of the movement is filmed.  The camera on its tracks follows the men as they attack the French lines.  Tonight, for instance, the soldiers start from the protection of a barn and advance to a house containing a machine gun nest.  After the company disbands in the morning, the art directors will move the house from the left side of the arena to the right and place some

other objective on the left and tomorrow night the
army will fight through the house and across the
field to the next point.   Different, gaunt trees will
take the place of the seared cluster of branches
that are there tonight.   The surface of the field
will be changed.   The advantage is in the perma-
nency of the lights and the camera track.   There
is no variation in the amount of illumination from
scene to scene and the even movement of the camera on the huge aluminum boom will give the action
a fluidity that otherwise could not be attained.

The intensive press coverage was deemed necessary
for the good of the picture, but Whale found the regular presence of the press both irritating and disruptive.   His tactics
in directing his company during the battle scenes were closely scrutinized by reporters who understood little of what he
was attempting to do.   "He was a goddamn good director and
he knew <u>exactly</u> what he wanted, " actor Larry Blake recalled.
"You could never say to him 'Why do you want me to do
this?' because he would explain it to you so thoroughly.   The
camera would be so close that you could see nothing on the
screen but my face.   Whale would lean in and say, 'Now
Larry, we will make him very, very cold and very hard.
Remember what you're doing. ...   Remember you're a Jew
and they don't like you ... ' right up to the time he hollered
'Action!'   You couldn't possibly make a mistake. "

Whale's sets were always very low-key and serious,
while some other directors--used to press attention--enjoyed
the visitors and did their best to entertain them.   Whale
found it difficult to relate to most of them.   He no doubt
impressed some as an aloof British snob, and his uniform
was, therefore, the subject of occasional printed jibes.   Furious at some, Whale had the offenders barred from the set
and received more catcalls.

Inwardly, he was also concerned about the amount of
pressure the Nazis might apply to the new owners to stop the
picture.   There were rumors that Cheever Cowdin, during
his frantic days of mustering enough capital to buy Laemmle
out, had German money in Universal.   In addition, the company, under Laemmle, had had a thriving operation in Berlin
that produced European products under Joseph Pasternak, until Hitler's rise to power caused production to cease when
Pasternak fled the country, via Vienna and Budapest, to the
United States.   Universal sold its holdings to Tobis-Rota, and

was $357,600 in the red by September 1936.   Hopes reported-
ly existed that the new owners might be able to revive German Universal, which had been lying dormant, and observers
could only speculate what influence Hitler might have with the
company under such conditions.   Charles Rogers maintained
a stiff posture against concerns of political tampering, but
he was a company man, and Whale knew better than to trust
him.

In spite of all the problems (John Mescall's drinking
forced his replacement by George Robinson about halfway
through production), Whale was pleased with what he was getting.   "He makes a picture like a composer writes a symphony," enthused Dimitri Tiomkin, who was writing the score.
"He takes a theme.   At first he touches it lightly--just enough
to acquaint you with it.   Then he emphasizes it--a little--oh,
just a little stronger.   Then he develops--dramatically, forcefully!   Then comes the climax!   It is wonderful!   His picture
is a symphony of many themes!"

Undaunted, he pushed on, but began to detect a soften-
ing of the front office's hard-line attitudes as the budget
inched toward $1 million.   Filming fell more than two weeks
behind; the production department noted his average had fallen
to only two pages per day and felt he was now insisting upon
"excessive coverage" in light of the situation.   By the time
filming finally wrapped on April 21, after 73 days, Universal
had reported a second quarter loss of $105,069 after a first
quarter loss of almost four times that amount.   Roger's ambitious expansion and production plans, announced at the time
of the transfer of power, were considerably contracted, and
a new look was taken at the hasty decision to wholly disregard the possibility of losing most all the European market
for all future Universal products.

Whale was concerned about the possible attempt to
dilute some of the stronger statements the film had to make
in order to appease the Germans, and Ted Kent saw little of
him as the editing progressed.   Kent recalled,

Whale had a battle scene--a key scene--that he
wanted to work closely with me on.   He was conferring over some matter with the studio that I

[Opposite:]   A special traveling camera crane was built to
shoot the opening battle scenes of The Road Back (1937).

wasn't aware of, and told me not to touch it until
he could go over it with me.    Some time passed,
and I didn't hear from him.
     One day, the front office called and wanted to
know what was holding things up.    I told them what
Whale had said, and they told me to go ahead and
cut it anyway.
     Then I talked to Whale, and he said to wait.
Another few days passed, and I got another call
from the management.    They wanted to know what
was going on, and I told them that Mr. Whale had
asked me to wait for him.    They said, "Forget
about Whale.    Who's paying your salary?    Finish
the picture, " so I cut it without him.
     Finally, I guess they called him and told him
that it was finished and he could come down and
take a look at it.    Generally, he was very pleased
with the way I had handled it, and only had a couple
of minor suggestions to make.

At the time of its initial screening, The Road Back
was close to what Whale had desired to attain, and his principal concern was in keeping the film in that same condition until it was ready for release.    David Lewis thought it was
very good at that point, but not a great film.    "That was because it wasn't a great story, " he said.    "Remarque was a
man with only one great story in him, and that was All Quiet.
Jimmy had done the best he could with it, as had Sherriff. "

Life magazine previewed The Road Back in its uncut
condition, and of the opening battle scenes, when the company
was ordered to attack on the eve of the Armistice, it wrote,
"The next twelve minutes of The Road Back are the most
cruel war scenes ever filmed by Hollywood. "

Life featured The Road Back as its "Movie of the
Week" in late June, but by that time the damage had been
done.    After several sneak previews, the worst that Whale
feared happened.    He was ordered to reshoot portions of the
film that were too finely done--to strong for Nazi consump-
tion.    The decision was made to try to gain German acceptance at all costs, and Whale, faced with a situation he never
had encountered before, was outraged.    The studio commissioned writer Charles Kenyon to adapt some new scenes to
replace old ones in the Sherriff script, and Whale thought
them weak, unfunny ("The idea was to show how much fun
war really was, " said David Lewis), and steadfastly refused

to shoot them.   "He had a great hatred for the Germans, "
said Larry Blake.   "He never would have done that. "   In all,
the studio deemed some 21 separate cuts to be necessary,
most of them to be replaced with Kenyon's lame comedy
scenes featuring Andy Devine and Slim Summerville.

Whale stood his ground, but his reasoning attempts
with Rogers--that the Germans wouldn't find the film acceptable under any conditions and that tampering could only hurt
the domestic business it might do--fell upon deaf ears.
Rogers was Cowdin's man, and Cowdin was the one who determined that the film would be cut.

David Lewis was upset about the altering plans and
wished he could do something to help.   He called David O.
Selznick about the matter, who became furious at the thought
of Adolph Hitler dictating policy to any American studio.
Immediately, he called Cheever Cowdin in New York to threat-
en him with public exposure and all the pressure that Selznick
could muster.   Cowdin was unimpressed with Selznick, but
angry that anyone would attempt to threaten him and blamed
the troublesome, $75, 000-a-picture Whale for the hassle.

"He probably told Selznick to go screw off, " suggested
David Lewis, "and he did exactly that.   Nothing further was
said. "

Universal's anger at Whale was intensified by the Selznick incident and they proceeded to make-over the film with
a new director (Ted Sloman), and a new editor (Charles
Maynard--Ted Kent's assistant).

After the opening battle, the Armistice is signed and
the company, glad that it is over, starts for home.   The film
follows the grim misfortunes they encounter when they get
there.   Andy Devine returns to school, to be handed a toy
gun the teacher had taken away from him years earlier.
Slim Summerville marries the mayor's daughter after saving
her father and his shop from a hungry mob's attack.

Goaded by hunger, a mob besieges City Hall and Larry
Blake, the radical, steps forward to speak for them, only to
be killed at the command of his old Captain.

The wistful Maurice Murphy returns to his betrothed,
only to be confronted by her infidelity with a war profiteer,
whom he then kills.   Murphy is tried and convicted as John

King tells the court that he was taught to kill men who never did him any harm, but could not kill a man who had ruined his life as the man he had shot.

Needless to say, this was all highly objectionable to the Fascist dictatorship of Germany, not to mention the film's ending, featuring a grotesque dwarf drilling Nazi-like schoolboys for the next war.

On Sunday, June 6, 1937, Universal rushed a print of the newly emasculated Road Back to New York for inspection by German ambassador Hans Luther before his return to Berlin, but to no avail.  Luther refused to view the film and it opened to its world premiere on June 17, minus its director, its punch, and its approval by the Hitler regime.  Frank Nugent reported in the New York Times,

> It is Universal's "The Road Back," not Erich Maria Remarque's, that they presented last night at the Globe.  Remarque's "The Road Back" was a savage and bitter sifting of the ashes of war, the poignant record of the lives of a group of young German soldiers who tried to find the road back to life after they had spent four years with death. Universal's "The Road Back" is not that.  It is an approximation of the novel; it is touched occasionally with the author's bleak spirit.  But most of the time, it goes its own Hollywooden-headed way, playing up the comedy, melodramatizing rather than dramatizing, reaching at the last toward a bafflingly inconclusive conclusion.
>
> Better to study the film, I reread the novel a few days ago, and now I have read the R. C. Sherriff script from which the picture was made.  The two ran almost parallel; the elisions and deletions were excusable.  It is obvious, then, that something must have gone out of it between the time the script was entrusted to director James Whale and the two hours last night when the picture flowed across the Globe's screen.  I do not believe Mr. Whale was at fault; the weakness is in the casting, in cast, and in editing.
>
> It is distressing to watch the mutilation of a great theme.  Remarque was not writing a comedy;

[Opposite:]   Larry Blake in The Road Back (1937).

Universal appears not to have recognized that.  Remarque was not writing a satire; Universal has not
realized that either.   When he studied the tragic
young men who came home from the war only to
see things that they fought for go slipping through
their fingers, only to realize with mounting bitter-
ness and helplessness that there was no way back
to normalcy for them, Remarque had touched a
theme as universal as the literature he was creat-
ing.   Universal has narrowed it and cheapened it
and made it pointless.

As though it were dealing with a routing comedy
of the trenches, it elected Andy Devine to play
Willy; it chose Slim Summerville to be an antic
Tjaden.   The armistice itself has become a matter
of comedy.   The agonizing journey home--of which
Remarque wrote with longing and prayer--has been
told in terms of slapstick, of French tavern revels
and soldiers' choruses.   That bitter moment when
the street rowdies, breathing revolutionary fire,
set upon the ill Ludwig, beat him and tore off his
lieutenant's chevrons is saved from tragedy by the
appearance of Willy, clutching an apple which he pre-
tends is a hand grenade.

Variety's "Kauf" wrote,

> There is one great scene in which Captain von
> Hagen (John Emery) dismisses what is left of his
> battalion, 30-odd men, and the ghosts of the hun-
> dreds, dimly outlined, also line up.
>   There is another fine scene in which the hungry
> embittered masses of a small town riot.   Still an-
> other in which hoodlums attack the puzzled soldiers
> because the latter can't understand why they should
> tear off their chevrons and decorations.
>   Against which is a series of minor blunders
> befuddling the whole issue.   Andy Devine is per-
> mitted to indulge in much silly comedy, as also
> Slim Summerville.   This ingredient of the picture
> has been very poorly handled.
>   The last two or three reels are also too thin.
> They lead nowhere and soften up incredibly.   Then,
> like a pop gun after a bombardment, the picture is
> over.

None of the reviews dismissed the film totally, but

concurred that the film had some excellent material that had
obviously been taken apart and toned down.  Whale was sick
at the sight of what had been done, but could do nothing.  He
was not a type to reveal the full, true story to the press,
and there could only be speculation as to what happened within the walls of Universal City.  Whale held the agony inside
himself, and even Ted Kent was unaware of what was done to
the film after he had finished with it; the tampering was done
quietly but effectively.  Whale requested a release from his
contract with the studio, which was denied.  The thought of
buying himself free of it was unthinkable.

The press seemed to understand that the fault was not
the director's, however little they knew of the film's history.
They could see great care and style in much of it, and did
not grab the chance to dump the blame on James Whale; rather, the problems were noted as existing, and the only suspi-
cions were cast upon "Universal" and whatever that implied.

The week The Road Back opened in New York, German diplomatic representatives formally promised to respect
international protocol in future dealings with the American
film industry when the State Department followed up on the
complaints of German meddling with the picture.  Dr. Gyssling, who threatened the blacklist, said that he had been under orders from the Ministry of Propaganda.  The ambassador, Hans Dieckhoff, explained that neither he nor his predecessor had honored Universal's continued requests to view the
film on the grounds that they had no authority to pass judgment on it, and formally apologized.

All was forgotten, but the film was nonetheless ruined.
And so was Whale's position with the "New" Universal.

David Lewis was terribly concerned about his friend's
impasse with the new regime at Universal and did all that he
could to turn Whale's attention--his churning energies--else-
where.  Lewis, at the time, had moved from M-G-M to
Warner Bros., ending months of inactivity following Irving
Thalberg's death.  When James Whale's strong position at
the "New Universal" began to crumble, Lewis explored the
possibilities of a picture for him at Warner's.

Hal Wallis, then head of production at the studio, was
interested in Whale, as was Mervyn LeRoy, whom Lewis had
also come to know.  At length, Whale was engaged at Warner
Bros. to direct The Great Garrick for LeRoy, under an inde-

pendent production agreement he had with the studio.  Garrick was his fourth picture, the first one that he did not plan
to direct personally.

With a screenplay by Ernst Vajda and Rowland Leigh,
The Great Garrick was a vastly entertaining story based upon
the legendary actor of the latter eighteenth century--David
Garrick--who is invited from England to France to play a
season at the Comedie Française.  In his farewell speech
at the Royal Theatre in Drury Lane, Garrick implies that
the French need a "lesson" in acting from him and proceeds
to walk into an elaborately prepared revenge that his hosts
arrange for him upon getting wind of his supposed remarks.

Happily, Whale was able to move almost directly from
The Road Back at Universal into preparation for The Great
Garrick, which began shooting in mid-June 1937 and continued
through July 29.  Once again, Whale was in a position of respect and control, to the extent that he was within a friendly,
though unfamiliar, environment.  The film was an elegant adventure into classical theatrics, and Whale made it smoothly,
with a fine eye toward detail and an unrelenting care with his
camera.  It moved with great freedom and frequency, and although the film was not overly expensive for its type, there
was more polish evident in its making at Warners than there
would have been at Universal.

The cast was excellent, but not as uniquely a Whale
cast as most before it.  Brian Aherne played the dashing
Garrick; Olivia de Havilland was the innocent woman who became involved with Garrick--he thinking that she was part
of the Comedie Française trick.  Edward Everett Horton was
Garrick's manservant, and Melville Cooper headed a supporting cast that included Lionel Atwill, Lana Turner, Marie Wil-
son, Fritz Lieber, E. E. Clive, Harry Davenport, and Jack
Norton.

While Whale was at work on The Great Garrick, the
death of his friend Colin Clive occurred on June 25, 1937,
after a year-long battle with the complications arising from
pneumonia and alcoholism.  Whale lost one of his favorite
actors, whose career he had been almost wholly responsible
for.  An Episcopalian service was scheduled in Hollywood
for Tuesday, June 27, before Clive's widow had the body re-

[Opposite:]  Whale directing The Great Garrick (1937).

turned to Britain for burial.    Whale declined to attend or to
be included as an honorary pallbearer.    Said David Lewis,

> He hated funerals and everyone's morbid pre-
> occupation with death.   He wouldn't go to cemeteries,
> and he refused to acknowledge services of any kind.
> I, for instance, was very close to Norma Shearer
> after Irving Thalberg's death, and I would regularly
> accompany her to Forest Lawn to visit the crypt.
> Jimmy would get furious.    "Oh, stop it!" he would
> exclaim.    "Keep away from that place!"
> I would go anyway, but there were few things
> that irritated him more.

One thing that did irritate him more was The Road
Back, which popped up to haunt him when he wasn't occupied
at Warners.    To Whale's everlasting dismay, the film was
doing record business in its first nine openings, and Universal had poured thousands of dollars into great billboard cam-
paigns and full-page ads in the leading trade publications.
"$2.00 Top on Broadway!" they shouted.    "The Most Talked
About Film of the Year!"

Whale's mutilated masterpiece was being sold with
carefully edited review quotes that made it sound like the
greatest picture ever made--certainly greater than Milestone's
All Quiet on the Western Front.    What burned Whale was
that he felt he had made a terrifically fine film of The Road
Back before it was taken away and butchered.    The ads sold
the film as if it were still in its original form.    The attention it was getting after its release was like adding insult to
injury; yet few knew the real story.    Whale simply wished it
would go away, and Universal along with it.

In late July, The Road Back finally came west.    For
its Los Angeles opening it was heavily touted.    Customary
for big pictures was the placement of a multi-page ad in
either The Hollywood Reporter or Variety (often both), with
each page bearing the name of a major participant in the
picture's production (i.e.--the producer would buy a full page,
blank except for the film's logo at the bottom and his name
in the center), and sometimes quoting reviews, etc.    Whale
rarely bothered with these ads himself, and certainly didn't
plan to buy one for the disowned Road Back.    However, he
fully expected Charles Kenyon to cut himself in for a full
share of the screenplay credit, and decided to strike a blow
for artistic purity.

In the middle of the July 21, 1937, edition of The Hollywood Reporter was a ten-page insert for The Road Back. Within the ten pages was a full-page ad that read:

"Charles Kenyon
In Collaboration With
R. C. Sherriff
Wrote The Screen Play For
Erich Maria Remarque's
THE ROAD BACK"

The ad on the opposite page to this read:

"'Render To Caesar The Things That Are Caesar's'
*
This Page Is A Tribute To
R. C. SHERRIFF
For His Screen Play And Dialogue
Based On
Erich Maria Remarque's
THE ROAD BACK
*
James Whale"

Whale was grateful for the position he enjoyed at Warner Bros. and he liked Mervyn LeRoy.  He considered it likely there would be other pictures at Warners, and fully expected The Great Garrick to wipe his slate clean, make a lot of money, and to show Cheever Cowdin just whom he was treating like dirt.  After a visit to the set, Douglas W. Churchill wrote,

> James Whale is directing and the attitude that was evident during the recent filming of "The Road Back" seems to have disappeared.  The whole episode was a distasteful one to Whale.  When he started out, he dressed in an army officer's uniform and equipped his assistants similarly, according to their rank in the troupe.  The attire apparently affected his conduct and he was roundly thwacked in print by correspondents who visited the sets and those who were barred.  Now he may be described as almost amiable.

The film was previewed for the press on September 24, 1937, at Warner's Hollywood Theatre, where the reception was very favorable.  The Great Garrick glowed with

Olivia de Havilland and Brian Aherne in The Great Garrick
(1937).

polish and style; it compared favorably to Whale's best
works.   It was a whimsical, delightful work that everyone
seemed to enjoy, and they were all convinced that it would
be a big success.

Whale's billing clause, in conjunction with LeRoy's
position as producer, was interestingly handled.   The Great
Garrick was billed as "A James Whale Production," "Personally Supervised By Mervyn LeRoy."   On the film itself,
Whale's direction card appeared toward the front of the opening titles, and LeRoy's came at the last of the credits, the
position normally reserved for the director's name.   In all
of the ads for the picture, LeRoy's name was generally
larger and more prominent than Whale's, although the line,
"A James Whale Production," was always present.

"Here is no ponderous biography," Frank Nugent said
in his New York Times review, "worshipful, solemnly paced,
leaning heavily upon the encyclopedia, but a jestful and romantic piece which has drawn its hero to life while employing a gay fiction as its model. This might have happened,
explains Ernst Vajda, its author, in the prologue. If it did,
so much the better; if it did not, Garrick missed a joyous
adventure."

Despite the favorable press, The Great Garrick did
poor business and both Warners and LeRoy cooled toward
Whale. At $75,000 a picture, he was a costly property to
utilize if he wasn't going to make hits like Show Boat and
Frankenstein. Whale was severly disappointed, but pushed
on toward doing a picture with Carl Laemmle, Jr. at M-G-M,
where Laemmle had recently signed on as a producer. The
Great Garrick soon disappeared from view, being the first
picture Whale had directed that had not been based on a book
or play.

Junior Laemmle's deal with Metro had been reported
in the trade press in late April, after he had broken off ne-
gotiations with United Artists (they wanted him for one film;
he wanted to make three). The new pact involved the sale
of two of his properties to the studio: a stage play called
Nine Officers; and another, The Amazing Dr. Clitterhouse,
about a man working on a book about the criminal mind who
became a criminal himself, which Laemmle hoped to produce
with Whale directing. Laemmle signed onto the Culver City
lot on June 1, while expecting Whale to join him when finished with Garrick.

The Amazing Dr. Clitterhouse, unfortunately, had also
been acquired by Warner Bros. in a complex deal that erupted
into a dispute between the studios over who actually controlled
the screen rights. In the end, Warners won out and the film
was made by Anatole Litvak with Edward G. Robinson and
Humphrey Bogart.

Forced to scuttle immediate plans to make Dr. Clitter-
house, Laemmle had M-G-M buy his father's greatest silent
success, The Hunchback of Notre Dame, for Paul Muni. In
addition to the money involved, Metro loaned Robert Mont-
gomery to Universal for one film, but decided against remaking the story and passed it along to RKO. Laemmle's interest in filming Marcel Pagnol's Fanny, about a young girl left
with child by an adventure-seeking sailor, came to the fore-

The making of Port of Seven Seas (1938) was a trying experience.  Here Whale confers with an attentive Maureen O'Sullivan and a disgruntled Wallace Beery.

front.  The play was part of the French trilogy that included
Marius and Cesar, and the idea was to condense elements of
all three into one script, while carefully avoiding censorship
problems.

Once Whale's commitment to M-G-M was made, problems began to arise.  As in David Lewis' case, Junior Laemmle had been engaged by Louis B. Mayer, and the resentment that Laemmle felt among the production powers at the
studio was strong.  Laemmle had never worked outside the
comfortable atmosphere of his own Universal before, and
could feel himself being squeezed out.  The family-like poli-
tics made outsiders like Laemmle feel most unwelcome at
M-G-M; after a scant two months of such nonsense, he gained
a release from his contract and backed out of Fanny, indicat-
ing that he would turn his attentions to the stage instead.  In
his place, the producer of Fanny became Henry Henigson, who

had worked with Laemmle at Universal for years, and had returned to work under him at Metro.

When Whale finished with The Great Garrick, therefore, the situation he anticipated at M-G-M had changed greatly. Henigson was a nice man, but not much of a producer, and the Preston Sturges script was roundly disappointing. Whale was unhappy, but there wasn't much he could do but make the best of it.

At M-G-M, Whale was not his own man; the production was controlled by a faceless committee of sorts, and pronouncements filtered down from the higher-ups with vague purpose but iron-clad enforcement. Things went from bad to worse when Wallace Beery was assigned to the picture as its star. He was horribly miscast. The whole affair was treated as a "B" picture. Aside from Beery as the grog-shop proprietor father of sailor John Beal, Maureen O'Sullivan was the girl, and Frank Morgan was the man who gave his name to the pregnant and unmarried heroine until the father returned to see the error of his ways.

Hence, Whale became the director of a misbegotten Wallace Beery vehicle that he knew was terrible to start with. Things grew even more unpleasant as matters progressed. Wallace Beery was a member of the M-G-M family, and he hated Whale from the beginning as much as Whale hated him. Whale was distant in dealing with the actor, and the actor retaliated by making his chore as tough as possible. He exercised veto power over Whale whenever he pleased. Whale had never encountered such an outrageous situation before, and after the damaging experience of The Road Back and the disappointment of The Great Garrick, it proved to be a very depressing affair. He finished with the film as early as he could, but the outlook was bleak for the future; he was still on contract to make two more pictures at Universal.

Fanny began filming in early December of 1937 as Madelon, and then became Man of the Waterfront. It was completed in late January 1938 and placed on the release schedule for April 1 as Life on the Waterfront. The film and its star had so little appeal, however, that it was shelved after completion and not shown until a week's engagement at New York's Capitol Theatre in late July under the title Port of Seven Seas. Business for the engagement was brutally poor ($10,000 for the week in a house that seated over 5,000, with a live stage show), and the film found only scant bookings on the lower halves of double bills.

"I'm glad to get out of there!" Whale told Ted Kent upon his return to Universal.   "I'm not going to the previews or anything.   To Hell with them!"

## CHAPTER EIGHT

The atmosphere was decidedly cool when James Whale returned to Universal early in 1938. At first, the studio had wanted to "squeeze" the contract--to negotiate a cash settlement for Whale's release--but as losses mounted and Charles Rogers' position as the head of production began to deteriorate, they did relent in order to save the $150,000 sum they would otherwise be compelled to pay him. Whale, however, changed his mind and refused to rescind, demanding the contract's fulfillment, and in retaliation was given two low-grade "B" pictures to make to finish off his obligation. Universal would certainly not trust him with a large-budgeted film like The Road Back again; his salary amounted to the largest single factor within the cost projections for each.

"They weren't just 'B's,'" David Lewis emphasized, "they were stinking 'B's.' The scripts were awful, and Jimmy just wanted to get finished with them and get out of there."

The two projects, which Whale dubbed his "punishment pictures," were shot back-to-back in the spring of 1938. The first was called Sinners in Paradise, a story of the survivors of an airplane crash on a tropical island. The second was a quasi-remake of The Kiss Before the Mirror, entitled Suspicion.

Whale found himself with assigned casts and assigned crews--he took whom he got, and that was that. Instead of Ted Kent, he was given Maurice Wright as the editor. George Robinson was assigned as cameraman instead of John Mescall. His cast for Sinners was Madge Evans, John Boles, and Bruce Cabot. He did what he could.

"A director like Lewis Milestone, " said David Lewis,
"wouldn't have been terribly bothered by such a situation.
He would have done the films and simply made sure that they
cost the studio a hell of a lot more than they were planning
on. Jimmy wasn't the type that could do that, but Universal
didn't know it. "

Shooting began on Sinners in Paradise during the first
week of March, and Suspicion, after a week's preparation,
started exactly one month later. Both were budgeted in the
$235, 000 to $275, 000 range and scheduled for twenty days
apiece. On the first, despite filming outdoors, Whale aver-
aged six pages a day. When it became apparent he would go
over the anticipated finish date of March 31, he drove his
cast through a marathon 18-hour session that wound the picture up at 3:00 a. m. , April 1--three hours over schedule
and $1000 under budget. He began Suspicion the following
week and moved with even greater speed. Wrote M. F.
Murphy, Universal Production Manager, in his weekly status
report, "It appears to us Mr. Whale is endeavoring to prove
he can be the fastest-shooting director in the organization. "
Suspicion finished four days ahead of schedule--and a full
$30, 000 under budget.

For Suspicion, the studio borrowed Warren William
from M-G-M for the old Frank Morgan part, and Gail Patrick,
who was excellent as Carole Lombard's sister in My Man Godfrey, was borrowed from Paramount to play his wife. William's character, this time around, was made the District
Attorney prosecuting Ralph Morgan's murder case, rather
than defending him.

In retrospect, the two "punishment pictures" were not
badly done. Whale, as always, did his best for them, but
they were not made under the most pleasant conditions. The
reviews were generally kind, but reserved, and they soon
went the way of Port of Seven Seas and Impatient Maiden.
Whale felt he should be making pictures like Show Boat and
One More River, instead of Madge Evans vehicles. In mid-
May, however, while Suspicion was filming, he did get the
satisfaction of seeing Charles Rogers replaced as Executive

[Opposite:] Milburn Stone, Morgan Conway, Marion Martin,
Nana Bryant, Bruce Cabot, Gene Lockhart, Donald Barry,
Madge Evans, and Charlotte Wynters in Sinners in Paradise
(1938).

Warren William and Gail Patrick in <u>Wives Under Suspicion</u>
(1938).

Vice-President in Charge of Production by RKO's former
Western Division Manager, Cliff Work.   The move didn't
change matters much--Cheever Cowdin was still Chairman
of the Board, and Nate J. Blumberg was still President.
Whale had little desire to remain at his old studio any longer.

　　　Interestingly enough, about that same time Universal
decided to reissue <u>Frankenstein,</u> along with <u>All Quiet on the
Western Front</u>, <u>Lady Tubbs,</u> and Love Before Breakfast; if
the new product couldn't pull enough business, the older stuff
would.   "The top grosser of all time!" raved the trade ads.
"The power thriller they can't resist!   Karloff!   Colin Clive!
Mae Clarke!   Boles!"

　　　The "power thriller of all time" still retained its title
of "the top grosser of them all, " but the studio didn't seem
to be interested in retaining the services of the man who
made it.

Whale left Universal after finishing with Wives Under
Suspicion (as it came to be known), and did not expect to return. Based on the success of the reissue, they made plans
to make a second sequel with Boris Karloff entitled Son of
Frankenstein. Whale was not offered the film, and wouldn't
have done it had he been. He fully expected the slump in
his career to be a temporary one; merely a season of bad--
very bad--luck. The new Frankenstein film was made in
November of that year as part of a multi-picture deal with
producer-director Rowland V. Lee, and the cast was weighted
with Basil Rathbone and Bela Lugosi. Karloff received second
billing, but his character was--once again--unspeaking, and
served to be little more than a menacing prop who spent most
of his time in a semi-coma on an old operating table. The
three were fun to watch together, but Lee was fond of long
shots that showed off the imaginatively lit, but simple, limbo-
like sets that gave an air of great size to the production.
Whale's loving close-ups were missed, and the Monster--as
he would be throughout the rest of the series--was just a
dumb, sleepy brute to occupy the background.

The Bride of Frankenstein remains the only one of
the eight films Universal finally made that was about the
Monster. Karloff, who realized where the idea was going,
declined to appear as the Monster in any more of them and
Son of Frankenstein was the last to be accorded "A" picture
status.

When Whale left Universal, he wasn't in much demand
elsewhere. People who were not familiar with the situation
were inclined to assume that Whale was slipping, getting difficult, and that he cost a lot more money than he was worth.
The Road Back's problems were indirectly associated with
him. In addition, Whale had never followed a policy of rigor-
ous self-promotion and was simply not in the minds of the industry as much as other directors of similar stature.

He was vain, but never boasted. As he approached
his fiftieth birthday, his hair was totally white--as it had
been for some time--and he hated it. He would fret into the
mirror about getting older and working less. His creative
energies--his drive--were as strong as ever, but since leaving the friendly atmosphere and occupation of the Laemmle
Universal, the outlet of regular film making no longer existed. Socially, he had a small sphere of friends and maintained a regular routine of little variation. He impressed
people by bringing them to his home for an excellent dinner,

but entertained scantly.  So bland was his existence, in fact, that he began to tell stories--he loved to tell stories--that he would lift directly from the life of David Lewis.  Lewis, as a producer at Warners, had many friends and a busy schedule.  As Whale would hear of his daily activities, he would adapt them to his own life.  Lewis then would hear his day pass before him as Whale drolled on to dinner guests, leaving him with nothing to say for himself.  "My life became his, " he said without exaggeration.

It wasn't until after the first of the year that another picture was secured for Whale.  Edward Small, an actor and agent turned independent producer, had entered into a five-picture agreement with the troubled United Artists in late 1938.  The first two were relatively small and inexpensive productions:  The Duke of West Point, with Louis Hayward and Joan Fontaine; and The King of the Turf, a middling racetrack story, both written by George Bruce and directed by Alfred E. Green.  Small's major film of the pact would be his third, a massive, detailed, wordy Bruce screenplay based on an episode in Alexandre Dumas' The Three Musketeers that came to be known as The Man in the Iron Mask.  Swashbucklers were bigger than ever, and Small intended his film to give Warners' The Adventures of Robin Hood a run for its money.

"Eddie Small used to say, " remembered Alan Napier, "that to make any picture a success, you had to have a scene where the villain comes up behind the girl and drapes a beautiful string of pearls around her neck.  That was the scene that sold the picture; he was a rather crude man, but he knew that melodrama was the thing. "

Bruce's script was so melodramatically pleasing, Small thought, that he made him a writer-producer and gave him Kit Carson, Adventurer to work on.  The screenplay was impressively heavy, and the film itself would be as impressive as possible.  Small was sold on James Whale to direct The Man in the Iron Mask; he met Whale's standard rate and agreed to a percentage of the profits over the initial few years of release.

Filming commenced over 47 sets built at the General Service Studios in Hollywood during the last week in February of 1939.  This time, Whale's problem was the script Small so loved.

"Bruce was a man who couldn't stop writing," said
David Lewis. "If they had shot it verbatim, it would have
been six hours long."

Cuttings and revisions were necessary to the point
that George Bruce was present on the set during most of production, but Small tended to side with his writer when dis-
putes arose. It was clear to Whale that Small was intent on
making a producer's film and would exercise control as to
his own conceptions and tastes, not Whale's. There was not
the time or atmosphere to carefully arrange the beautiful
moving shots and angles that had so distinguished his earlier
pictures, and although the credits read, "Edward Small presents The Alexandre Dumas Classic, The Man in the Iron
Mask - A James Whale Production," few of Whale's distinctive touches were apparent. In the old days, Whale had enjoyed the simple luxury of being able to prepare his day's
work before he arrived on the set, but with the script being
rewritten as filming went along, this was hardly possible.
Even if he were able to, there was no strong indication that
Small would accept what he wanted to do. Consequently,
Whale proceeded to drive--head down--straight into the problems and push to finish the film as efficiently as possible.
The time and atmosphere did not exist to make The Man in
the Iron Mask as stylishly unique a film as James Whale
could have.

"Small had a thing against directors," Louis Hayward,
who played the twin brothers, recalled. "He was on the set
a lot and would interfere. He'd stand at the back of the
stage and yell 'That's not right!' He was never happy."

Whale found Small's cast to be acceptable, but not ex-
traordinary. Joan Bennett was the love interest. Warren
William played the dashing D'Artagnan, and the supporting
cast boasted Alan Hale, Joseph Schildkraut, Walter Kingsford,
Miles Mander, Bert Roach, Marion Martin, Montagu Love,
Doris Kenyon, Albert Dekker, and Reginald Barlow.

Whale and Hayward got along, but not well. "I think
perhaps he was a little more important than all of us," the
actor suggested. "I think he disliked me. I thought he disliked everyone."

Whale barely directed Hayward, except to point with
his cigar and say, "Move there, will you?" When Hayward
disagreed with Whale, Small always backed him. "I camped

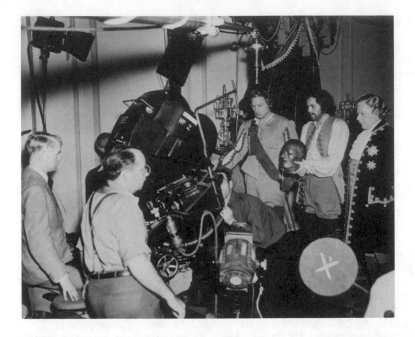

Above and below:  Setting up a shot with Warren William, Louis Hayward,  and Walter Kingsford for <u>The Man in the Iron Mask</u> (1939).

Whale grew detached as filming progressed on The Man in
the Iron Mask.   Louis Hayward was convinced Whale didn't
like him.

it.   I think that caused a certain resentment on Jimmy's
part. "   Whale's interest in the film obviously waned under
Small's domination.   Toward the end of his involvement,
when it became evident Small might fire him, Whale sat under the camera, bouncing his leg and smoking his cigar, un-
caring if the smoke showed up on film.   He made it clear
he didn't need the work:   "Listen Hayward, I've saved my
berries. "

        When Small did fire him, George Bruce was allowed
to direct nine days of retakes himself.   Hayward called to
mind the experience of working with Colin Clive on The Woman I Love.   They shot all Clive's scenes in the morning, as
he was drunk by noon; he had to be held up for over-the-
shoulder shots.   "My dear sir, " he told the young actor,
"get out of this business.   It'll kill you ... it'll kill you. "

Predictably, the film's reviews complained of its wordy nature and melodramatic tone, but still had to give it credit for its rapport with the audiences.

"For the record," post-scripted Frank Nugent, "the picture was well received by a bumper matinee attendance, which proves that romance is not dead, even though it's inclined to be dull."

The Man in the Iron Mask did very good business in a year of stiff competition (Gone with the Wind, The Wizard of Oz, Stagecoach, Dark Victory, Good-Bye, Mr. Chips, Mr. Smith Goes to Washington, and, of course, Robin Hood). Whale, with his percentage, made a great deal of money off it, although he was not very proud of it. Small later did a follow-up for Bennett and Hayward called The Son of Monte Cristo.

After finishing with The Man in the Iron Mask, Whale sat back and waited for offers. He had trouble occupying himself around the house; he was not a great reader, and preferred to go to the movies. He loved the movies, and wanted to soak all of them up; he wasn't a jealous man, and offered little criticism of the works of others. He felt that all art should be accepted for itself, and any film that gave him pleasure was good enough.

Whale's boredom and his fondness for new films combined to create a problem for David Lewis at Warner Bros.: Jack Warner liked to have his creative forces around him at the studio previews to help gauge the audience responses, and Lewis generally went. Whale loved previews, and would go to any that he heard about. Warner, who disliked Whale, saw him at one and had a fit. Whale was an outsider, and Warner was very sensitive about other industry people seeing his new unreleased films, possibly before needed corrections had been made.

"Jack didn't like anyone else around the people he cared about," said Lewis, "and I told Jimmy on several occasions to stay away from the previews unless it was one of my pictures."

Whale considered Warner's mandates to be of little concern, however, and one night drove all the way to Newport Beach--roughly 90 minutes from Pacific Palisades--to see a preview of The Old Maid with Bette Davis.

"We were in the lobby talking during intermission, "
Lewis recalled, "and I glanced over to the stairs.  With
Warner watching, down from the balcony comes Jimmy Whale,
smoking a big cigar and oblivious to everyone. "

Warner was furious.  Lewis discovered the next day
that Whale was regularly getting the preview locations and
times from Lewis' own secretary, who would phone Whale
whenever the information passed her desk.

Offers of new pictures for Whale were not forthcoming.
Even after the success of Man in the Iron Mask, there was
little renewed interest in him.   Observed Alan Napier,

> Jimmy had always had his greater success in
> working with fellow Englishmen and his manner-
> isms--his style--his sexuality--were simply ac-
> cepted as being part of him.  It was just Jimmy
> Whale, and that was that.
> In America, there was a different attitude to-
> ward a person like Jimmy, and it was probably
> much harder to deal with the bigger American ac-
> tors for him.  When his name came up, possibly
> someone would simply say, "Oh, can't we get some-
> one else?"
> Jimmy was good, but he wasn't good enough to
> transcend those attitudes.

Indeed, it took an association of friends, not a clamor
of producers anxious to engage the director of The Man in the
Iron Mask, to bring about Green Hell, which proved to be
Whale's last completed feature.

Around David Lewis were the three elements of the production:  Harry E. Edington, the producer; Frances Marion,
the writer; and Whale, the director.  All were Lewis' friends;
they came together through him to make a motion picture of
Marion's original screenplay, a safari adventure that Lewis
backed away from when he read it:  "It was awful. "  He
added,

> Frances Marion was one of my dearest friends.
> She was the one responsible for my going to Thal-
> berg at M-G-M, and she was, without a doubt, one
> of the world's worst writers.  She and Jimmy Hilton
> once wrote a script for Camille that was so bad it
> was embarrassing.  Irving liked her because she

was a "ditch digger." There had to be someone to
poke out the story--to dig the ditches that other
writers could work into usable screenplays. That
was Frances Marion.

Whale knew the script was substandard and cliché-
ridden, but he was anxious to work again and privately distressed by the lack of interest in him after Iron Mask. Green
Hell sounded like a good story, the faults of which he felt he
could handle.

Arrangements were made to make the film under Edington's banner of Famous Productions, in association with Universal, which didn't bother Whale. This time, he drove
through the gates with renewed vigor. He would be in firm
control again, and it would be up to Edington to deal with
Cliff Work and the other company executives. With him
again would be Ted Kent to cut it, Joe McDonough as assistant director, Karl Freund on camera, and Helen McCaffrey,
who worked on most all of his films as the script supervisor.

Green Hell was planned as a major production, budgeted at just under $700,000. The plot simply concerned an
expedition of adventurers in the upper Amazon searching for
a lost Inca treasure. For it, an interior jungle set covering
45,000 square feet and an Inca Temple 125 feet high and 225
feet across were built. A major hand-picked cast assembled:
Joan Bennett and Alan Hale were in it, as were Douglas Fairbanks, Jr., John Howard, George Sanders, George Bancroft,
and Vincent Price. The six-week shooting schedule began in
August 1939, and Whale's enthusiasm was boundless.

"I read the script," recalled Ted Kent, "and I didn't
think it was very good. I saw Whale on the set during the
first day of shooting, and asked him what he thought of it.
'Very good,' he said. 'Great.' So I figured that he knew
what he was doing, and didn't say any more about it."

"Jimmy had changed since I had known him in England," said Alan Napier, who came to California in 1939 and
visited the Green Hell set. "He seemed to have developed a
tremendous sort of 'power' complex. His attitude was, 'I
can do anything, you see,' and I suspect that he had grown
to deal with people less tactfully than before."

Whale worked away at Green Hell, trying to get
around the dialogue to make as stylish an adventure as he

Whale's studio portrait, Universal, 1939.

could.  "It was one of the funniest films ever shot anywhere
in the world, " Vincent Price once recalled.  "About five of
the worst pictures ever made are all in that one picture. "

Filming began slowly, owing to problems in lighting
the massive jungle set that completely occupied one of the
largest stages.  Whale ultimately fell eleven days behind, re-
sorting to shooting nights to retain Alan Hale, who was on
call at Warner Bros. in the daytime.  When it was finished
and cut, they took Green Hell to San Francisco for a preview.

"It was a Saturday night, " remembered Ted Kent,
"and they had booked the preview into a theatre showing Stanley and Livingston.  Whale was furious!  He said, 'Who's
responsible for this?' and had the film pulled.  The theatre
manager had the preview signs out, but he wouldn't let them
run it. "

Whale was worried about the reception of Green Hell,
and badly wanted it to be a success.  They checked around
and finally found a theatre in Oakland that would take it for
the next evening.  Whale stationed himself in the seat behind
Kent, and started his crossed leg bouncing.  After about ten
minutes of film, he leaned forward and tapped Kent on the
shoulder.

"They like it, " he said hopefully.

Kent nodded his agreement.  Green Hell opened by introducing members of the Fairbanks expedition, as they were
preparing to descend into the jungles in the fall of 1922.

"What are you running away from?" Gene Garrick
asked George Sanders on the eve of their last day in Ta-
batinga.

"Boredom, " he answered.  "There are too many wom-
en in the world. "

"Just a charming but tired cavalier, " Fairbanks observed.

"If there weren't any women in the world, men would
get more work done, " said Alan Hale.

"Sure, " injected John Howard, "but if there weren't
any women, there might not be any men. "

"And no work either!" Sanders added.

"Here's to adventure!" Fairbanks offered.

"Skoll!" shouted Hale.

The audience began to titter.   Vincent Price asked
Fairbanks at one point, "Tell me Brandy, is it possible to be
in love with two women at the same time, and in your heart
be faithful to each, and yet want to be free of both of them?"

Problems began to mount.   Joan Bennett played Price's
wife in the film, and she followed them into the jungle, but
was overcome by fever.   When she was discovered by the
men, her husband had died of poison dart wounds.   Upon her
recovery, she took up with both Sanders and Fairbanks.

Bennett liked Fairbanks better, though, and became
terribly distressed when he soon faced the same painful death
as her husband.   As she talked with Dr. Hale about mercifully doing away with him, the audience grew increasingly
restless.

"Would it be wrong?" she asked.

"There can be no evil in mercy, " he replied.

"Dr. Loren, " she urged,  "quickly now--before he
wakes. "

He prepared a needle.

"Quickly, " she hissed.

The audience began to laugh openly.

"Let me do it!" she finally blurted.

The audience roared; they could no longer contain
themselves.   Ted Kent turned to address Whale.   His seat
was empty.

The last third of the picture, a native siege against
the miraculously recovered leader and his band of men, was
received as pure comedy.

Green Hell did more to hurt James Whale's career

A tense moment from the remarkably silly <u>Green Hell</u> (1940).
Alan Hale, John Howard, and George Sanders comfort Douglas
Fairbanks, Jr.


than help it.    No one denied that it was well-made; it was
just silly.    Additional editing and an extra day of retakes
took care of the "Let me do it!" sequence, but it was too
little, too late.    The <u>New York Times</u> dubbed it, "... the
best worst picture of the year, " and Frances Marion wanted
her name taken off of it.    The others argued, however, that
she was just as much to blame as anyone else, possibly
more so.    <u>Green Hell</u> became her last motion picture writing
credit.

          Whale settled into what looked like an uneasy retire-
ment.    No new offers were tendered, and he moped around
the house during the days with virtually nothing to do.    One
day, David Lewis drove to Michael's Art Supply and bought
a supply of canvas, paints, and a good easel.    He returned
to Amalfi Drive with his car full of materials.

"What's that?" Whale asked.

"Gift," Lewis answered.

"Surprise?"

"No, gift."

Whale was enchanted. He took to the gear like old, forgotten friends and painted long hours. Soon, his pictures were all over the house, and he eventually bought a plot of land behind and below the house--across from Gladys Cooper's --where he built a studio in which to work.

Whale spent most of 1940 painting, occasionally going away for a few days, or motoring to lunch with friends. He attended the movies whenever the mood struck him and would work-out in a local gym when he felt that he needed toning up. He liked driving up the California coast to Santa Barbara or perhaps San Francisco. He drove a Cadillac, and would bring back fabulous gifts for his friends, something he was not inclined to do when at home.

As far as the motion picture industry was concerned, Whale was a very disillusioned man. His career had gone sour in four years' time, and he was at a loss to understand how to deal with the situation. He still had a need to work, but not for money.

> He was enormously proud of being so rich [said Alan Napier, who had been a more successful actor than Whale in the twenties]. When I visited his beautiful home, it was as if he was saying, "My dear boy, you've come to the right place."
> We had dinner together on a couple of occasions in California, but his life-style didn't fit in with mine. One's social contacts are often influenced by one's wife; mine wasn't Jimmy's cup of tea, and he wasn't hers. She was a very forthright, straight Englishwoman, not the type of woman that Jimmy would get along with.
> At dinner, he'd talk about "the old days," and whether so-n-so was really homosexual or not. Jimmy had a rather nasty way of implying things without coming right out and saying them--cocking his eyebrow with that wicked smile of his....

Late in 1940, plans for another film began to develop
for Whale, but he was actually not in a receptive mood for
such a project.   The deal was promoted by a man named
Bert Allenberg, who was the partner of David Lewis' agent,
Phil Berg.   Allenberg had tentatively arranged an agreement
with Columbia's Harry Cohn, who was always interested in
getting top talent (or formerly top talent) at reduced rates.

The film was They Dare Not Love, a story of Nazi
persecution in Austria, written by Ernst Vadja and Charles
Bennett.   Whale was against doing the film after meeting the
legendarily crude Cohn, whom he disliked intensely.   Allenberg was adamant, however, and argued that the film would
help serve to revive Whale's flagging career.

Whale's fee at Columbia was a mere $30,000 and his
cast consisted of George Brent; Martha Scott, whom Columbia was carefully trying to build after her debut in Sol Lesser's Our Town; and Whale's old friend Paul Lukas.   Production began at the first of the new year and quickly became a tragic replay of the Port of Seven Seas affair.   Brent
disliked Whale in much the same way that Wallace Beery had,
and the screenplay was a poor one.   Filming churned turbu-
lently along until some night shooting took place on Thursday,
January 23.   The next day, it was noted in Variety that Martha Scott had "caught a cold" and the director was shooting
around her.   The following day--Saturday--Whale received
a phone call advising him not to bother to come in again,
and he was replaced later that day by Charles Vidor.

Production resumed on Monday morning, with a diplomatic statement from the studio in the morning trades, noting
that Whale had gotten the flu, as had both Scott and Brent.

James Whale was fed-up with Hollywood and film making.   They Dare Not Love managed to kill whatever ambitions
he entertained about returning to the studios, or his hope
that he could some day acquire another position of comfort
and respect similar to the old Universal days.   He turned
his back on motion picture production and never worked at it
again.

[Opposite:]   George Brent and Martha Scott in They Dare Not
Love.

# CHAPTER NINE

James Whale regressed into a daily regimen, continuing to paint. He attempted a portrait of his friend David Lewis, but complained that his subject could not refrain from moving. He never seemed to get it right and eventually painted over it. Later, as a birthday gift, he painted Lewis' mother with considerably greater success.

His business investments, directed by George Lovett, were consistently successful. Whale, Lovett always contended, had an instinct about such things. When he would propose a purchase of land or stock, Whale either responded positively or not at all. Later developments usually proved him correct.

With the eruption of World War II, Whale involved himself with various war activities, including a British orphans' organization in which his friend Gladys Cooper was involved. He sponsored an orphan, would write letters to him, and had him to the house for dinner on at least one occasion. Whale was an entirely apolitical creature, although he always remained devoted to England and the Crown. If a label could be placed on him, he would have been a conservative who liked Roosevelt, Churchill, famous people, and especially royalty. Generally, he adopted the views of George Lovett--who was a Republican--but held no firm positions of his own. David Lewis, by contrast, was a liberal Democrat.

In the summer of 1942, deciding that induction was imminent, Lewis enlisted in the United States Air Force. His absence from Amalfi Drive made Whale all the more

restless.  Whale took to almost daily correspondence with his
friend, reporting the drab atmosphere at home and betraying
the inactivity and boredom:

> The two days seem like 20 years since you went
> away, and the house and every simple thing in it
> shrieks for you.  I suppose we shall all get used
> to it--I sincerely hope so--Sigrid and Cecile just
> keep going, and I've got about as much as I can
> do to appear nonchalant.

*

> Your Mom just rang me up and asked if I had heard
> from her son D.  I said, "Hasn't he writ?" and
> she said, "He's only my son you know!"
> You ba-ad boy--you should really drop a line to
> your ma.
> Has Pantages applied for a commission?  He's
> not a bad guy, but I don't like him very much.
> He's too much like George Cukor!

*

> I've been taking my little walks, but haven't been
> able to settle down to do much painting.  Lenore
> Coffee was an awful bore last night, but I didn't
> particularly want to talk to the other folks, so I
> was rather glad to sit and just listen to her gab
> gab.

*

> Well, everything is oky-dok here--the puppies are
> back home again--I think I could have shot Hazel if
> they had got lost this time.  I told you they got out
> last Sunday morning.  She yelled out, "You better
> get up Mr. Whale--the dogs are out."
> I rushed out and she was all in a dither and
> trembling like a jelly at Xmas.  "They're over at
> Gladys Cooper's place," she gasped.
> I got in my car and no sign of them could I see.
> Soon, Hazel came down and said, "Not there--
> they're at Gladys Cooper's place."
> I said, "This IS Gladys Cooper's place!"
> "Oh, I didn't mean there," she said.  "I meant
> over the road."
> I called Simon and Chucky, and heard a rustling,
> and there was Simon trying to get through to the
> canyon below.  I nabbed him, and called Chucky,

and heard another rustling.    Neither of them could
get through the box hedge!!
    We ought to give her gardener something for
Christmas for making such a good box hedge.

*

I hear George Cukor is a Major--did Goering tell
you?

*

Judy rang up while I was out for a walk,  and asked
me to go down for a chat,  but when the time came,
I didn't feel up to a night chat,  so I rang up and
said I'd look in for a cocktail soon.

*

I took on a mood,  and have painted my bedroom
over--it looked quite lovely and only cost $2. 75.
Last time it cost $90. 00.
    I do so hope the officers' training school soon
materializes--I wouldn't feel so bad then,  but the
thought of you cleaning windows almost did me in
. . . .

*

The Duchess sent the other two dogs up,  and said
she expected you to call her up.
    Cecile said,  "After all Mr. Lewis has done for
her,  if she can't afford 15 cents,  it's just too bad
--she's just an old bitch!!

*

Charley Glett of General Service Studios rang up
today,  and asked me if I had read the contract.
I told him yes,  and asked him how many lawyers
he had to protect him from me.    I told him I
should have to ask the Myron Selznick office to
look over it.    I don't really care much,  but if
they are going to protect themselves to such an extent,  I must have a little protection too--don't you
think?

*

It was nice to hear your voice again--it seemed
like ages since I had heard a friendly sound.  When
are you coming home?

In 1942-43, Whale became involved in a local little theatre group, working to produce plays in a small 100-seat theatre in the Santa Monica Canyon.  Many of his friends, including Gladys Cooper and Doris Lloyd, worked without compensation with the purpose of entertaining the visiting servicemen.  All pitched in to build scenery, handle lighting and technical effects, and to perform.  Whale generally directed the plays, and worked at building the sets that he, of course, designed himself.  Privately, he had always wished he had been more successful in the portion of his career in which he was an actor, and once undertook to play a part in one of his plays in the Canyon, to demonstrate his talents to the visiting David Lewis.  "He mugged horribly," Lewis remembered, "and was absolutely terrible.  He asked me afterward what I thought, and I told him.  He knew that he wasn't very good, but he enjoyed it immensely. "

Once, Whale directed Sara Allgood in a revival of J. M. Synge's Irish play Deirdre of the Sorrows at the Canyon theatre.  She was going to re-create a role she had originally played in 1910, and was rather sensitive about her age.  She repeatedly asked to have the lights dimmed to help compensate for her wrinkles.  "She finally insisted on reducing the illumination to the point where they were playing to one candlelight, " Whale later said.  "You could just barely see her shadowy figure moving about the set. "

Occasionally, David Lewis was able to get home.  At one point, he was released to produce Frenchman's Creek at Paramount.  Whale busied himself with his theatre, fussed around the house, and painted when he felt like it.  He ate a good breakfast, a light lunch, and, as always, dinner was at seven, sharp.  It usually consisted of meat and a vegetable, a glass of wine, coffee, and a sweet for dessert.  He never ate between meals, and could not tolerate hard liquor.  One martini was bad; two and he was out.  David Lewis introduced him to "gimlets, " made of gin and Rose's lime, and he was comfortable with them.  He carried himself regally, had his clothes made in England.  He wore no jewelry, however, other than a family cameo on his little finger.  His status symbol was his cigar.  He smoked three a day:  one after lunch, one mid-afternoon, and one after dinner--the biggest, best Havanas he could buy.  In between, he smoked Lucky Strikes, but switched to Chesterfields when Lewis did so.

Whale was a terribly reserved man; he always sought

Whale enjoyed an occasional motor trip up the California coast.

to keep a lid on untoward emotions.  Once, when he sank into a deep fit of depression, it took nearly two weeks for
Lewis to discover--quite by accident--that Whale's beloved
mother had died.  Grief had to be hidden.  He'd sulk; let it
boil.  Nothing ever came out.

Finally, late in 1944, Whale ventured east to direct
another play on Broadway.  It was a melodrama; a murder
thriller entitled Hand in Glove.  It had a psychological angle
to it, like Kiss Before the Mirror, and was written in a prologue and three acts by Charles K. Freeman and Gerald
Savory from the latter's novel, Hughie Roddis.  Whale liked
the play because of its English setting and diverse Cock-
ney characters.  It opened to generally good notices on December 4 at the Playhouse.  Lewis Nichols observed,

> In a prologue, a young man is seen strangling
> a girl, and during the course of the evening, he
> strangles one or two more.  The townspeople, aided
> by the guilty man, attach the blame to an idiot boy
> but Scotland Yard arrived eventually to straighten
> out the matter.
> As the young Jack the Ripper George Lloyd is
> giving an excellent performance.  The character is
> somewhat similar to the leading figure of "Thunder
> Rock, " and playing it, Mr. Lloyd darts about the
> stage, speaks softly and obviously is dangerous
> after dark.  As the Scotland Yard man, Aubrey
> Mather also is excellent.  This detective is calm,
> also big and bald, and could come from Center
> Street after acquiring an English accent.  The oth-
> er important part is played by Skelton Knaggs.  His
> portrait of the idiot looks like something made up
> by the late Lon Chaney, and while there may be
> too much of it, there can be no doubt it is the fin-
> al stage of realism.
> There are perhaps too many characters in "Hand
> in Glove, " and some of them are a shade pat.  Iso-
> bel Elsom is good as the keeper of the boarding
> house in which the events take place, and Jean Bel-
> lows and Islay Benson are a couple of attractive
> victims for a young man who likes to murder his
> girls.  Robin Craven, however, has a touch job to
> make anything but a stock job of the usual police
> sergeant, and St. Clair Bayfield has equal trouble
> with a retired school teacher and current boarder.
> James Whale has come on from Hollywood to direct

190                                              James Whale

and has done a thorough job, and Samuel Leve's
settings of a Yorkshore room are effective. "Hand
in Glove" starts off on its best foot, the initial
murder being one of the play's best moments.

Disappointingly, Hand in Glove was not a great hit.
Whale returned home with no further engagements.

He considered himself pretty much forgotten by 1947,
when Curtis Harrington, then a young post-graduate studying
film at UCLA, sought him out.   Recalled Harrington,

> The reason I wanted to meet him was through
> my love for horror films.   One of my earliest
> childhood memories was a big color billboard for
> The Bride of Frankenstein.   I saw it somewhere,
> and without any idea of what it was about, I said
> to my mother, "I want to see that. "
> It was the artwork that fascinated me so, but
> she would never let me go to a horror film.   When
> I got older, I discovered his work--I remember
> seeing The Old Dark House at the Paramount The-
> atre in Los Angeles in the late thirties--and I
> wanted to meet him.

Whale invited Harrington to dinner occasionally, and
at times he would also play bridge at the house.

> I did talk to him about his films, but not at great
> length.   It's hard to describe his attitude toward
> his own work.   He was a tremendous wit, and he
> treated anything like that very lightly.   He had no
> great pose as an artist; to me, his films were much
> more artistic than anything about him, or the way
> he presented himself.   If you praised his work, he
> was very self-disparaging, very modest, very un-
> pretentious.   It was hard to get anything serious
> about his work out of him.
> At least he could live in high style, if he couldn't
> make films in high style.   He had a wonderful cook
> and a maid--Anna and Johanna were their names (he
> always thought that was so funny--the rhyming names)
> --and he served magnificent dinners.   He was pret-
> ty much of a self-starter, and after a meal he
> would hold court.   We would all just sit back and
> listen to him deliver his witty comments about any-
> thing he pleased.   He had favorite stories he would

tell, and occasionally he would come forth with an anecdote about the making of one of his films.

One time, Harrington was seized with the idea of introducing Whale to another friend of English background, writer Christopher Isherwood. The plan failed to work.

> I mentioned it to Jimmy one day, and he said, "Fine, bring Christopher to dinner." David Lewis was there, and it was just the four of us. Christopher, at the time, tended to drink a little. He was a rather pugnacious drunk, and he had seemed to have had a couple of drinks already when I picked him up. Well, they didn't hit it off at all, and I felt responsible.
>
> Christopher just sat at the table drinking, and saying nasty things to James Whale. I was so embarrassed. I don't know why Isherwood took an immediate dislike to James, but he had always identified himself with left-wing concepts, while James was just the opposite. At that point, he certainly had little money--living in a little place in the Santa Monica Canyon--and here he was coming to the great home of this rich, famous movie director, who was sitting there like a king. It was like two different worlds clashing.
>
> The veneer of social affability just left Christopher entirely, and he said absolutely poisonous things. At one point, we were talking about making some kind of experimental film that Christopher would write and I would direct.
>
> Christopher said, "Yes ... and there'll be a part for you in it, Jimmy. We'll have a scene where we'll have the camera on a manhole. The cover will open up, and, Jimmy, you will rise up out of it."
>
> Whale took it all with great grace and charm. I sat back in absolute horror!

Rarely did Whale seriously consider working again, but in 1949, he did become involved in a project planned for television. He was no longer interested in theatrical motion pictures, and had turned down a contract offered him by David O. Selznick for $1,000 a week. Selznick then specialized in packaging talent (i.e.--a star, director, and script), which he would sell to various studios at a profit. Whale toyed with the idea, but that was all.

Television, however, was a vast new frontier, and it seemed to promise much freedom in development and experimentation. Whale became associated with Huntington Hartford's Theasquare Productions as a director, along with John Brahm. The idea was to develop short stories and one-act plays to the inexpensive film medium, for distribution to individual stations. The idea was also to showcase Hartford's new wife, actress Marjorie Steele. Whale's property was a one-act play by William Saroyan, Hello Out There, which he had directed in the Canyon.

The play was a grim love story set in a small-town jail cell somewhere on the southwestern prairie, in which a roustabout gambler is trapped for allegedly raping a local citizen. The principal theme was loneliness and isolation.

The 41-minute film Whale directed was shot at KTTV Television in Hollywood--where the Hartford company was based--in a matter of several days at a cost of approximately $40,000. The cast featured Harry Morgan, Lee Patrick, and Marjorie Steele. The one set was designed by Whale to great effect. "The film was very, very expressionistic," said Curtis Harrington, "and one could sense his trademark--that tremendous influence of German expressionism--moreso than in any of his later features."

The picture was previewed before a gathering of notables that included Charles Chaplin, John Huston, Jean Renoir, and Saroyan himself, but it was said that Hartford was displeased with his wife's performance and the film/television idea for distribution never developed.

"Marjorie wasn't that bad," Harrington added, "but I was impressed by the absolutely dreadful performance of Harry Morgan. I think Jimmy made an awful mistake in allowing it. He was terrible."

Hello Out There was never released, although two other short films made by Hartford, The Secret Sharer, directed by Brahm, and The Bride Comes to Yellow Sky, directed by Bretaigne Windust, were theatrically released by RKO in 1951 as a feature called Face to Face.

*    *    *

As he grew older, James Whale began to lose control
of himself.  He spent most of the 1950's desperately trying
to hold his life together, and maintaining a purpose for living.
"He was torn in a million ways, " said David Lewis.  "He
had such fantasies of youth and beauty.  They were preying
on him.  He had made his money, but he was a tormented
man. "

The energies within Whale were strong, but increasingly lacked direction.  He tired of painting, and Lewis
bought him a camera, for which he would muster little interest.  The suggestion was made that he should perhaps write
a novel--his sister's story--but he could not concentrate, and
after playing with the idea only slightly, refused.

Producer William Dozier even approached him with an
idea for a feature based upon H. G. Wells' Food of the Gods,
which Whale had wanted to make in the thirties.  A meeting
was arranged between the two but Whale--in the end--simply
could not summon the interest to follow through and the option was allowed to lapse.

Late in 1950, Franklin Lacey, a young playwright who
later co-authored the book for The Music Man, approached
Whale with a comedy he had written, titled Pagan in the Parlour.  It was a silly play about a sea captain's two spinster
daughters in Britain who discovered that a third, from somewhere in the South Seas, had come to visit.  Whale took a
liking to it, and directed a production of it at the Pasadena
Playhouse in February 1951.

At home, he became increasingly difficult to get along
with.  The relationship between David Lewis and Whale began to deteriorate.  In 1951 Whale decided to go to Europe,
where he planned to stage Pagan in the Parlour, although he
used the play merely as an excuse for going.  He wanted
Lewis to accompany him; when Lewis declined, he left by
himself.  His tour was an extended one, taking him to Paris,
where he looked up Curtis Harrington, who was living in
France at the time.  Whale's intentions were simply to enjoy himself, and to visit all the important art galleries.

Said Harrington,

> I had been dropping him cards occasionally, and
> he seemed to have no trouble finding me when he
> got to Paris.  He really didn't know anyone there,

RAYMOND VOINQUEL PARIS

Whale in Paris, 1951.

so we had a number of dinners together. I remember that I was there with no visible means of support, and virtually no money. I was only surviving because my parents would occasionally send me a small sum of money.

I was living in a tiny Left-Bank hotel, and I never will forget that James, one night, took me to dinner, and handed me 20,000 francs, which was about $100-$150; it was like a fortune to me. He said, "This is for you. I don't know how you do it, but I think it's wonderful, and I want you to have it."

While in Paris, Whale met a young man called Pierre Foegel, of whom he grew fond. He engaged Foegel as his secretary-chauffeur-companion for the duration of his trip. They lingered in Paris almost a month, then visited Italy and Spain.

"He spent a great deal of time in the galleries," Foegel remembered, "especially when he found a painting that drew his interest. He would sit there and concentrate very hard on it. He would analyze the technique of the artist, and study his use of color. He was particularly interested in the rendering of china, porcelain, and glasswork. He wanted to find the secret of the painting's effect, and then he'd apply it to his own work.

"His own glasswork was fantastic. There was great mood in his paintings, and depth and warmth. He was very impressed by the old Dutch school of painting, with the rich browns, and also the light colors with the impressionistic."

In August Whale advanced to England and produced Pagan in the Parlour, first at the Royal Theatre in Bath, then at the Wimbledon, where it opened on September 22. The audiences were good, but the play was not a success. It marked Whale's last directorial project.

He spent some time in London after that, and again crossed paths with Curtis Harrington. Harrington and Gavin Lambert, then the editor of Sight and Sound magazine, proposed an evening in honor of Whale in conjunction with the British Film Institute. "We showed The Old Dark House," Harrington related. "At that time, there was a perfectly good print available in London. We announced the tribute and he came through me, because I was the only one who knew him.

"I remember sitting there and watching the scene where Eva Moore talks and her face becomes more and more distorted with those wonderful cuts.  That was very imaginative film making, and I would say to him, 'Oh, that's so wonderful, Jimmy.'

"And he would sit there and say, 'Don't you think it's a little dated and kind of corny?'"

Whale was satisfied with his past works, but maintained little interest in them otherwise.  He didn't enjoy seeing many of them again, because he could always find things that didn't turn out the way he had planned--things he could have done better.  He found it difficult to seriously consider the subject of film, as it was for him another life, a period long ago.

Whale returned to California in early 1953, planning to have Pierre Foegel follow.  He proposed to David Lewis that the studio be enlarged so that Lewis could live in it.  Lewis balked and decided to move out, though the house was his.  Years before, when Whale had bought the land below the house and had some additions to the main structure made, he had requested and received Lewis' permission to put the house in his name.  Legally, it belonged to Whale, and he became uncharacteristically vindictive.  "If you leave," he told Lewis, "you'll leave with nothing."

"Then I leave with nothing," he replied.

Lewis took an apartment in Bel Air, and later bought a house on Mulholland Drive.  Foegel arrived soon after that, and remained for five months before returning to France to settle some personal business.  Whale enlarged and updated the servants' quarters and, after Lewis' new home, installed a swimming pool next to the studio, although he couldn't swim.  "But you hate pools," Lewis said to him.

"I can look at it, can't I?" Whale shot back.

Later, he felt very remorseful over his actions against Lewis, and had some investment properties put in his friend's name.

"I understood Jimmy," said Lewis.  "I knew how to live with him; I knew his difficulties, and I knew how to avoid them.  In fact, he always treated me as if I were twenty years older than he was."

For a while, Whale threw parties and maintained the company of younger acquaintances, with many of whom he found little in common.  The crowd he kept were people totally different from his social sphere of a few years previous.  He had built the pool principally for entertaining.  He occasionally sunbathed by it, or waded in the shallow end, but privately he feared it.  "He was living a hedonistic existence, " Lewis said of the period, "and hating it. "

Whale no longer knew what he wanted of life.  He was 65 years old, and, in a sense, in pursuit of his fantasies.  One night, when Lewis was visiting with a friend, Whale produced a small diary of pornographic fantasies, from which he read aloud.  When Lewis openly expressed his disgust, Whale became quite upset.

Pierre Foegel's return to Amalfi Drive seemed to somewhat stabilize Whale's activities.  There was talk of producing a fantastic operetta based upon the stories of Max Beerbohm and Ray Bradbury, for which Whale would design the sets and costumes.  He made some sketches for Charles Laughton, who planned to direct the production with Elsa Lanchester performing, but the project was never realized. Whale regressed into his daily routines, and stayed there. He was not interested in working and considered himself totally retired.  On a normal day, he would rise at 7:00 a.m. and have his orange juice.  Then he would shave and shower, and have breakfast.  Around 8:30 a.m., he would go down to the studio, where he would read the paper and paint.  "His painting was according to his mood of the day, " Pierre Foegel observed.  "He loved to paint flowers and still-lifes, and he also tried a few copies.  He'd say, 'Well, today I'm going to paint something like Degas, ' or he would go through an art book or magazine and say, 'I think I'll try to paint that. '

"Then he'd look at it when it was finished and say, 'It's alright, ' and paint over it when he ran short of canvas. Sometimes, he'd work at two or three at once. "

At 1:00 p.m., he'd emerge from the studio and return to the house, where his lunch would generally consist of cold cuts, salad, tea, or a bottle of beer when it was hot. Then he would go back to the studio, or possibly sunbathe (Whale tanned well), and perhaps some friends would stop by for conversation.  Dinner was at 7:00 p.m., and then he would watch television, or sometimes go to a movie.  He was also fond of playing Scrabble, or bridge.  Once in a

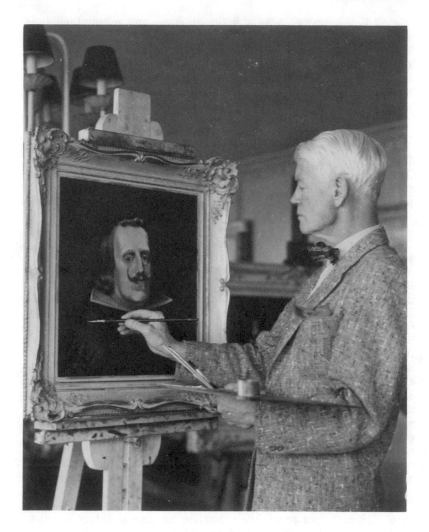

Whale at work in his studio, circa 1955.

while, he would watch a movie on television, but his favorite programs were the comedy-variety shows of Jimmy Durante and George Gobel.

Whale calmly accepted his destiny, possibly better than some of his friends did later.  He motored to Palm Springs, or San Francisco, or Yosemite, and would occasionally visit friends like Junior Laemmle.  His cigars became his trademark, and he used them as props and symbols of his assumed snobbery.  "If he wanted to show you something," said Pierre Foegel, "he'd take the end of his cigar and point, or use it to draw a picture in the air. "

One night, when a fire threatened to destroy his entire house, Whale maintained his placid demeanor with little effort.  According to Foegel,

> We didn't know how it started.  It was in the garage.  Both our cars were in there, side by side. I had a '47 Cadillac, and he had a '54 Ninety-eight Convertible.  We had retired about 11:00 p. m. and about 1:00 a. m., the maid started screaming "Fire!"
> We rushed down to the garage, which was attached to the house, and it was pretty well engulfed.  The door was burned through.  I took a garden hose after it, but there was little to be done. The gas tank on my car blew up then, and it just lifted the whole thing about three feet in the air. There was a great wall of flames, and I hit the panic button.
> I ran inside, got a suitcase, and started cramming whatever I could into it.  I loaded up all of my stuff, and threw it out on the lawn; it looked as if the whole house was going to go up.  The servants--we had two girls whose quarters were right next to the garage--did the same thing.
> Mr. Whale, by contrast, did one thing:  he walked into the house, went to the buffet in the dining room, took his box of cigars, put it under his arm, and walked back outside.

The Pacific Palisades fire department arrived, and was able to extinguish the blaze quickly.  Whale was insured; as long as his cigars were safe, he enjoyed the excitement. "Pierre ..., " he drolled as he pulled a cigar out of the box, "you got a light?"

It was in the latter part of 1956, at the age of 67, that Whale's excellent health began to crumble with the first of a series of mild strokes. "We were having dinner one night," Foegel recalled, "and all of a sudden, he said, 'Ummmmm ... ,' and I said, 'What's the matter?'

"He said, 'I don't know. I feel strange.'

"The color in his face changed. I asked him if he wanted to lie down. 'Should I call the doctor?'

"'No, I'm feeling better now.'

"It just happened for a couple of minutes, and then it took a few days for the effects to show. There was a slight coordination problem, and his mood changed a bit. Finally, he saw a doctor, but there wasn't much that could be done."

A few months passed, and then one morning, possibly as a result of a cerebral hemorrhage or some similar damage to the blood vessels of the brain, he suffered another stroke. Pierre Foegel was unattainable by phone; a call was placed to David Lewis at M-G-M, where he was supervising some dubbing for <u>Raintree County</u> with Elizabeth Taylor. However, the message was held for him until the session was finished. By that time, it was too late. The maid had summoned a neighbor to get him to a doctor--not his own-- and although he returned home later that day, his hospitalization was imminent.

Whale entered St. John's Hospital, where he was placed under observation and sedation. He was treated as if he were crazy: he was reportedly given shock treatment, which was wrong. There was a pressure on a portion of his brain, but none of his motor abilities seemed to be affected. He was exceedingly nervous and high-strung. His painting talents suffered; he could do little more than read, but his concentration was very limited. Finally, he was transferred to a convalescent hospital, where he was under constant medical supervision. He was virtually isolated from his friends, and suffered greatly from the inner energies he had always possessed, but could no longer contain. He could do nothing to expend these energies; he was constantly drugged and frightened--not of death, but of further life under illness. He feared the future, advancing age, and the probability that he would only grow worse.

Early in 1957, his condition stabilized, and he was allowed to return home. With him came a nurse and regular medication. He puttered around the house, but there was nothing to do. He would watch television, if the mood struck him, but he could no longer paint or drive. He found himself unable to conduct the long, flowing, witty conversations he took such pleasure in, and could turn his attention toward reading matter for only a short period of time.

Once in a great while, he seemed to rally, and once again was his old self. On one such occasion, he was talking with his nurse, Lenore Coffee, and David Lewis. "This is the old Jimmy, " Lewis thought. "He's feeling better. " Whale was laughing and in high spirits. Suddenly, he said, "I'm going to give each of you $10, 000. " It was not a characteristic thing for him to say.

"This isn't Jimmy, " said Coffee to Lewis. "He's feeling worse. "

He suffered fits of depression and loneliness, as Foegel--during the day--managed a service station at Third and Crescent Heights, and David Lewis could visit only occasionally. As Memorial Day approached, Whale got in the habit of taking his own medicine and gave his nurse the holiday off.

On Wednesday, May 29, 1957, Whale rose as usual, took his medication, shaved, and dressed in a favorite suit and tie. After breakfast, he made his way down to his studio, where he sat down at his desk and took a piece of personal stationery from the drawer. It was an expensive bond, folded in half--booklike--with his address printed at the head:

James Whale
788 South Amalfi Drive
Pacific Palisades, California
EXbrook 5-5844

He produced a fountain pen and began to write. Rapidly, but with great decisiveness:

To ALL I LOVE,

Do not grieve for me--My nerves are all shot and for the last year I have been in agony day and night--except when I sleep with sleeping pills--and

any peace I have by day is when I am drugged by
pills.

I have had a wonderful life but it is over and
my nerves get worse and I am afraid they will have
to take me away--so please forgive me--all those I
love and may God forgive me too, but I cannot bear
the agony and it is best for everyone this way.

The future is just old age and pain. Goodbye
all and thank you for all your love. I must have
peace and this is the only way.

He signed it "Jimmy," and then paused to read it
over once. He thought for a moment, and then began to
write on the back of the first page:

p. s. --

Do not let my family come--my last wish is to
be cremated so nobody will grieve over my grave--
no one is to blame. I have wonderful friends and
they do all they can for me, but my heart is in
my mouth all the time and I have no peace. I
cannot keep still and the future would be worse.
My financial affairs are all in order and I hope
will help my loved ones to forget a little. It will
be a great shock but I pray they will be given
strength to come through and be happy for my release from this constant fear. I've tried very hard
all I know for a year and it gets worse inside so
please take comfort in knowing I will not suffer
any more.

"J. "

He carefully folded the note in half, and put it into
an unsealed envelope on which he wrote, "To Those Whom I
Love," and laid it--face up--on the blotter. He then walked
out to the edge of the pool at the shallow end and threw himself in--head first--striking his forehead against the bottom,
and knocking himself unconscious.

# CHAPTER TEN

About 1:15 p. m. that afternoon, Pierre Foegel received a call from James Whale's cook. When he had failed to answer her intercom call for lunch, she had gone down to the studio to investigate. "Mr. Whale is in the pool, " she told Foegel in an urgent tone of voice.

"That's okay, " he replied, seeing it as a positive sign. "Let him enjoy himself--can't hurt him. "

"No, no, " she stressed. "He's at the bottom of the pool. "

"I jumped in my car, " said Foegel, "and drove like a maniac. I went by George Lovett's office on La Cienega, picked him up, and made it to the house in record time. I had just enough time to dive in and get the body onto the deck before the police and fire department arrived. "

It was hard for either Lovett or Foegel to think clearly, but when the maid handed Lovett the note, which she had found, he quickly showed it to Foegel and pocketed it. "Nobody must know about this, " he said.

David Lewis didn't find out until that night, when he was shown the note by Lovett. "George went to pieces, " he said, "and it fell upon me to make the funeral arrangements. "

A niece and nephew flew in from England. The funeral took place at 11:00 a. m. the following Monday, at the Wayside Chapel in West L. A. The service was uneventful, ex-

cept for a headstrong funeral director's decision to counter-
mand David Lewis' orders for a closed casket:   when Lewis
entered the chapel and walked toward the front to inspect the
arrangements, he was greeted face-to-face with Whale, who
had been propped up at a 30° angle within the coffin!   "My
legs went limp, " he said,   "and I damn near fainted on the
spot. "

In attendance were Carl Laemmle, Jr. ,  Mary Forbes,
Charles Brackett, Doris Lloyd, and her sister Milba, among
others.   For James Whale, who had no religious convictions
of any kind, Judith Anderson simply read the 23rd Psalm.
The body was cremated, and his remains were intombed in
nitch 20076 of the Columbarium of Memory at the Great
Mausoleum, Forest Lawn, Glendale, just a hallway from
Irving Thalberg, Jean Harlow, and Alexander Pantages.   The
tablet read:

JAMES
WHALE
1893-1957

The will had been quickly drawn by George Lovett
and was not a good one.   As it stood, the house on Amalfi
Drive was divided between David Lewis and Pierre Foegel,
and trust funds were set up for each.   A substantial portion
of the estate went to the family, and taxes, and some friends
were left sums of $1, 000 each, including Doris Zinkeisen,
Una O'Connor, Doris Lloyd, and Gladys Cooper.   In all, the
estate was valued at a little over $600, 000.

*    *    *

In the year that followed James Whale's death, Frankenstein was shown on Los Angeles television for the first time.
Over the years it has proven to be an attraction of lasting
magnitude for any station licensed to show it.   In his obitu-
aries, the headlines usually noted that he had directed the
film, above all others, although, ironically, Hell's Angels
was generally mentioned, as well as The Road Back, in lieu
of The Bride of Frankenstein, One More River, and The Kiss
Before the Mirror.

It has taken many years since his death for James
Whale to be recognized as someone other than the man who

directed Frankenstein.   A great problem was the unavailabil-
ity of his relatively few films.   Journey's End had been
bought in the 1930's by M-G-M for a remake that never ma-
terialized, as had Waterloo Bridge, which was remade in
1940; Show Boat, re-done in color in 1951; and Port of Seven
Seas, remade by Warner Bros. in 1961 as Fanny.

Others, such as The Road Back and The Old Dark
House were involved in copyright entanglements, where the
studio had been afforded the film rights to a story for only
a limited number of years.

Still others, like Impatient Maiden, The Kiss Before
the Mirror, One More River, and By Candlelight were simply
obscure to the point that few people cared to see them--and
some, in fact, were considered lost.

The house on Amalfi was sold, and the land containing the pool and the studio was sub-divided to make two more
lots.   Carl Laemmle, Jr. had six trees planted in Israel in
Whale's name, and his paintings were distributed among his
friends.   A coroner's autopsy determined the death to be accidental and nothing more was said.

George Lovett turned the note over to his lawyer for
safe keeping, and it was given to David Lewis several years
later, after Lovett's own death.   "For God's sake, destroy
this!" the lawyer told him as he plucked it from a file and
handed it over.

Lewis, who had seen it only once, read "To Those
Whom I Love" on the envelope and put it into his coat pocket.
He said nothing, but to destroy it would be unthinkable.   When
he arrived home later that day, he carefully wrapped the note
with some other important papers he kept, and stored the
package in the back of a closet, where it has remained ever
since.

## FORTUNATO and THE LADY FROM ALFAQUEQUE

Court Theatre - October 22, 1928.   Two one-act plays by Serafin and Joaquin Alvarez Quintero.   Translated from Spanish by Helen and Harley Granville-Barker.   Produced by Anmer Hall.   Settings and Direction by James Whale.

### Fortunato

| | |
|---|---|
| Don Victorio | Fewlass Llewellyn |
| Monica | Elsie French |
| Alberto | John Gielgud |
| Constanza | Ann Trevor |
| Fortunato | O. B. Clarence |
| Amaranta | Miriam Lewes |
| Gorguera | Harold Young |
| A Dressmaker's Assistant | Catharina Ferraz |
| A Blind Man | Eric H. Messiter |
| Conchita | Maris Marden |
| A Sister of Mercy | May Congdon |
| Another Sister of Mercy | Peggy Rae |
| An Old Gentleman | Ernest Haines |
| A Lame Beggar | John Fernald |
| Ines | Isobel Pargiter |

### The Lady from Alfaqueque

| | |
|---|---|
| Don Pascual | Eric Stanley |
| Rosita | Ann Trevor |
| Alberta | Margaret Webster |

Realito                                Geoffery Wincott
Fernandita                             Gillian Scaife
Blanca                                 Molly Rankin
Noblejas                               Anthony Ireland
Adoración                              Gracie Leigh
Felipe Rivas                           John Gielgud
Paloma                                 Virginia Isham

## THE DREAMERS

"Q" Theatre--November 12, 1928.  A play by Anthony
Merryn.  Settings and Direction by James Whale.

Margaret                               Clare Harris
Tom                                    Sydney Seaward
Clarisse                               Gwen Ffrangeon-Davies
Vivian                                 Ernest Milton

## JOURNEY'S END

Apollo Theatre--December 10, 1928.  A play by R. C.
Sherriff.  "The Stage Society" (Two Performances).  Settings
and Direction by James Whale.

Captain Hardy                          David Horne
Lieutenant Osborne                     George Zucco
Private Mason                          Alexander Field
Second Lieutenant Raleigh              Maurice Evans
Captain Stanhope                       Laurence Olivier
Second Lieutenant Trotter              Melville Cooper
Second Lieutenant Hibbert              Robert Speaight
The Company Sergeant-Major             Percy Walsh
The Colonel                            H. G. Stoker
A German Soldier                       Geoffrey Wincott


Savoy Theatre--January 21, 1929.  Produced by Maurice Browne.  Presented with the original cast except:

Captain Stanhope                       Colin Clive
The Company Sergeant-Major             Reginald Smith


Henry Miller's Theatre--March 22, 1929.  A play by
R. C. Sherriff.  Produced by Gilbert Miller.  Settings and
Direction by James Whale.

| | |
|---|---|
| Captain Hardy | Evelyn Roberts |
| Lieutenant Osborne | Leon Quartermaine |
| Private Mason | Victor Stanley |
| Second Lieutenant Raleigh | Derek Williams |
| Captain Stanhope | Colin Keith-Johnston |
| Second Lieutenant Trotter | Henry Wenman |
| Second Lieutenant Hibbert | Jack Hawkins |
| The Company Sergeant-Major | Sidney Seaward |
| The Colonel | Eric Stanley |
| A German Soldier | Geoffrey Wincott |

(Mr. Whale also directed the Chicago company of Journey's End in August/September 1929 with Richard Bird as Captain Stanhope, and a revival in July/August 1930, again with Richard Bird. )

## THE LOVE DOCTOR

| | |
|---|---|
| Director | Melville Brown |
| Cinematographer | Edward Cronjager |
| From the play The Boomerang by Winchell Smith and Victor Mapes | |
| Adaptation | Guy Bolton and J. Walter Ruben |
| Dialogue | Guy Bolton |
| Titles | Herman J. Mankiewicz |
| Dialogue Director | James Whale |
| Assistant Director | Henry Hathaway |
| Film Editor | Otto Ludwig |
| Art Director | Van Nest Polglase |
| Sound Recording | Earl Hayman |
| Make Up | James Collins |
| Released in both silent and sound versions | |
| Production and Distribution | Paramount |
| Release Date | September 1929 |
| Running Time | 60 Minutes |

| | |
|---|---|
| Dr. Gerald Sumner | Richard Dix |
| Virginia Moore | June Collyer |
| Bud Woodbridge | Morgan Farley |
| Grace Taylor | Miriam Seegar |
| Mrs. Woodbridge | Winifred Harris |
| Preston De Witt | Lawford Davidson |
| Lucy | Gail Henry |

## A HUNDRED YEARS OLD

Lyceum Theatre--October 1, 1929.   A play by Serafin and Joaquin Alvarez Quintero.   Translated from Spanish by Helen and Harley Granville-Barker.   Produced by Gilbert Miller.   Directed by James Whale.

| | |
|---|---|
| Manuel | Arthur Lewis |
| Carmen Campos | Georgia Harvey |
| Dona Marciala | Katharine Grey |
| Don Evaristo | Fred Tiden |
| Papa Juan | Otis Skinner |
| Dona Filomena | Octavia Kenmore |
| Eulalia | Mary Howard |
| Trino | Hardie Albright |
| Currita | Mary Arbeny |
| Rosa | Veronica Rey |
| Antonon | Charles Dalton |
| Alonso | Gerald Hamer |

## HELL'S ANGELS

| | |
|---|---|
| Director | Howard Hughes (uncredited: James Whale) |
| Producer | Howard Hughes |
| Cinematographer (Air Footage) | Harry Perry |
| Cinematographer (Dialogue) | Gaetano Gaudio |
| Original Story | Howard Hughes, Marshall Neilan, and Joseph Moncure March |
| Adaptation | Harry Behn and Howard Estabrook |
| Dialogue | Joseph Moncure March |
| Dialogue Director | James Whale |
| Assistant Directors | Reginald Callow and William J. Scully |
| Production Assistant | Charles Stallings |
| Assistant Cinematographers | E. Burton Steene, Harry Zech, Jockey Feindel, Fred R. Eldridge, Jack MacKenzie, Paul Perry, Roy Greiner, Dewey Wrigley, Elmer Dyer, Pliny Goodfriend, Alvin Wyckoff, Sam Landers, William Tuers, Glenn |

| | |
|---|---|
| | Kershner, Donald Keyes, Roy Klaffki, Paul Ivano, Charles Boyle, Herman Schoop, L. Guy Wilky, John Silver, Edward Snyder, Edward Kull, Jack Greenhalgh, Henry Cronjager, Edward Cohen, Jack Breamer, and Ernest Laszlo |
| Film Editors | Douglas Biggs, Perry Hollingsworth, and Frank Lawrence |
| Art Director | Julian Boone Fleming |
| Technical Engineer | E. Roy Davidson |
| Music | Hugo Riesenfeld |
| Sound Recording | Lodge Cunningham |
| Aeronautical Technician | J. B. Alexander |
| German Technicians | Julius Schroeder, A. K. Graves, and K. Arnstein |

Released in black and white with a Technicolor sequence

| | |
|---|---|
| Studio | Metropolitan |
| Production | Caddo Company |
| Distribution | United Artists |
| Release Date | May 1930 |
| Running Time | 135 Minutes |

| | |
|---|---|
| Monte Rutledge | Ben Lyon |
| Roy Rutledge | James Hall |
| Helen | Jean Harlow |
| Karl Armstedt | John Darrow |
| Baron von Kranz | Lucien Prival |
| Lieutenant von Bruen | Frank Clark |
| "Baldy" | Roy Wilson |
| Captain Redfield | Douglas Gilmore |
| Baroness von Kranz | Jane Winton |
| Lady Randolph | Evelyn Hall |
| Staff Major | William B. Davidson |
| RFC Squadron Commander | Wyndham Standing |
| Gretchen | Lena Malena |
| Zeppelin Commander | Carl von Haartmann |
| Elliot | Stephen Carr |
| Von Schieben | Hans Joby |
| Marryat | Pat Somerset |
| Girl Selling Kisses | Marilyn Morgan |
| Von Richter | William von Brinken |
| 1st Officer of Zeppelin | F. Schumann-Heink |

## JOURNEY'S END

| | |
|---|---|
| Director | James Whale |
| Producer | George Pearson |
| Cinematographer | Benjamin Kline |
| From the play Journey's End by | R. C. Sherriff |
| Adaptation and Dialogue | Joseph Moncure March |
| Assistant Director | M. K. Wilson |
| Production Assistant | Gerald L. G. Samson |
| Film Editor | Claude Berkeley |
| Art Director | Hervey Libbert |
| Sound Recording | Buddy Myers |
| Technical Advisor | Colonel George Magee |
| Production (England) | Gainsborough and Welsh-Pearson-Elder Ltd. |
| Production (United States) | Tiffany-Stahl |
| Distribution (England) | Gainsborough |
| Distribution (United States) | Tiffany |
| Release Date | April 1930 |
| Running Time | 125 Minutes |

| | |
|---|---|
| Captain Stanhope | Colin Clive |
| Lieutenant Osborne | Ian MacLaren |
| Second Lieutenant Raleigh | David Manners |
| Second Lieutenant Hibbert | Anthony Bushell |
| Second Lieutenant Trotter | Billy Bevan |
| Private Mason | Charles Gerrard |
| Captain Hardy | Robert A'Dair |
| Sergeant Major | Thomas Whiteley |
| The Colonel | Jack Pitcairn |
| A German Boy | Warner Klinger |
| Corporal Ross | Leslie Sketchley |

## BADGER'S GREEN

Prince of Wales Theatre--June 12, 1930.   A play by R. C. Sherriff.   Produced by Maurice Browne.   Settings and Direction by James Whale.

| | |
|---|---|
| Doctor Wetherby | Horace Hodges |
| Major Forrester | Louis Goodrich |
| Mr. Twigg | Sebastian Smith |
| Mr. Butler | Felix Aylmer |
| Mr. Rogers | Frederick Burtwell |
| Dickie Wetherby | Robert Douglas |
| Mrs. Wetherby | Margaret Scudamore |

| Mrs. Forrester | Hilda Sims |
|---|---|
| Mr. Butler's Secretary | Maisie Darrell |
| Mary | Kathleen Harrison |

## THE VIOLET and ONE, TWO, THREE!

Henry Miller's Theatre--September 29, 1930.   Two one-act plays by Ferenc Molnar.   The Violet translated by Arthur Richman.   One, Two, Three! translated by Sidney Howard.   Produced by Gilbert Miller.   Directed by James Whale.

### The Violet

| Miss Roboz | Natica de Acosta |
|---|---|
| The Producer-Manager | A. P. Kaye |
| John | Johnnie Brewer |
| Miss Markus | Aldeah Wise |
| The Composer | Reginald Mason |
| Miss Rakolnoki | Joan Carr |
| Miss Szell | Sue Moore |
| Ilona Stobri | Ruth Gordon |

### One, Two, Three!

| Nordson | Arthur Byron |
|---|---|
| Nordson's Secretary | George H. Trader |
| Nordson's Valet | Norbert Humphreys |
| Lydia | Audray Dale |
| Anton Schuh | John Williams |
| Miss Kuno | Aldeah Wise |
| Miss Posner | Eileen Byron |
| Miss Brasch | Joan Carr |
| Miss Petrowitsch | Natica de Acosta |
| Dr. Pinsky | Frederick Roland |
| A Haberdasher | Johnnie Brewer |
| Mr. Osso | J. P. Wilson |
| Mr. Ciring | George Fogle |
| Dr. Wolff | Harold Thomas |
| A Barber | Isidor Marcil |
| Count Van Dubois-Schottenburg | Reginald Mason |
| Dr. Faber | Robert Noble |
| Kaldoorian | Donald MacMillan |
| Miss Lind | Fifi Laynee |
| Karl | Forbes Herbert Dawson |
| Felix | Colin Hunter |

Calleon                                    Maurice Cass
Kristian                                   Frank Rothe
Ferdinand                                  Carl Del Mel

## WATERLOO BRIDGE

| | |
|---|---|
| Director | James Whale |
| Producer | Carl Laemmle, Jr. |
| Cinematographer | Arthur Edeson |
| From the play Waterloo Bridge by Robert E. Sherwood | |
| Screenplay | Benn W. Levy |
| Continuity | Thomas Reed |
| Assistant Director | Joseph A. McDonough |
| Film Editor | Clarence Kolster |
| Art Director | Charles D. Hall |
| Sound Recording | William Hedgecock |
| Make Up | Jack P. Pierce |
| Production and Distribution | Universal |
| Release Date | September 1931 |
| Running Time | 73 minutes |

| | |
|---|---|
| Myra | Mae Clarke |
| Roy Cronin | Kent Douglass |
| Kitty | Doris Lloyd |
| Mrs. Hobley | Ethel Griffies |
| Mrs. Wetherby | Enid Bennett |
| Major Wetherby | Frederick Kerr |
| Janet | Bette Davis |
| Old Woman | Rita Carlisle |

## FRANKENSTEIN

| | |
|---|---|
| Director | James Whale |
| Producer | Carl Laemmle, Jr. |
| Cinematographer | Arthur Edeson |
| From the novel Frankenstein, or The Modern Prometheus by Mary W. Shelley and the play Frankenstein by Peggy Webling | |
| Adaptation | John L. Balderston |
| Screenplay | Robert Florey, Garrett Fort, and Francis Edwards Faragoh |
| Continuity | Thomas Reed |
| Assistant Director | Joseph A. McDonough |

| Film Editor | Clarence Kolster |
| Art Director | Charles D.  Hall |
| Special Electrical Properties | Kenneth Strickfaden |
| Sound Recording | William Hedgecock |
| Make Up | Jack P.  Pierce |
| Technical Advisor | Dr.  Cecil Reynolds |
| Production and Distribution | Universal |
| Release Date | December 1931 |
| Running Time | 71 Minutes |

| Henry Frankenstein | Colin Clive |
| Elizabeth | Mae Clarke |
| Victor Moritz | John Boles |
| The Monster | Boris Karloff |
| Dr.  Waldman | Edward Van Sloan |
| Baron Frankenstein | Frederick Kerr |
| Fritz | Dwight Frye |
| Burgomaster Vogel | Lionel Belmore |
| Maria | Marilyn Harris |
| Ludwig | Michael Mark |
| Bridesmaid | Arletta Duncan |
| Villager | Francis Ford |

## IMPATIENT MAIDEN

| Director | James Whale |
| Producer | Carl Laemmle,  Jr. |
| Cinematographer | Arthur Edeson |
| From the novel Impatient Virgin by Donald Henderson Clark |
| Screenplay | Richard L.  Schayer and Winnifred Dunn |
| Continuity | Thomas Reed |
| Assistant Director | Joseph A.  McDonough |
| Film Editor | Clarence Kolster |
| Art Director | Charles D.  Hall |
| Sound Recording | William Hedgecock |
| Make Up | Jack P.  Pierce |
| Production and Distribution | Universal |
| Release Date | March 1932 |
| Running Time | 78 Minutes |

| Dr.  Myron Brown | Lew Ayres |
| Ruth Robbins | Mae Clarke |
| Betty Merrick | Una Merkel |
| Albert Hartman | John Halliday |
| Clarence Howe | Andy Devine |

Dr. Wildox                    Oscar Apfel
Nurse Lovett                  Ethel Griffies
Mrs. Gilman                   Helen Jerome Eddy
Mr. Gilman                    Bert Roach
Mrs. Rosy                     Cecil Cunningham
Little Girl                   Marilyn Harris


## THE OLD DARK HOUSE

Director                      James Whale
Producer                      Carl Laemmle, Jr.
Cinematographer               Arthur Edeson
From the novel Benighted by J. B. Priestley
Screenplay                    Benn W. Levy
Additional Dialogue           R. C. Sherriff
Assistant Director            Joseph A. McDonough
Film Editor                   Clarence Kolster
Art Director                  Charles D. Hall
Sound Recording               William Hedgecock
Make Up                       Jack P. Pierce
Production and Distribution    Universal
Release Date                  October 1932
Running Time                  70 Minutes

Morgan                        Boris Karloff
Roger Penderel                Melvyn Douglas
Sir William Porterhouse       Charles Laughton
Margaret Waverton             Gloria Stuart
Philip Waverton               Raymond Massey
Horace Femm                   Ernest Thesiger
Gladys DuCane                 Lilian Bond
Rebecca Femm                  Eva Moore
Saul Femm                     Brember Wills
Sir Roderick                  Elspeth Dudgeon


## THE KISS BEFORE THE MIRROR

Director                      James Whale
Producer                      Carl Laemmle, Jr.
Cinematographer               Karl Freund
From the play The Kiss Before the Mirror by Ladislaus
    Fodor
Screenplay                    William Anthony McGuire
Assistant Director            M. Mancke
Film Editor                   Ted Kent

| | |
|---|---|
| Art Director | Charles D. Hall |
| Sound Recording | Gilbert Kurland |
| Make Up | Jack P. Pierce |
| Production and Distribution | Universal |
| Release Date | March 1933 |
| Running Time | 67 Minutes |

| | |
|---|---|
| Maria Held | Nancy Carroll |
| Dr. Paul Held | Frank Morgan |
| Dr. Walter Bernsdorf | Paul Lukas |
| Frau Bernsdorf | Gloria Stuart |
| Bachelor | Walter Pidgeon |
| Hilda | Jean Dixon |
| Maria's Lover | Donald Cook |
| Schultz | Charles Grapewin |
| Hilda's Lover | Allen Conner |
| Prosecutor | Wallis Clark |

## THE INVISIBLE MAN

| | |
|---|---|
| Director | James Whale |
| Producer | Carl Laemmle, Jr. |
| Cinematographer | Arthur Edeson |
| Special Effects | John P. Fulton (with John Mescall) |
| From the novel The Invisible Man by H. G. Wells | |
| Screenplay | R. C. Sherriff |
| Assistant Director | Joseph A. McDonough |
| Film Editor | Ted Kent |
| Art Director | Charles D. Hall |
| Sound Recording | William Hedgecock |
| Music | Heinz Roemheld |
| Make Up | Jack P. Pierce |
| Production and Distribution | Universal |
| Release Date | November 1933 |
| Running Time | 70 Minutes |

| | |
|---|---|
| Jack Griffin | Claude Rains |
| Flora Cranley | Gloria Stuart |
| Dr. Cranley | Henry Travers |
| Dr. Kemp | William Harrigan |
| Mrs. Hall | Una O'Connor |
| Mr. Hall | Forrester Harvey |
| Chief of Police | Holmes Herbert |
| Jaffers | E. E. Clive |

| | |
|---|---|
| Chief of Detectives | Dudley Digges |
| Inspector Bird | Harry Stubbs |
| Inspector Lane | Donald Stuart |
| Milly | Merle Tottenham |
| Reporter | Dwight Frye |
| Townsman | John Carradine |
| Townsman | Walter Brennan |

## BY CANDLELIGHT

| | |
|---|---|
| Director | James Whale |
| Producer | Carl Laemmle, Jr. |
| Cinematographer | John Mescall |
| From the play Candle Light by Sigfried Geyer | |
| Screenplay | Hans Kraly, F. Hugh Herbert, Karen de Wolf, and Ruth Cummings |
| Assistant Director | William Reith |
| Film Editor | Ted Kent |
| Art Director | Charles D. Hall |
| Music | W. Franke Harling |
| Make Up | Jack P. Pierce |
| Production and Distribution | Universal |
| Release Date | January 1934 |
| Running Time | 70 Minutes |

| | |
|---|---|
| Marie | Elissa Landi |
| Josef | Paul Lukas |
| Prince von Rommer | Nils Asther |
| Countess von Rischenheim | Dorothy Revier |
| Count von Rischenheim | Lawrence Grant |
| Baroness von Ballin | Esther Ralston |
| Baron von Ballin | Warburton Gamble |
| Ann | Lois January |

## ONE MORE RIVER

| | |
|---|---|
| Director | James Whale |
| Producer | Carl Laemmle, Jr. |
| Cinematographer | John Mescall |
| Special Effects | John P. Fulton |
| From the novel Over The River by John Galsworthy | |
| Screenplay | R. C. Sherriff |
| Assistant Director | Joseph A. McDonough |
| Film Editor | Ted Kent |

| | |
|---|---|
| Art Director | Charles D. Hall |
| Make Up | Jack P. Pierce |
| Production and Distribution | Universal |
| Release Date | August 1934 |
| Running Time | 90 Minutes |

| | |
|---|---|
| Lady Clare Corven | Diana Wynyard |
| Sir Gerald Corven | Colin Clive |
| Tony Croom | Frank Lawton |
| Dinny Charwell | Jane Wyatt |
| Lady Mont | Mrs. Patrick Campbell |
| David Dornford | Reginald Denny |
| General Charwell | C. Aubrey Smith |
| Sir Lawrence Mont | Henry Stephenson |
| Brough | Lionel Atwill |
| Forsyte | Alan Mowbray |
| Lady Charwell | Kathleen Howard |
| Judge | Gilbert Emery |
| Chayne | E. E. Clive |
| Blore | Robert Greig |
| Benjy | Gunnis Davis |
| Mrs. Purdy | Tempe Pigott |

## THE BRIDE OF FRANKENSTEIN

| | |
|---|---|
| Director | James Whale |
| Producer | Carl Laemmle, Jr. |
| Cinematographer | John Mescall |
| Special Effects | John P. Fulton |
| From the novel Frankenstein or The Modern Prometheus by Mary W. Shelley | |
| Screenplay | William Hurlbut and John L. Balderston |
| Assistant Director | M. Mancke |
| Film Editor | Ted Kent |
| Art Director | Charles D. Hall |
| Special Electrical Properties | Kenneth Strickfaden |
| Music | Franz Waxman |
| Musical Director | Constantin Bakaleinikoff |
| Make Up | Jack P. Pierce |
| Production and Distribution | Universal |
| Release Date | April 1935 |
| Running Time | 75 Minutes |
| Academy Award Nomination for Best Sound Recording | |

| | |
|---|---|
| The Monster | Boris Karloff |
| Henry Frankenstein | Colin Clive |
| Mary and The Bride | Elsa Lanchester |
| Dr. Pretorius | Ernest Thesiger |
| The Hermit | O. P. Heggie |
| Minnie | Una O'Connor |
| Elizabeth | Valerie Hobson |
| Lord Byron | Gavin Gordon |
| Percy Shelley | Douglas Walton |
| The Burgomaster | E. E. Clive |
| Otto | Lucien Prival |
| Karl | Dwight Frye |
| Hans | Reginald Barlow |
| Han's Wife | Mary Gordon |
| Shepherdess | Anne Darling |
| Uncle Glutz | Gunnis David |
| Auntie Glutz | Tempe Pigott |
| Ludwig | Ted Billings |
| Rudy | Neil Fitzgerald |
| Neighbor | Walter Brennan |
| Hunter | John Carradine |
| King | Monty Montague |
| Queen | Joan Woodbury |
| Archbishop | Norman Ainsley |
| Devil | Peter Shaw |
| Baby | Billy Barty |
| Ballerina | Kansas De Forest |
| Mermaid | Josephine McKim |
| Girl | Helen Parrish |

## REMEMBER LAST NIGHT?

| | |
|---|---|
| Director | James Whale |
| Producer | Carl Laemmle, Jr. |
| Cinematographer | Joseph Valentine |
| From the novel The Hangover Murders by Adam Hobhouse | |
| Screenplay | Doris Malloy, Harry Clork, and Dan Totheroh |
| Additional Dialogue | Benn W. Levy |
| Assistant Director | Scott Beal |
| Film Editor | Ted Kent |
| Art Director | Charles D. Hall |
| Music | Franz Waxman |
| Musical Director | Constantin Bakaleinikoff |
| Make Up | Jack P. Pierce |
| Production and Distribution | Universal |

| | |
|---|---|
| Release Date | November 1935 |
| Running Time | 85 Minutes |

| | |
|---|---|
| Danny Harrison | Edward Arnold |
| Carlotta Milburn | Constance Cummings |
| Bette Huling | Sally Eilers |
| Tony Milburn | Robert Young |
| Fred Flannagan | Robert Armstrong |
| Jack Whitridge | Reginald Denny |
| Billy Arnold | Monroe Owsley |
| Vic Huling | George Meeker |
| Maxie | Edward Brophy |
| Baptiste | Jack La Rue |
| Penny Whitridge | Louise Henry |
| Professor Jones | Gustav von Seyffertitz |
| Faronea | Gergory Ratoff |
| Phelps | Arthur Treacher |
| Mme. Bouclier | Rafaela Ottiano |
| Photographer | E. E. Clive |

## SHOW BOAT

| | |
|---|---|
| Director | James Whale |
| Producer | Carl Laemmle, Jr. |
| Cinematographer | John Mescall (uncredited: Leon Shamroy) |
| Special Effects | John P. Fulton |

From the novel Show Boat by Edna Ferber and the stage musical by Oscar Hammerstein II and Jerome Kern

| | |
|---|---|
| Screenplay | Oscar Hammerstein II |
| Lyrics | Oscar Hammerstein II |
| Music | Jerome Kern |
| Songs (In Order of Appearance) | "Make Believe Love" |
| | "Ol' Man River" |
| | "Can't Help Lovin' Dat Man of Mine" |
| | "I Have the Room Above Her" |
| | "Gallavantin' Around" |
| | "You Are Love" |
| | "Ah Still Suits Me" |
| | "My Bill" |
| | "Good-Bye My Lady Love" (Joseph Howard) |
| | "After the Ball" (Charles K. Harris) |

| | |
|---|---|
| Assistant Director | Joseph A. McDonough |
| Film Editors | Ted Kent and Bernard Burton |
| Art Director | Charles D. Hall |
| Musical Director | Victor Baravelle |
| Make Up | Jack P. Pierce |
| Production and Distribution | Universal |
| Release Date | May 1936 |
| Running Time | 110 Minutes |
| | |
| Magnolia Hawks | Irene Dunne |
| Captain Andy Hawks | Charles Winninger |
| Gaylord Ravenal | Allan Jones |
| Joe | Paul Robeson |
| Julie | Helen Morgan |
| Parthy | Helen Westley |
| Steve | Donald Cook |
| Ellie | Queenie Smith |
| Frank Schultz | Sammy White |
| Queenie | Hattie McDaniel |
| Rubberface | Francis X. Mahoney |
| Sheriff Vallon | Charles Middleton |
| Pete | Arthur Hohl |
| Windy | J. Farrell MacDonald |
| Green | Charles Wilson |
| Kim | Sunnie O'Dea |
| Kim (as a child) | Marilyn Knowlden |
| Kim (as a baby) | Patricia Barry |
| Landlady | Mae Beatty |
| Janitor | Clarence Muse |
| Jeb | Stanley Fields |
| Englishman | E. E. Clive |
| Negro | Eddie Anderson |
| Woman | Helen Jerome Eddy |
| Little Girl | Marilyn Harris |

## THE ROAD BACK

| | |
|---|---|
| Director | James Whale (uncredited: Ted Sloman) |
| Executive Producer | Charles R. Rogers |
| Associate Producer | J. Edmund Grainger |
| Cinematographers | John Mescall and George Robinson |
| Special Effects | John P. Fulton |

From the novel The Road Back by Erich Maria Remarque

| | |
|---|---|
| Screenplay | R. C. Sherriff and Charles Kenyon |
| Assistant Director | Joseph A. McDonough |
| Film Editor | Ted Kent (uncredited: Charles Maynard) |
| Art Director | Jack Otterson |
| Music | Dimitri Tiomkin |
| Musical Director | Charles Previn |
| Make Up | Jack P. Pierce |
| Production and Distribution | Universal |
| Release Date | June 1937 |
| Running Time | 79 Minutes |
| | |
| Ernst | John King |
| Ludwig | Richard Cromwell |
| Tjaden | Slim Summerville |
| Willy | Andy Devine |
| Lucy | Barbara Read |
| Angelina | Louise Fazenda |
| Wessling | Noah Beery, Jr. |
| Albert | Maurice Murphy |
| Von Hagen | John Emery |
| Mayor | Etienne Girardot |
| Prosecutor | Lionel Atwill |
| Bethke | Henry Hunter |
| Weil | Larry Blake |
| Giesicke | Henry Hunter |
| Maria | Greta Gynt |
| Ernst's Mother | Spring Byington |
| Ernst's Aunt | Laura Hope Crews |
| Ernst's Father | Frank Reicher |
| Heinrich | Arthur Hohl |
| Mr. Markheim | Al Shean |
| Defense Attorney | Samuel S. Hinds |
| Manager | Reginald Barlow |
| General | E. E. Clive |
| President | Edward Van Sloan |
| Street Cleaner | Francis Ford |
| Small Man | Dwight Frye |
| French Girl | Dorothy Granger |
| Woman | Tempe Pigott |
| Door Keeper | Tiny Sandford |

## THE GREAT GARRICK

| | |
|---|---|
| Director | James Whale |

| | |
|---|---|
| Producer | Mervyn Le Roy |
| Cinematographer | Ernest Haller |
| Original Story and Screenplay | Ernst Vadja |
| Additional Dialogue | Rowland Leigh |
| Assistant Director | Sherry Shrourds |
| Film Editor | Warren Low |
| Art Director | Anton Grot |
| Music | Adolph Deutsch |
| Musical Director | Leo F. Forbstein |
| Make Up | Perc Westmore |
| Production and Distribution | Warner Bros. |
| Release Date | September 1937 |
| Running Time | 89 Minutes |

| | |
|---|---|
| David Garrick | Brian Aherne |
| Germaine | Olivia de Havilland |
| Tubby | Edward Everett Horton |
| M. Picard | Melville Cooper |
| Beaumarchais | Lionel Atwill |
| Sir Joshua Reynolds | Henry O'Neill |
| Basset | Luis Alberni |
| Auber | Lana Turner |
| Nicolle | Marie Wilson |
| Molee | Linda Perry |
| Horatio | Fritz Leiber |
| Jean Cabot | Etienne Girardot |
| Mme. Moreau | Dorothy Tree |
| M. Janin | Craig Reynolds |
| Le Brun | Albert Van Dekker |
| Innkeeper | Paul Everton |
| M. Noverre | Trevor Bardette |
| Thierre | Milton Owen |
| M. Moreau | Chester Clute |
| Vendor | E. E. Clive |
| Drunk | Jack Norton |
| Innkeeper of "Turk's Head" | Harry Davenport |

## PORT OF SEVEN SEAS

| | |
|---|---|
| Director | James Whale |
| Producer | Henry Henigson (uncredited: Carl Laemmle, Jr. ) |
| Cinematographer | Karl Freund |
| From Fanny by Marcel Pagnol | |
| Screenplay | Preston Sturges (uncredited: Ernst Vadja) |
| Montage | Slavko Vorkapich |

| | |
|---|---|
| Assistant Director | Joseph A. McDonough |
| Film Editor | Frederick Smith |
| Art Director | Cedric Gibbons |
| Music | Franz Waxman |
| Musical Director | Nat Finston |
| Make Up | Jack Dawn |
| Production and Distribution | Metro-Goldwyn-Mayer |
| Release Date | June 1938 |
| Running Time | 81 Minutes |

| | |
|---|---|
| César | Wallace Beery |
| Panisse | Frank Morgan |
| Madelon | Maureen O'Sullivan |
| Marius | John Beal |
| Honorine | Jessie Ralph |
| Claudine | Cora Witherspoon |
| Bruneau | Etienne Girardot |
| Captain Escartefigue | E. Allyn Warren |
| Boy | Robert Spindola |
| Customer | Doris Lloyd |
| Man | Jack Latham |
| Postman | Paul Panzer |
| Arab Rug Seller | Jerry Colonna |
| Bird Seller | Fred Malatesta |
| Chinese Peddler | Moy Ming |
| Organ Grinder | George Humbert |

## SINNERS IN PARADISE

| | |
|---|---|
| Director | James Whale |
| Producer | Ken Goldsmith |
| Cinematographer | George Robinson |
| Original Story | Harold Buckley |
| Screenplay | Lester Cole, Harold Buckley, and Louis Stevens (uncredited: Robert Lee Johnson) |
| Assistant Director | Fred Frank |
| Film Editor | Maurice Wright |
| Art Director | Jack Otterson |
| Musical Director | Charles Previn |
| Make Up | Jack P. Pierce |
| Production and Distribution | Universal |
| Release Date | May 1938 |
| Running Time | 65 Minutes |

| | |
|---|---|
| Anne Wesson | Madge Evans |
| Jim Taylor | John Boles |
| Robert Malone | Bruce Cabot |
| Iris Compton | Marion Martin |
| Senator Corey | Gene Lockhart |
| Thelma Chase | Charlotte Wynters |
| Mrs. Franklin Sydney | Nana Bryant |
| Honeyman | Milburn Stone |
| Jessup | Donald Barry |
| Harrison Brand | Morgan Conway |
| Ping | Willie Fung |
| Marshall | Dwight Frye |
| Captain | Jason Robards |
| Radio Announcer | William Lundigan |

## WIVES UNDER SUSPICION

| | |
|---|---|
| Director | James Whale |
| Producer | J. Edmund Grainger |
| Cinematographer | George Robinson |

From the play The Kiss Before the Mirror by Ladislaus Fodor

| | |
|---|---|
| Screenplay | Myles Connolly |
| Assistant Director | Fred Frank |
| Film Editor | Maurice Wright |
| Art Director | Jack Otterson |
| Musical Director | Charles Previn |
| Make Up | Jack P. Pierce |
| Production and Distribution | Universal |
| Release Date | June 1938 |
| Running Time | 68 Minutes |

| | |
|---|---|
| Jim Stowell | Warren William |
| Lucy Stowell | Gail Patrick |
| Phil | William Lundigan |
| Elizabeth | Constance Moore |
| Shaw Mac Allen | Ralph Morgan |
| Sharpy | Cecil Cunningham |
| Dave Allison | Jonathan Hale |
| Dave Marrow | Samuel S. Hinds |
| Creola | Lillian Yarbo |
| Kirk | Milburn Stone |
| Jenks | James Flavin |
| Judge Johnson | Edward Stanley |

## THE MAN IN THE IRON MASK

| | |
|---|---|
| Director | James Whale |
| Producer | Edward Small |
| Cinematographer | Robert Planck |
| From the novel The Three Musketeers by Alexandre Dumas | |
| Screenplay | George Bruce |
| Second Unit Director | Cullen Tate |
| Assistant Director | Edgar Anderson |
| Fencing Director | Fred Cavens |
| Film Editor | Grant Whytock |
| Art Director | Jack Du Casse Schulze |
| Music | Lucien Moraweck |
| Musical Director | Lud Gluskin |
| Make Up | Paul Stanhope |
| Studio | General Service |
| Production | Edward Small Productions/ United Artists |
| Distribution | United Artists |
| Release Date | July 1939 |
| Running Time | 110 Minutes |
| Academy Award Nomination for Best Original Musical Score | |

| | |
|---|---|
| Louis XIV and Philippe of Gascony | Louis Hayward |
| Maria Theresa | Joan Bennett |
| D'Artagnan | Warren William |
| Fouquet | Joseph Schildkraut |
| Parthos | Alan Hale |
| Colbert | Walter Kingsford |
| Aramis | Miles Mander |
| Athos | Bert Roach |
| Mlle. de la Valliere | Marion Martin |
| Spanish Ambassador | Montague Love |
| Queen Anne | Doris Kenyon |
| Louis XIII | Albert Dekker |
| Cardinal Richelieu | Nigel de Brulier |
| Commandant of Bastille | William Royle |
| Lord High Constable of France | Boyd Invin |
| Cardinal | Howard Brooks |
| Jean Paul | Reginald Barlow |
| Second Officer | Peter Cushing |

## GREEN HELL

| | |
|---|---|
| Director | James Whale |

| | |
|---|---|
| Producer | Harry Edington |
| Cinematographer | Karl Freund |
| Original Story and Screenplay | Frances Marion |
| Additional Dialogue | Harry Hervey |
| Assistant Director | Joseph A. McDonough |
| Film Editor | Ted Kent |
| Art Director | Jack Otterson |
| Musical Director | Charles Previn |
| Make Up | Jack P. Pierce |
| Production | Famous Productions/Universal |
| Distribution | Universal |
| Release Date | January 1940 |
| Running Time | 87 Minutes |

| | |
|---|---|
| Keith Brandon | Douglas Fairbanks, Jr. |
| Stephanie Richardson | Joan Bennett |
| Hal Scott | John Howard |
| Forrester | George Sanders |
| Dr. Loren | Alan Hale |
| Tex Morgan | George Bancroft |
| David Richardson | Vincent Price |
| Graham | Gene Garrick |
| Gracco | Frances McDonald |
| Mala | Ray Mala |
| Santos | Peter Bronte |
| Native Girl | Lupita Tovar |

## THEY DARE NOT LOVE

| | |
|---|---|
| Director | James Whale (uncredited: Charles Vidor) |
| Producer | Samuel Bischoff |
| Cinematographer | Franz Planer |
| Original Story | James Edward Grant |
| Screenplay | Charles Bennett and Ernst Vadja |
| Assistant Director | William Mull |
| Film Editor | Al Clark |
| Art Director | Lionel Banks |
| Music | Morris Stoloff |
| Make Up | Clay Campbell |
| Production and Distribution | Columbia |
| Release Date | April 1941 |
| Running Time | 75 Minutes |

| | |
|---|---|
| Prince Kurt von Rotenberg | George Brent |
| Maria Keller | Martha Scott |
| Baron von Heising | Paul Lukas |
| Professor Keller | Egon Brewher |
| Baron Shafter | Roman Bohnen |
| Captain Wilhelm Ehrhardt | Edgar Barrier |
| Barbara Murdock | Kay Linaker |
| Captain | Frank Reicher |
| Blond Officer | Lloyd Bridges |
| Radio Officer | Phillip Van Zandt |

## HAND IN GLOVE

Playhouse Theatre--December 4, 1944.  A play by Charles K. Freeman and Gerald Savory.  From the novel Hughie Roddis by Gerald Savory.  Settings by Samuel Leve. Produced by Arthur Edison.  Directed by James Whale.

| | |
|---|---|
| Jenny | Jean Bellows |
| Mr. Ramskill | George Lloyd |
| Auntie B. | Isobel Elsom |
| Hughie | Skelton Knaggs |
| Mr. Forsythe | St. Clair Bayfield |
| Mrs. Willis | Viola Rosche |
| Lily Willis | Islay Benson |
| Curly Latham | Victor Beecroft |
| Purple Cap | Almon Bruce |
| Bowler Hat | Todd Stanton |
| Sergeant | Robin Craven |
| Chief Constable | Wallace Widdecombe |
| Man From London | Aubrey Mather |

## HELLO OUT THERE

| | |
|---|---|
| Director | James Whale |
| Producer | Huntington Hartford |
| Cinematographer | Karl Struss |
| From the one-act play Hello Out There by William Saroyan | |
| Screenplay | George Tobin |
| Film Editor | Otto Mayer |
| Art Director | Edward Ilou |
| Make Up | Gustav Norin |
| Studio | KTTV Television |
| Production | Theasquare Productions |

Production Date                  1949
Running Time                     41 Minutes

(Hello Out There was originally intended for television distribution, but was never commercially released.  In 1951, RKO
released two other short stories also produced by the same
company:   The Secret Sharer by Joseph Conrad, with James
Mason and Gene Lockhart, directed by John Brahm; and The
Bride Comes to Yellow Sky by Stephen Crane, with Robert
Preston and Marjorie Steele, directed by Bretaigne Windust,
under the collective title Face to Face. )

The Roustabout                   Harry Morgan
The Woman                        Lee Patrick
The Sheriff's Wife               Marjorie Steele


## PAGAN IN THE PARLOUR

        Wimbledon Theatre--September 22, 1952.   A play by
Franklin Lacey.   Settings and Costumes by Doris Zinkeisen.
Directed by James Whale.

Dolly                            Catherine Lacey
Isavelle                         Moyna MacGill
Eve                              Ann Summers
Mrs. Peters                      Phyllis Baker
Terry                            Joss Ackland
Dan                              William Mervyn
Ezra                             Horace Kenney
Noo-ga                           Hermione Baddeley
Maitland                         Aubrey Mather
Mrs. Maitland                    Una Venning
Miss Babbacombe                  Lally Bowers
Minnie                           Ruth Goring

# BIBLIOGRAPHY

Balcon, Michael. A Lifetime of Films. London: Hutchinson, 1969.

Brosnan, John. The Horror People. New York: St. Martin's Press, 1976.

Browne, Maurice. Too Late to Lament. London: Victor Gollancz, 1955.

Dietrich, Noah, and Thomas, Bob. Howard, The Amazing Mr. Hughes. Greenwich, Conn. : Fawcett, 1972.

Drinkwater, John. The Life and Adventures of Carl Laemmle. New York: G. P. Putnam's Sons, 1931.

Gielgud, John. Early Stages. London: Macmillan, 1939.

Lanchester, Elsa. Charles Laughton and I. London: Faber and Faber, 1938.

Pearson, George. Flashback. London: George Allen & Unwin, 1957.

Sherriff, R. C. Journey's End. London: Victor Gollancz, 1929.

Sherriff, R. C. No Leading Lady. London: Victor Gollancz, 1968.

Webster, Margaret. The Same Only Different. London: Victor Gollancz, 1969.

231

Whittemore, Don, and Cecchettini, Philip Alan.  Passport to
    Hollywood.  New York:  McGraw-Hill, 1976.